The Vietnam Experience

Flags Into Battle

by Michael Casey, Clark Dougan, Samuel Lipsman, Jack Sweetman, Stephen Weiss, and the editors of Boston Publishing Company

Boston Publishing Company / Boston, MA

Boston Publishing Company

President and Publisher: Robert J. George
Vice President: Richard S. Perkins, Jr.
Editor-in-Chief: Robert Manning
Managing Editor: Paul Dreyfus
Marketing Director: Jeanne Gibson

Series Editor: Samuel Lipsman
Senior Editor: Gordon Hardy
Design Director: Lisa Bogle
Senior Picture Editor: Julene Fischer
Senior Writer: Denis Kennedy

Picture Editor: Lanng Tamura
Picture Coordinator/Researcher:
Rebecca Black

Text Researcher: Michael Hathaway

Editorial Production: Theresa Slomkowski
Business Staff: Amy Pelletier, Amy Wilson

Special contributors to this volume:
Text Research: Katharine Brady, Jason
Brown, Matthew Hong, Kenneth Jacobson,
Steven W. Lipari, Jonathan Mark, Jennifer
Smith, Michael Youmans
Design: Sherry Fatla, Lynne Weygint
Picture Research: Robert Ebbs, Shirley L.
Green (Washington, D.C.), Kate Lewin (Paris)

Editorial Production: Dalia Lipkin, Patricia
Leal Welch

About the editors and authors:

Editor-in-Chief: *Robert Manning*, a long-time journalist, has previously been editor-in-chief of the *Atlantic Monthly* magazine and its press. He served as assistant secretary of state for public affairs under Presidents John F. Kennedy and Lyndon B. Johnson. He has also been a fellow at the Institute of Politics at the John F. Kennedy School of Government at Harvard University.

Authors: *Michael Casey*, author of the chapters on the 1st Aviation Brigade and the 101st Airborne Division, is formerly a researcher for *The Vietnam Experience*. He is a graduate of Harvard College. *Clark Dougan* (1st Cavalry Division), a former Watson and Danforth fellow, has taught history at Kenyon College. He received his M.A. and M.Phil. at Yale University. *Samuel Lipsman* (MACV and support commands), series editor at Boston Publishing Company, is a former Fulbright Scholar. He received his M.A. and M.Phil. in history at Yale. *Jack Sweetman* (Navy) is a member of the history faculty at the U.S. Naval Academy. His publications include *American Naval History: An Illustrated Chronology*. *Stephen Weiss* (Air Force, 3d Marine Division, and 1st Marine Division) has been a fellow at the Newberry Library in Chicago. An American historian, he received his M.A. and M.Phil. at Yale. Messrs. Dougan, Lipsman, and Weiss have coauthored other volumes in *The Vietnam Experience*.

Historical Consultants: Chief Historical Consultant *Shelby L. Stanton*, a Vietnam veteran and former captain in the U.S. Army Special Forces, is currently a fellow at the Georgetown Center for Strategic and International Studies. His books include *Vietnam Order of Battle* and *The Rise and Fall of an American Army*. Mr.

Stanton also reviewed the pictures and provided material for the illustrations on pages 42–5. *Vincent H. Demma*, a historian with the U.S. Army Center of Military History, read the chapters on the U.S. Army. *John F. Guilmartin, Jr.*, who read the chapter on the Air Force, is currently senior secretary of the Navy Research Fellowship at the U.S. Navy War College. *Edward J. Marolda*, who read and reviewed pictures for the Navy chapter, heads the Contemporary History Branch of the U.S. Naval Historical Center. *Jack Shulimson*, head of the Histories Section, U.S. Marine Corps Historical Center, read the chapters on the Marines.

Picture Consultants: *Glen Sweeting* reviewed the Air Force material. A twenty-year veteran of the U.S. Air Force, he has served with the Air Force Historical Division and the National Air and Space Museum of the Smithsonian Institution. *Alan Archambault*, who reviewed material on the Marines, is a military artist and researcher.

Cover Photo:
American, divisional, and brigade flags are dipped in salute as the 1st Brigade, 101st Airborne Division, arrives in Vietnam on July 29, 1965.

Library of Congress Catalog Card Number: 87-071309
ISBN: 0-939526-22-0

10 9 8 7 6
5 4 3 2 1

Contents

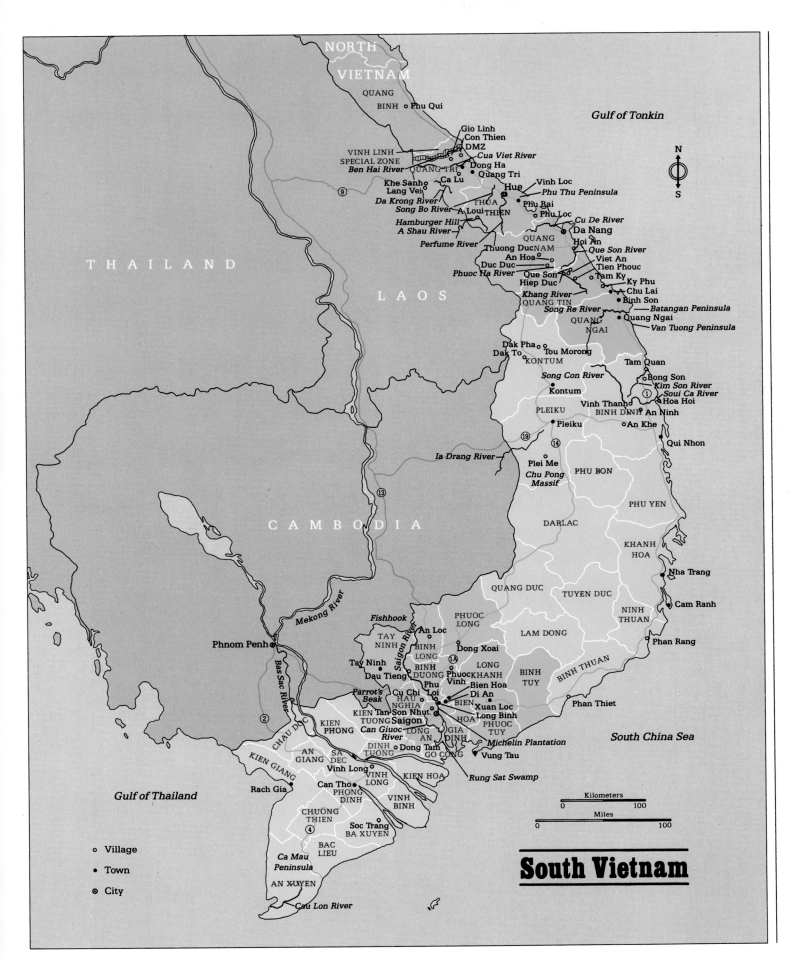

South Vietnam

- ○ Village
- ● Town
- ◉ City

NORTH VIETNAM

QUANG BINH • Phu Qui

Gulf of Tonkin

Gio Linh
Con Thien
DMZ
VINH LINH
SPECIAL ZONE
Cua Viet River
Ben Hai River
QUANG TRI
Dong Ha
Quang Tri
Khe Sanh
Lang Vei
Ca Lu
Hue
Vinh Loc
Phu Thu Peninsula
Da Krong River
Song Bo River
THUA THIEN
Phu Bai
Phu Loc
A Loui
Hamburger Hill
A Shau River
Perfume River
Cu De River
Da Nang
Hoi An
Thuong Duc NAM
An Hoa
Duc Duc
QUANG
Que Son River
Viet An
Tien Phouc
Phuoc Ha River
Que Son
Hiep Duc
Tam Ky
Ky Phu
Chu Lai
Khang River
QUANG TIN
Binh Son
Song Re River
Batangan Peninsula
Quang Ngai
QUANG NGAI
Van Tuong Peninsula

THAILAND

LAOS

Dak Pha
Dak To
Tou Morong
KONTUM
Tam Quan
Song Con River
Bong Son
Kim Son River
Soui Ca River
Kontum
Hoa Hoi
Vinh Thanh
BINH DINH
An Ninh
PLEIKU
An Khe
Pleiku
Qui Nhon
Ia Drang River
Plei Me
Chu Pong Massif
PHU BON
PHU YEN

CAMBODIA

DARLAC
KHANH HOA
Nha Trang
Mekong River
QUANG DUC
TUYEN DUC
NINH THUAN
Cam Ranh
PHUOC LONG
LAM DONG
Phan Rang
Fishhook
An Loc
Bas Sac River
TAY NINH
BINH LONG
Dong Xoai
Saigon River
BINH DUONG
LONG KHANH
BINH TUY
Phnom Penh
Tay Ninh
Dau Tieng
Phuoc Vinh
Phu Loi
Cu Chi
Bien Hoa
Di An
CHAU DOC
Parrot's Beak
HAU NGHIA
Son Nhut
BIEN HOA
Xuan Loc
Long Binh
Phan Thiet
KIEN TUONG
Tan
Saigon
LONG AN
GIA DINH
PHUOC TUY
Can Giuoc River
Michelin Plantation
South China Sea
KIEN PHONG
AN GIANG
SA DEC
DINH TUONG
Dong Tam
GO CONG
Vung Tau
Rung Sat Swamp
Vinh Long
VINH LONG
KIEN HOA
KIEN GIANG
Rach Gia
Can Tho
PHONG DINH
VINH BINH

Gulf of Thailand

CHUONG THIEN
Soc Trang
BA XUYEN
BAC LIEU
Ca Mau Peninsula
AN XUYEN
Cau Lon River

Kilometers
0   100
Miles
0   100

5

Command and Control

Like much of American policy in Vietnam, the decisions that established the relationships that commanded, controlled, and supported the U.S. combat troops in Vietnam evolved as much from unpredictable events inside South Vietnam as from careful Pentagon planning. While standard military doctrine governed the establishment of American military commands in Vietnam, they had to adapt to the evolving crisis in South Vietnam as well as the ever-increasing American role in that conflict.

A military command that was intended only to oversee an advisory effort in Southeast Asia grew to one that controlled more than half a million uniformed American servicemen and women. In addition, the military in Vietnam was given command over thousands of civilian government officials as well. To be sure, the resulting command structure had its share of problems, but it remains a tribute to the talents of American military management that a viable system of command and control emerged so quickly.

MACV

At the top of the American chain of command in Vietnam stood the ubiquitous institution of MACV (or "Mack-Vee," as it was always referred to by civilians and troops alike), whose commander bore the ponderous title COMUSMACV. By 1968 the Military Assistance Command, Vietnam, had under its control not only all of the U.S. servicemen and women serving in South Vietnam but also many civilian agencies in that country. The power of MACV was probably greater than that of the U.S. Embassy in Saigon and, with its ability to telephone the White House directly, it may even have overshadowed the Pentagon in its influence on critical decisions. It had not always been so.

MACV could trace its ancestry to the small group of men—only 128 in all—who established the Military Assistance Advisory Group (MAAG), Indochina, on September 17, 1950. The task of this group was to supervise the ever-increasing flow of U.S. aid to the French and to the nascent armies of Indochina that they commanded in their fight against the Ho Chi Minh-led Vietminh. With the signing of the Geneva accords in 1954 and the ebbing of French influence in South Vietnam, on November 1, 1955, the MAAG, Indochina, was rechristened the Military Assistance Advisory Group, Vietnam. The Geneva accords limited its authorized strength to 888 advisers, whose chief function was to train the independent South Vietnamese armed forces.

The MAAG was a unified command; that is, it controlled personnel from all branches of the armed services. It had been established by and was directly subordinate to the military command in the Pacific and its commander, known as CINCPAC, who maintained overall responsibility for American military policy in eastern Asia. During the 1950s, CINCPAC's attention was drawn increasingly to South Vietnam. In the early 1960s, CINCPAC assigned to Lieutenant General Paul D. Harkins, deputy commander in chief, U.S. Army, Pacific, responsibility for developing contingency plans in the event that American combat operations in Vietnam became necessary.

The likelihood of such intervention increased as the insurgency in South Vietnam developed and intensified during those years. In 1961 President John F. Kennedy chose to surpass the Geneva-imposed ceiling on advisers, and their number doubled by the end of the year to more than 1,600. More important, the advisers' duties expanded far beyond barracks-style training. They became intimately involved in combat operations, advising South

Preceding page. *President Lyndon Johnson ends high–level discussions with the MACV commander, Gen. William Westmoreland, at Cam Ranh Bay in November 1966.*

The headquarters of the Military Assistance Command, Vietnam, sprawls across the grounds of Tan Son Nhut Air Force Base on the outskirts of Saigon.

An IBM 360 computer (below) spews out information on the security status of Vietnam's hamlets in the only photograph ever taken of this computer—the most powerful of its era. MACV officials (right) then analyze the data to assess the progress of the pacification program.

Military Assistance Command, Vietnam

1965

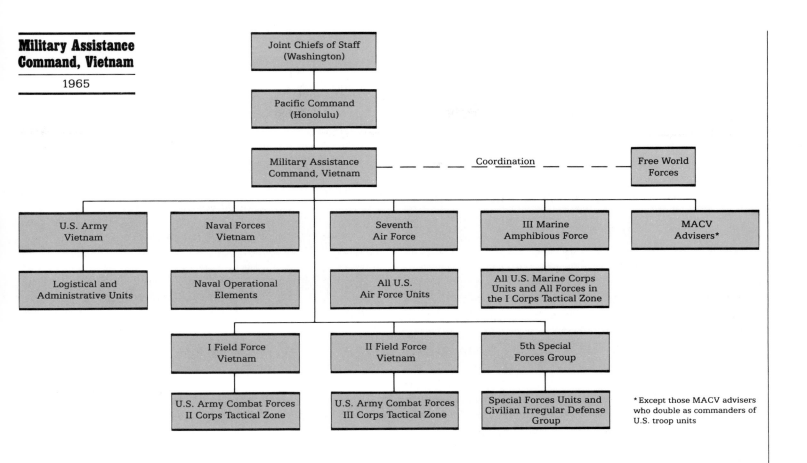

Joint Chiefs of Staff (Washington)
→ Pacific Command (Honolulu)
→ Military Assistance Command, Vietnam — — Coordination — — Free World Forces

- U.S. Army Vietnam
  - Logistical and Administrative Units
- Naval Forces Vietnam
  - Naval Operational Elements
- Seventh Air Force
  - All U.S. Air Force Units
- III Marine Amphibious Force
  - All U.S. Marine Corps Units and All Forces in the I Corps Tactical Zone
- MACV Advisers*

- I Field Force Vietnam
  - U.S. Army Combat Forces II Corps Tactical Zone
- II Field Force Vietnam
  - U.S. Army Combat Forces III Corps Tactical Zone
- 5th Special Forces Group
  - Special Forces Units and Civilian Irregular Defense Group

*Except those MACV advisers who double as commanders of U.S. troop units

MACV's first commander, Gen. Paul D. Harkins (right), discusses the advisory effort with Army Chief of Staff Gen. George H. Decker during a visit to Vietnam in 1962.

COMUSMACV, Gen. William Westmoreland, inspects a 1st Infantry Division pacification project near a Vietcong-controlled village in 1966.

Vietnamese officers in the field. At the urging of the Pentagon and with the approval of President Kennedy, CINCPAC Admiral Harry D. Felt ordered the creation of the Military Assistance Command, Vietnam. On February 18, 1962, MACV assumed control of the growing combat support role of the American forces in Vietnam as well as continuing contingency planning for any deeper U.S. involvement. It was thus only natural that General Harkins should become the first COMUSMACV.

MACV was considered a temporary command, necessary only for the duration of the immediate crisis in Vietnam. MAAG, Vietnam, was thus neither disbanded nor merged with MACV but rather retained its own charter, concentrating on the training of the South Vietnamese armed forces. By 1964, however, it had become clear that MACV's "temporary" life would be considerably longer than expected, and in May MACV absorbed the functions of MAAG, Vietnam. MACV took responsibility not only for the command of American personnel engaged in combat but also for training the Vietnamese forces. To many, at least in hindsight, it was one responsibility too many.

MACV's goal was to achieve the standing American objective in Vietnam: the creation of an independent and secure South Vietnam, capable of defending itself against internal subversion or foreign aggression. The attainment of this objective required that the South Vietnamese armed forces eventually become capable of defending the country on their own. When in 1965 America began sending increasing numbers of its own troops to shoulder the burden

of defending South Vietnam, MACV became caught between its responsibilities as the command headquarters of American forces and as a MAAG—to the detriment of both.

Like its MAAG predecessor, MACV operated as a "subordinate unified command," according to a doctrine known as the Joint Chiefs of Staff Unified Command Plan. It was "subordinate" because it remained under the Pacific command umbrella. This became a technicality, however, when in Washington the importance of the war in Vietnam came to overshadow the Pacific command. As a consequence, the Joint Chiefs of Staff often by-passed CINCPAC when communicating with COMUSMACV. And sometimes, although General William Westmoreland, who succeeded General Harkins in June 1964, reported that it was "seldom" the case, the president actually ignored the JCS in favor of a direct relationship with MACV.

MACV's relationship to its subordinate commands was equally complex. Under the concept of unified command the individual branches of the armed services retained administrative *command* of their own troops and were called "component commands." But to maintain unity of effort within the combat zone, MACV exercised operational *control* over all military personnel assigned to Vietnam.

The four branches of the armed forces thus contributed four component commands to MACV: Naval Forces, Vietnam; the 7th Air Force; the III Marine Amphibious Force (III MAF); and the largest of all, U.S. Army, Vietnam (USARV). Each of these component commands maintained its own separate logistical and administrative units.

The third commander of U.S. forces in Vietnam, Gen. Creighton W. Abrams, listens intently to a February 1969 briefing in his Saigon office.

Gen. Frederick Weyand, America's last MACV commander, attends a memorial service for the war dead in a Buddhist temple in Saigon in 1972.

The largest component command, USARV, presented particular organizational problems for MACV. In accordance with the thinking of the JCS, the head of MACV also commanded his own Army component. In practice, however, each COMUSMACV delegated day-to-day command of USARV to the deputy commander.

But this delegation of authority did not extend to army combat units. MACV chose to exercise direct control over these troops by the creation of subordinate field force commands independent of USARV. Each field force controlled operations in areas defined by South Vietnam's Corps Tactical Zones, which divided the country into four regions for the exercise of military command. Thus, I Field Force controlled all Army units operating in II Corps while II Field Force commanded those in III Corps and, with the introduction of American combat troops in the Mekong Delta area in 1967, also in IV Corps. In contrast, MACV exercised only indirect operational control over the Navy, Air Force, and Marine combat forces. For example, MACV's orders to individual Marine units were issued through the component command, III MAF.

Deputy commanders, the de facto commanders, of USARV, disagreed about the wisdom of this decision, which made USARV little more than an administrative and a logistical command. Lieutenant General Bruce Palmer, Jr., who served as deputy commander, USARV from 1967 to 1968, argued forcefully that field command of Army troops should have passed through USARV. His successor, Lieutenant General Frank T. Mildren, who served until mid-

1970, disagreed, believing that USARV's logistical and administrative responsibilities were so vast that it could not undertake any additional command responsibilities.

The advisory effort continued after it was absorbed by MACV in 1964, but it was drawn into the MACV chain of command. The commanders of the field forces became the corps' senior advisers, and army advisers served under their command. The advisory effort was responsible for the assignment and control of American military advisers attached to South Vietnamese units. It grew only slowly during the early years of the buildup of American troops but began to expand rapidly in late 1967 when American policy first began to reemphasize development of the South Vietnamese forces. From a total of less than 5,000 advisers in 1964, the advisory effort reached a peak of nearly 10,000 by 1969. With the development of President Richard Nixon's Vietnamization policy, the work of the advisers became one of MACV's highest priorities. Some of the most dedicated American servicemen—most of them volunteers—served as advisers during those years. Many of them had already served one or more tours of duty in Southeast Asia with regular American combat units and returned to share their knowledge and experience with their South Vietnamese counterparts.

In May 1967, MACV assumed control of another newly created component command, MACV-CORDS, or Civil Operations and Rural Development Support. CORDS pulled together the various civilian and military agencies working on the pacification effort into a single agency.

Military adviser Capt. Vernon Gillespie of the 5th Special Forces Group addresses Montagnard troops in 1964.

Civilian agencies were thus placed directly in the military chain of control, although each one, like each branch of the armed forces, still remained under the ultimate command of its Washington headquarters. To ensure that the new relationship worked smoothly, General Westmoreland and his successors, generals Creighton Abrams and Frederick Weyand, delegated most of their authority to the CORDS' civilian commanders.

Besides these component commands, MACV also controlled other smaller components of the U.S. effort in Vietnam. One of MACV's earliest commands was over the 5th Special Forces Group—the Green Berets—whose work with the South Vietnamese Civilian Irregular Defense Group predated the arrival of U.S. combat troops. The 5th Special Forces Group also joined the Air Force, Navy, and CIA in contributing personnel to the Studies and Observation Group, which conducted clandestine operations in Laos, Cambodia, and even North Vietnam.

In charge of such disparate elements, it is not surprising that MACV headquarters at Tan Son Nhut, on the outskirts of Saigon, took on the atmosphere of the corporate headquarters of a giant conglomerate directing its far-flung subsidiaries. And like a corporate headquarters, much of what MACV learned about the war came not from firsthand experience but from the flood of reports and data that its component commands sent to it. For while MACV was responsible for overall strategic planning, most tactical decisions were made at the divisional level or lower.

New technology only added to MACV's corporate style. It was perhaps inevitable that the availability of modern communications systems and data processing would create radical changes in the nature of a military headquarters. MACV could realistically request and reliably receive vast quantities of data on the performance of every American combat unit and many of the enemy's as well. More important, the most powerful computers of that era could process the information and make it available to the war's planners. For example, MACV fed every bit of information on the movement of enemy troops into its computers. The computers could then make "predictions" on the enemy's subsequent movement. The system worked perfectly except that the computers' predictions proved to be no more accurate than mere guesswork.

If the troops in the field looked upon such "advancements" in the art of warfare with little more than amusement, other developments at MACV headquarters left them bitter. MACV personnel enjoyed the use of tennis courts, golf courses, housing in expensive Saigon villas, even private bathrooms guarded by MPs to keep enlisted men out. These amenities created an atmosphere starkly at odds with the reality of warfare experienced by the average infantryman. Many servicemen, including field officers, complained loudly about the luxury of life at headquarters. Such complaints were not new to warfare, but MACV greatly expanded the gulf that separated life on the battlefield from that at headquarters.

Vietnam, it is said, represented a new type of warfare for the U.S. Armed Forces. It was therefore almost inevitable that it required the development of new concepts in command. Like much of what Americans tried in Vietnam, MACV achieved impressive successes as well as disappointing failures. The lessons learned from those experiences may, in fact, prove to be the most important product of those efforts.

Next to MACV itself, the U.S. Army, if only by its size, dominated the American presence in Vietnam, and the most forgotten soldiers of the Army were those who served in the support units directly subordinate to USARV. On the following pages the major support commands are described in an effort to present the wide range and importance of their activities.

The advisers. Left. Gen. James F. Hollingsworth (second from left), senior U.S. adviser in III Corps, confers with South Vietnamese officers during the counterattack after the NVA Easter offensive in April 1972. Below. A decade earlier Capt. Gerald Kilburn assists South Vietnamese forces in a battalion-size search for Vietcong guerrillas in the Mekong Delta.

U.S. Army Engineers

In 1965, when U.S. combat troops first landed in Vietnam, it was a country incapable of supporting American-styled military operations. Almost wholly lacking were airfields, paved roads, ports, pipelines, and, above all, bases to support operations. The men who provided these facilities for the Army were the U.S. Army Engineers. (Marine Corps engineers and Navy Seabees filled this need in I Corps.)

After a steady buildup, the engineers attained their final organizational form on December 1, 1966, with the establishment of the U.S. Army Engineer Command, Vietnam, a support command operating directly subordinate to USARV. The command consisted solely of the 18th Engineer Brigade until mid-1967 when the 20th Engineer Brigade joined it in the field. By early 1968 over 27,000 soldiers served in the engineer command, divided into the two brigades, six engineer groups, twelve construction battalions, and more than forty companies and detachments organized into combat battalions. In addition, each combat division controlled its own engineer combat battalion and each separate brigade an engineer company. In all, 5,000 army engineers served directly with divisions.

Engineers were divided into two main groups: construction engineers and combat engineers, with the vast majority serving in the former group. Construction engineers were primarily engaged in facilities construction, building the ports, airfields, and base camps required to house and support the U.S. Army in Vietnam. After mid-1968 they concentrated on building roads and bridges throughout the country. In addition, engineers built hospitals and schools and dug wells in their own civic action program.

Engineers were kept most busy building the base cantonments. Long before a U.S.-based division headed for Vietnam, engineers were busily constructing its new base camp. Starting with primitive tent cantonments that included no running water or electricity, these base camps were improved to include most of the amenities of stateside bases, including post exchange buildings. In some ways, the engineers' work may have been too good: MACV became concerned with the "homeyness" of many divisional headquarters that seemed in such contrast to the realities of war. So the Saigon command began to move divisions around to remind them that their stay was not permanent.

Combat engineers, as the name suggests, worked directly in support of tactical operations. Often preceding combat troops and thereby exposing themselves to constant danger, engineers hacked out landing zones, plowed roads, and cleared land to facilitate the movement of troops to operational zones. These tasks were the primary responsibility of divisional engineers, but the combat companies of the U.S. Engineer Command, Vietnam, were always available to provide extra manpower and support.

The contrast between "support" and "combat" troops in Vietnam was often misleading, seldom more so than with the engineers. Engineers were often engaged in road-clearing operations, any one of which could end in an enemy ambush. For example, in late November 1967, a platoon of combat engineers led by Sergeant John K. McDermott was ambushed near Kontum as the men attempted to make their way to Dak To during the heavy fighting for Hill 875. McDermott ordered a squad and a half to flee in their vehicles, while he and the remaining ten men attempted to hold off an estimated eighty Vietcong. Running low on ammunition, McDermott began a counterattack armed only with an ax. Fortunately, just at that moment, the platoon commander, First Lieutenant Ernest G. Bently, arrived with reinforcements. In the fighting, two of McDermott's men were killed and three more wounded.

During the Tet offensive, two months later, Army engineers took up arms throughout the country to defend their installations against enemy attacks. At Can Tho, twenty-nine men from the 69th Engineer Battalion joined a force making an air assault on the Vinh Long airfield, which was under heavy attack. They held their perimeter for ten hours without any casualties until the VC retreated.

Like most support commands, engineers continued their service in Vietnam until late in the Vietnamization process. Finally on April 30, 1972, the U.S. Army Engineer Command, Vietnam, was officially deactivated. A residual engineer force remained in Vietnam until 1973 under the command of the U.S. Army Engineer Group, Vietnam.

Members of Company B, 815th Engineer Battalion, begin laying the foundation for the warehouse of a logistical complex in Pleiku in April 1967.

Men of the 299th Engineer Battalion install a floating bridge to replace one damaged near Dak To in June 1969.

Above. A bridge constructed by the 70th Engineer Battalion in support of Operation MacArthur in late 1967 completes a section of Route 512 near Dak To. Below. Members of the 18th Engineer Brigade lay a culvert in support of the ARVN's invasion of Laos, Lam Son 719, in early 1971.

1st Logistical Command

No unit was more critical to the buildup of American forces in Vietnam than the 1st Logistical Command. Prior to 1965, the U.S. Army in Vietnam was supplied by the Army's Pacific Command through the small U.S. Army Support Group, Vietnam, which served under the 9th Logistical Command in Okinawa. With the deployment of division-sized units it quickly became apparent that the logistical effort required greater manpower and organization. As a result, the 1st Logistical Command, which had first been activated during the Korean War, was deployed from Fort Hood, Texas, and arrived in Saigon on April 1, 1965.

At that time, Vietnam possessed only two ports capable of supporting the ocean-going vessels that brought most American materiel to Vietnam: one in Da Nang that the U.S. Navy used to provide logistical support to the Marines in I Corps, the other in Saigon. Not wanting to absorb the capacity of the port of Saigon, which was needed to provide South Vietnam with most of its imported goods, USARV made the critical decision to build a major port at Cam Ranh Bay. Utilizing the DeLong pier, which operated by hydraulic lifting devices, Army engineers succeeded in completing the port at Cam Ranh in record time. Additional ports were soon constructed at Qui Nhon and a new one at Saigon, where the facility was named Newport. The results were astonishing. In mid-1965 the 1st Log Command, as it was commonly called, could process 70,000 tons of incoming materiel per month. One year later that figure had risen tenfold, to 700,000 tons a month, not counting critical items brought in by air.

An aerial view of the 506th Field Depot storage area at the Long Binh logistical complex on November 13, 1967.

The development of the ports played a large role in determining the organization of the 1st Logistical Command. Separate U.S. Army Support Commands were established in Saigon, Cam Ranh, Qui Nhon, and, in 1968, when Army units began to serve in I Corps, in Da Nang. Each support command operated independently in maintaining a flow of needed goods to the combat zones. The 1st Log maintained overall control and supervision through the Logistical Operations Control Center located at its Saigon headquarters.

That headquarters was originally located in a single villa, but as the command grew in size its activities were dispersed throughout the city, making coordination difficult. In late 1967, 1st Log moved its headquarters to the new compound at Long Binh, thirty kilometers northeast of Saigon, which became home for USARV. Long before that date, the 1st Log had become the largest single unit serving in Vietnam. By 1968 the number of men in the command had risen above 50,000.

The diversity of 1st Log activities was astounding. Under its command were truck units, boat companies, railroad facilities, and airlift and airdrop capabilities. Almost every piece of Army equipment sent to Vietnam was processed, transported, issued, and maintained by the 1st Log. Not only was the 1st Log responsible for providing the Army troops with the basic weapons of war, but it also clothed and fed them and supplied them with virtually every amenity available in Post Exchanges.

Many of the administrative functions of the 1st Log were accomplished through the aid of the era's most powerful computers, which attempted to keep track of the 700,000 tons of "imports" each month. But the size of the undertaking almost inevitably led to problems and abuses.

Among the major problems confronting the 1st Log Command was the responsibility for supervising a large civilian work force made up largely of Vietnamese citizens. While great care was taken to screen out security risks, inevitably mistakes were made, the extent of which may never be known. Some supplies intended for American and South Vietnamese troops wound up in enemy hands. In other cases the lure of high profits on the black market proved to be too much for hired civilian workers and even U.S. soldiers.

Equipment was also lost simply because the extent of the logistical effort precluded careful tracking of all materiel. This problem was further exacerbated during the Vietnamization process when the South Vietnamese proved less than able at mastering American managerial techniques.

Still, when it was finally redeployed to Fort Hood on December 7, 1970, the 1st Log could look back upon more than five years of distinguished service. Two of its number had won the Medal of Honor, and thousands of others had maintained the distinction of seeing the American Army the best supplied and best equipped in the world.

The 1st Log. Above left. *Members of the 1st Log Command at Qui Nhon secure a net of rations for helicopter delivery in 1965. Above right. PFC Billy Gibson of the 88th Service and Supply Command Support releases helicopter fuel into a* storage tank near Pleiku in early August 1967. Below. A *convoy of trucks from the 500th Transportation Group moves supplies overland during the same year.*

1st Signal Brigade

When the North Vietnamese plotted their Tet offensive of 1968 they made the destruction of South Vietnamese army units their first objective. But after two and one-half years of war against U.S. combat troops, they realized that to achieve their goal they would have to prevent the Americans from coming to the aid of the South Vietnamese. Virtually powerless to prevent reinforcement by helicopter, the enemy concluded—or hoped—that the Achilles' heel of the American effort was the complex communications system that made rapid response by U.S. troops possible. And so, when the Tet offensive erupted on January 31, 1968, signal installations became the most important American targets attacked by the Communists.

Joint Chiefs of Staff chairman General Earle Wheeler later called the offensive "a very near thing." If his assessment was correct, then the enemy got no closer because of the work of the 1st Signal Brigade. Although there were minor disruptions throughout Vietnam during the first weeks of the offensive, there were no serious communications failures. At Hue, for example, the communications system was knocked out for little more than thirty hours

The 1st Signal Brigade provided worldwide communications for the Army in Vietnam. Above. A Tropospheric Scatter Radio site near Da Nang connects Vietnam to the U.S. Strategic Communications network. Below. A communications van and antennas provide makeshift service in 1962.

after the power station was overrun by the NVA. During that period, critical communications were maintained through extemporized circuits. Members of the brigade worked round-the-clock to repair damaged circuits and wires, often while under attack. At Khe Sanh, Army Specialist William Hankinson kept circuits operating for forty hours until he was finally relieved. Of the six members of his team, two had been killed and three severely wounded by an NVA rocket attack.

The achievements at Tet were only one link in a chain of miracles performed by the 1st Signal Brigade. Although Army signal units had been in Vietnam since 1951 and by 1962 had established a sophisticated communications network in both Thailand and Vietnam, the 1st Signal Brigade did not arrive from Fort Gordon, Georgia, until April 1, 1966, serving as a command subordinate to USARV. Eventually growing to more than 20,000 men, it became the largest combat signal unit ever formed.

The brigade was divided into four groups. The 2d Signal Group provided communications for II and IV Corps, the 12th for I Corps, the 21st for III Corps, and the 160th Signal Group for the Saigon area. Additional signal units attached to each division and independent combat brigade provided communications within those units' Tactical Areas of Operations (TAORs). The 1st Signal Brigade was responsible for providing communications between the TAORs of combat units, between the four military zones in Vietnam, and between Vietnam and the rest of the world.

This latter function created unique command relationships for the 1st Signal Brigade. It not only served under the U.S. Army, Vietnam, but also independently as the command of the Vietnam combat theater in the Army's Strategic Communications Command, a part of the worldwide Defense Communications System. As part of this responsibility, the brigade maintained the interlocking communications network between Thailand and Vietnam that enabled those communications systems to tie into the Pentagon's worldwide network. In addition, the 1st Signal Brigade provided a hookup with the commercial telephone system within the United States.

The astonishing results provided unprecedented communications in wartime. To the annoyance of many generals, this system enabled the Pentagon, even the president, to communicate directly with virtually any commander in the field. But it also enabled a combat infantryman to learn of the birth of a son or daughter within minutes of the event and, if conditions permitted, even in the midst of a firefight.

When the 1st Signal Brigade departed Vietnam on November 7, 1972, it hoped that when peace finally came to South Vietnam the country would be blessed with one of the most sophisticated commercial communications networks in Southeast Asia. That these hopes were never realized does nothing to diminish the impressive tasks the brigade had performed in that country.

Above. *Men of the 362d Signal Company operate the main switchboard of a communications facility near Dalat in September 1969. Below. Men from Company B, 40th Signal Battalion, lay two cables simultaneously in a ditch near Cam Ranh Bay in January 1967.*

Above. *The 45th Surgical Hospital, a self-contained, transportable unit maintained by the 13th Medical Group, treats the wounded in Tay Ninh Province in late 1966. Below. The survivors of a helicopter crash receive treatment at the 93d Evacuation Hospital at Long Binh in April 1970.*

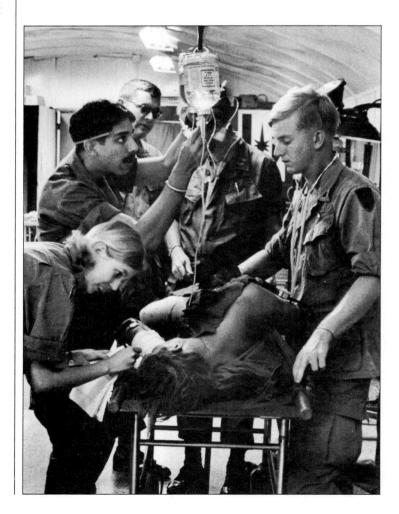

44th Medical Brigade

By any measure—casualty survival rates, disease rates, length of hospital stay—U.S. soldiers received better medical treatment in Vietnam than in any previous U.S. conflict, and the credit for this achievement belongs largely to the Army's medical service under the 44th Medical Brigade. Arriving in Vietnam in April 1966, the 44th eventually became a major subordinate command under USARV, bringing together the already large but disjointed medical effort. It had command and control responsibility for all Army medical support units not assigned to divisions or independent brigades.

From its headquarters at Long Binh, the 44th Medical Brigade commanded a vast network of personnel. At the beginning of 1967 it controlled 121 medical units and 7,830 men and women. These subordinate units operated either on a countrywide basis providing general medical support services or received assignment to a particular area of the country.

For area service, the 44th Brigade headquarters was the apex of a hierarchical system that provided direct medical support to battle casualties. Four medical groups were responsible for regions roughly equivalent to the military zones: the 43d and 55th in II Corps, the 67th in III Corps and later I Corps, and the 68th in III and IV Corps. By 1968 these four groups controlled four medical clearing battalions, six mobile army surgical hospital (MASH) units, eight field hospitals, ten evacuation hospitals, two surgical hospitals, a convalescent center, a POW hospital, and fourteen air ambulance and clearing companies.

These elements meshed to produce an efficient, effective medical service. On the front line, U.S. Army medics gave preliminary treatment to the wounded and called in helicopters. These air ambulances—nicknamed dustoffs for the call sign of one of the first medevac pilots—usually arrived in a matter of minutes and could pick up six to nine patients. Then they either carried the wounded to clearing stations, where they received short-term treatment or, with increasing frequency, flew them directly to the appropriate specialized hospital. This was accomplished by radio with the helicopter medic, the medical group regulating officer, and the brigade regulating officer, all coordinating to find the most suitable facility with the smallest surgical backlog. The inbound helicopter then informed the receiving hospital of its time of arrival, the nature of the casualties, and any special arrangements that would be needed.

Upon reaching a hospital, casualties had an excellent chance of living. Of all the wounded in Vietnam that reached Army medical facilities, 97.5 percent survived. Using ever-improving medical techniques against burns, shock, and head injuries, medical teams returned 40 percent of the wounded to active duty in Vietnam. Air Force hospital planes evacuated the more seriously wounded to hospitals in the United States, the Philippines, Okinawa, or Japan.

Along with caring for wounded and ill soldiers, personnel of the 44th Medical Brigade aided Vietnamese civilians, both formally in army programs and informally. Many Vietnamese injured during fighting received medical and surgical care at U.S. facilities.

The guerrilla nature of the war meant that almost anyone in the 44th could come under enemy attack. In 1968, for example, the Vietcong attacked the 3d Surgical Hospital at Dong Tam thirteen times. But the most vulnerable medical personnel were the dustoff crews who flew their unarmed helicopters into hostile areas during any and all weather. Two dustoff pilots, Major Patrick Brady and Chief Warrant Officer Michael J. Novosel, received Medals of Honor for their efforts at rescuing the wounded.

On March 1, 1970, the 44th Medical Brigade was officially deactivated and its subordinate units assigned to the U.S. Army Medical Command, Vietnam. Still, the advances in medical care made under the 44th Medical Brigade remained, not only in the thousands of lives it had saved in Vietnam but also in the innovations it brought back to the United States.

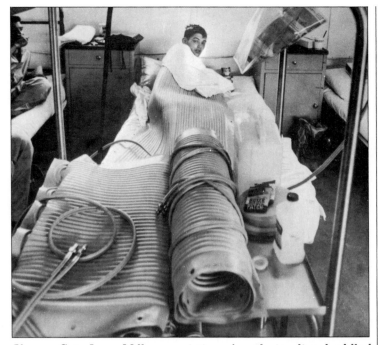

Above. *Sgt. Jerry Miller, a victim of malaria, lies huddled under a rubber blanket filled with water that can be cooled and heated to control his temperature at the Long Binh hospital in November 1967. Below. The survivors of a land mine are rushed to the same facility in April 1970.*

18th Military Police Brigade

The conflict in Vietnam modified the traditional roles of many U.S. units, combat and support alike, but it affected none more so than the Army's military police, the 18th Military Police Brigade. During the war the Army's MPs performed a greater range of duties than they had in any previous conflict, many going far beyond their normal law and order or traffic responsibilities. In a war without clearly defined fronts, the line between police work and infantry work blurred, and MPs often found themselves providing crucial combat support.

Although elements of the brigade were in Vietnam as early as 1962 when the 560th MP Company arrived, full military police groups and battalions were not organized until 1965 and 1966. The 18th Military Police Brigade itself was established in the United States in May 1966 and, after landing at Vung Tau in September, became a subordinate command of USARV, with its headquarters at Long Binh. It then took command of all army military police units in Vietnam. This included three Military Police Groups: the 8th, responsible for Army criminal investigations; the 16th, in charge of MP operations in I and II Corps; and the 89th,

A military policeman from the 173d Airborne Brigade gives water to a Vietcong prisoner while guarding others captured in November 1965.

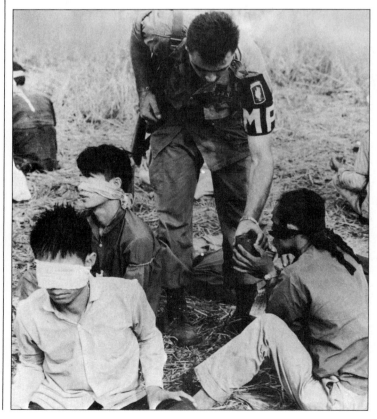

overseeing III and IV Corps. The brigade also included seven battalions and numerous assigned and attached units.

Its personnel enforced military law, orders, and regulations; controlled traffic and the travel of individuals; protected property; handled prisoners of war; and operated checkpoint and route security. A number of these police and traffic duties required ingenuity for they reflected specific conditions in Vietnam. For example, to inhibit Communist infiltration and resupply along South Vietnam's waterways, the brigade used a unique transportation company, the 458th, to patrol rivers and ports.

Similarly, when the sale and use of drugs became a major problem, especially following the Tet offensive, the brigade responded by establishing customs units and special drug suppression teams complete with narcotics-sniffing dogs. On the province level, narcotics squads joined forces with local South Vietnamese national police to patrol known areas of drug traffic and prostitution. In some provinces, such as Quang Tri, the success of the MPs caused a discernible economic recession in areas where the drug trade had flourished.

As part of their traffic responsibilities the MPs escorted convoys, a mission that in Vietnam became a major combat support duty. Because military trucks were vulnerable to ambush by guerrillas, the MPs escorted them with armored jeeps and commando cars. The escort teams frequently had to fight off small attacks and some larger battles developed, especially along the roads of the central highlands and west of Saigon.

The MPs used their normal infantry training as never before in Vietnam. In November 1967, the 18th Military Police Brigade received tactical responsibility for a forty-square-kilometer area surrounding the Long Binh post and Bien Hoa Air Base, the first time an MP unit was given such a large area of responsibility in a combat zone.

The military police assumed an even larger combat role as American combat units withdrew from Vietnam. When the 1st Infantry Division left Vietnam, the 300th MP Company took over its base camp at Di An. When the 3d Brigade, 82d Airborne Division, and then the 199th Light Infantry Brigade returned home, the 720th MP Battalion took charge at Phu Loi and Xuan Loc. Securing these areas was no small task. Sergeant Cal Strong noted at the time, "The 720th actually has 31,000 square miles of responsibility. That's a big load for any one battalion of men. Our B Company extends down into the Delta and there are no U.S. combat troops there at all."

The 18th Military Police Brigade kept its personnel in Vietnam longer than almost any other unit. Four of the brigade's battalions remained well into 1972. The brigade itself and its last battalion, the 716th, left South Vietnam on the last day of the U.S. troop withdrawal on March 29, 1973, and as one MP observed, most likely "only after checking the baggage of the others on the flight."

Above left. *MP Mike Griffin guards the entrance to a signal facility at Vung Chua Mountain in Binh Dinh Province in March 1972. Above right. An MP from the 615th MP Company, 18th MP Brigade, allows elements of the 11th Armored* Cavalry *to pass over a Saigon bridge during the attacks on the capital city in May 1968. Below. Men of the 516th MP battalion fire down Nguyen Binh Khien Street during the street fighting.*

The Limits of Air Power

No branch of the American military had a longer history in Vietnam than the United States Air Force. During World War II, U.S. Army Air Corps fighters and bombers lashed Japanese targets throughout French Indochina. After the war, USAF advisers, air crews, maintenance technicians, and supply experts assisted French forces in their doomed attempt to regain their colony and, following the creation of the Republic of Vietnam, took over the task of building the South Vietnamese Air Force (VNAF). Beginning in 1957, U.S. Air Force personnel constructed communications and radar facilities, upgraded airfields, and trained Vietnamese pilots in such American-supplied aircraft as the F-8 Bearcat, the A-1 Sky-raider, and the H-34 helicopter. But even as they labored to create a creditable deterrent to Communist aggression from the North, insurgency within South Vietnam drew the Americans back into combat in Southeast Asia.

John Kennedy entered the White House in January 1961, proclaiming his willingness to defend freedom

wherever it was threatened around the world. Determined to resist what he saw as a Soviet-inspired "war of national liberation" against South Vietnam, the new president ordered additional military assistance for the Saigon government. For the Air Force this meant the deployment of a detachment of the 507th Tactical Control Group to man a radar installation at Tan Son Nhut Air Base outside Saigon. Arriving in September 1961, the men of the 507th were quickly joined by elements of the 4400th Combat Crew Training Squadron—designated Farmgate—four RF-101 Voodoo reconnaissance aircraft, a squadron of sixteen C-123 assault transport planes, and a group of C-47 pilots known as the "Dirty Thirty" whose presence freed Vietnamese airmen for combat duties.

Together they comprised the 2d ADVON (Advanced Echelon) under the overall command of Brigadier General Rollen H. Anthis. By the summer of 1962, the USAF was carrying out transport, supply, and reconnaissance missions for the South Vietnamese army; training pilots; conducting defoliation flights; and operating a tactical air control system. In October, the 2d ADVON became the 2d Air Division.

At the same time, American pilots were assuming a much more direct role in the steadily expanding war. As early as December 1961, Secretary of Defense Robert S. McNamara had approved Farmgate combat missions provided a Vietnamese crewman rode along to maintain the facade of training. By the latter part of 1962, U.S. Air Force T-28 fighters and B-26 bombers were pounding Vietcong positions as part of a government drive into War Zone D north of Saigon. With the arrival of the 19th Tactical Air Support Squadron and the 1st Air Commando Squadron during the summer of 1963, the Americans began providing air support to ARVN offensives and embattled South Vietnamese outposts on a regular basis.

This commitment to battle stiffened South Vietnamese ground forces but also brought the Air Force a growing compendium of problems. There were disputes with the Army over control of U.S. aircraft in Vietnam and uncertainty over the effectiveness of air strikes, complaints about the limitations imposed by the Washington-mandated rules of engagement, and concerns over the frequency of civilian casualties. More serious were mounting losses of planes and pilots to enemy fire and worn-out parts. In March 1964, an exasperated Lieutenant General Joseph H. Moore proclaimed that "the 2d Air Division is practically flat out of business."

Indeed, as Communist military pressure on the Saigon government mounted during the latter part of 1963 and early 1964, the Air Force found itself pulled in two different directions. On the one hand, the steady expansion of VNAF air capabilities and Kennedy's reluctance to become more

---

Preceding page. Two B–52 Stratofortresses from Guam soar four miles above the sea toward South Vietnam's Iron Triangle, a VC stronghold west of Saigon, October 1965.

An F–105 Thunderchief takes off from Korat Air Base, Thailand, en route to a bombing mission over North Vietnam during the Rolling Thunder campaign, December 1966.

2d Air Division/7th Air Force*

Arrived Vietnam: October 8, 1962 *(2d Air Division)*   **Departed Vietnam:** March 29, 1973
*(Seventh Air Force superseded 2d Air Division
April 1, 1966)*

Unit Headquarters

Tan Son Nhut, South Vietnam   Oct. 1962–March 1973

Commanding Officers

Brig. Gen. Rollen H. Anthis *Oct. 1962*	Lt. Gen. Joseph H. Moore *Jan. 1964*	Gen. Lucius D. Clay, Jr. *Sep. 1970*
Brig. Gen. Robert R. Rowland *Dec. 1962*	Gen. William W. Momyer *July 1966*	Gen. John D. Lavelle *Aug. 1971*
Brig. Gen. Milton B. Adams *Dec. 1963*	Gen. George S. Brown *Aug. 1968*	Gen. John W. Vogt, Jr. *April 1972*

Major Subordinate Units

2d/13th Air Force (Udorn, Thailand)	56th Air Commando Wing (Special Ops. Wing	4258th Strategic Wing (307th SW in April '70)
7th/13th Air Force (Udorn, Thailand)	in Aug. '68)	6234th Tactical Fighter Wing (388th TFW in
Air Force Advisory Group	307th Strategic Wing	April '66)
834th Air Division	315th Tactical Airlift Wing (formerly 315th Air	6251st Tactical Fighter Wing
3d Tactical Fighter Wing	Commando Wing)	6252d Tactical Fighter Wing
8th Tactical Fighter Wing	355th Tactical Fighter Wing	3d Aero Rescue & Recovery Group
12th Tactical Fighter Wing	366th Tactical Fighter Wing	315th Troop Carrier Group (315th Air
14th Air Command Wing (14th Special Ops.	388th Tactical Fighter Wing	Commando G in March '65)
Wing in Aug. '68)	432d Tactical Reconnaissance Wing	504th Tactical Air Support Group
31st Tactical Fighter Wing	460th Tactical Reconnaissance Wing	505th Tactical Control Group
35th Tactical Fighter Wing	483d Tactical Airlift Wing	552d Airborne Early Warning Task Force
37th Tactical Fighter Wing	553d Reconnaissance Wing	1964th Communications Group
	633d Special Operations Wing	1974th Communications Group

1,737 KIA	3,457 WIA 941 MIA (2/85)	12 Medals of Honor

*Air operations were also conducted from Guam under control of the Strategic Air Command.

deeply involved in Southeast Asia produced steps toward disengagement. The first contingent of Air Force personnel left Vietnam at the end of 1963, and by March 1964, planning for the withdrawal of the 19th Tactical Air Support Squadron and the 1st Air Commando Squadron was completed. Two months later, Secretary McNamara ordered Air Force pilots to stop flying combat missions and to restrict their activity to training. At the same time, the growing infiltration of men and supplies down the Ho Chi Minh Trail persuaded Kennedy's successor, Lyndon Johnson, to consider bombing North Vietnam.

When North Vietnamese patrol boats and U.S. destroyers tangled in the Gulf of Tonkin in August 1964, Johnson ordered retaliatory air strikes carried out by the Navy and dispatched additional USAF aircraft to South Vietnam and Thailand. The only effect this show of force had on the Vietcong guerrillas who roamed the South Vietnamese countryside was to provoke a series of assaults on American installations, including a November 1 mortar attack on Bien Hoa airfield that left four Americans dead, five B-57 Canberras destroyed, and fifteen more heavily damaged.

Despite demands for a swift response from the Joint Chiefs of Staff, Johnson set up an interdepartmental working group under Assistant Secretary of State for Far Eastern Affairs William P. Bundy to review the president's options. The Bundy group rejected Air Force Chief of Staff General Curtis LeMay's call for massive air strikes, endorsing instead a program of tit for tat air reprisals against

the North that could be gradually escalated at a controlled rate. Two more enemy attacks against U.S. installations and the continued success of Vietcong military campaigns produced limited retaliatory air strikes in the North and a major policy decision. Convinced that Hanoi was "moving in for the kill," Johnson approved a program of "measured and limited air action against selected military targets in North Vietnam south of the nineteenth parallel." The operation was code-named Rolling Thunder.

Rolling Thunder

On March 2, 1965, twenty days after Johnson's approval, 104 Air Force fighter-bombers from airfields in South Vietnam and Thailand struck an ammunition depot at Xom Bang, sixty kilometers north of the DMZ. The coordinated assault virtually obliterated the target. But heavy enemy fire, compounded by confusion in the air, cost the Air Force six planes. Five of the pilots were rescued. The sixth, Lieutenant Hayden Lockhart, Jr., became the first USAF airman captured by the North Vietnamese.

Because of bad weather, the second Rolling Thunder mission did not take place until March 15. During the next two weeks, Air Force and Navy pilots divided their time between armed reconnaissance missions against transportation targets and the larger Alpha strikes against bridges and radar sites. Although successful, these sporadic assaults in the southern panhandle were frustrating to the military, which sought permission to attack more substantial targets farther north.

At the end of March the Joint Chiefs persuaded the president to authorize an expanded bombing program against North Vietnamese lines of communication (LOCs) as far north as the twentieth parallel. Beginning on April 3 with a thunderous strike against the Thanh Hoa railroad and highway bridge known as the Dragon's Jaw, the month-long "LOC-cut" campaign sent waves of American fighter-bombers against transportation targets in the southern half of North Vietnam. Although the Dragon's Jaw withstood the Air Force, by early May twenty-six other bridges; seven ferries; and hundreds of trucks, locomotives, and boxcars had been destroyed.

After a five-day bombing pause in mid-May, during which American diplomats tried in vain to establish contact with the North Vietnamese, Rolling Thunder resumed in earnest. To minimize confusion between Air Force and Navy carrier aircraft, North Vietnam was divided into six major "route packages," with longer-range USAF fighters generally assigned to inland targets while shorter-range Navy aircraft operated near the coast. The primary tactical strike aircraft employed by the Air Force during Rolling Thunder operations was the F-105 Thunderchief. Nicknamed the "Thud," the F-105 was fast and versatile—capable of carrying more than six tons of ordnance, extra fuel, or electronic gear. The F-4 Phantom was initially used to provide cover for strike aircraft but also was employed as an attack bomber. Used less frequently over North

---

Smoke billows from the remains of a North Vietnamese POL storage site following an attack by U.S. tactical fighter-bombers in March 1967.

Vietnam were the F-100 Supersabre, the F-104 Starfighter, and the B-57 Canberra light bomber. B-52 Stratofortresses appeared over North Vietnam for the first time in April 1966. To ensure their safety from the North's dangerous SA-2 missile sites, the high-altitude strategic bombers rarely flew against targets in North Vietnam.

Throughout the remainder of 1965, additional USAF squadrons—their three-month temporary duty assignments soon to become permanent—arrived in Indochina. By year's end the Air Force had more than 500 aircraft and 21,000 men at eight major air bases in South Vietnam, plus more men and machines in Thailand. The continuing buildup eventually required a larger organizational framework, and in April 1966, the 2d Air Division was replaced by the 7th Air Force. Operating out of Tan Son Nhut, the 7th (along with its component 7/13th Air Force based at Udorn, Thailand) directed tactical air operations in Southeast Asia, while the USAF's Strategic Air Command retained control of its B-52 bombers, aerial refueling tankers, and long-range reconnaissance jets.

Matching the somewhat fragmented nature of these command arrangements was the uneven progress of the air war against the North. The pace of bombing increased steadily—from 1,500 Air Force and Navy sorties in April 1965, to almost 4,000 in September before the northeast monsoon restricted flying—but not the overall dimensions of the campaign. Some new fixed targets were added to the list, and the area available for armed reconnaissance flights was cautiously enlarged. Few sorties were made into the key northeast quadrant near the Chinese border, however, and none into the restricted zone surrounding Hanoi and Haiphong. With the ground war in South Vietnam growing more ferocious with each passing month, the Joint Chiefs pressed for an intensification of raids against the North, arguing that the limitation of targets made it impossible for American air power to halt the flow of men and equipment south. In April 1966, Johnson partially lifted the geographic restrictions and in June finally approved a full-scale assault on North Vietnam's vital petroleum, oil, and lubricant (POL) depots.

On the morning of June 29 the POL campaign got under way. Twenty-four F-105s, each carrying eight 750-pound bombs, struggled into the air and headed toward a giant thirty-two-tank POL farm on the northern outskirts of the North Vietnamese capital. Assigned the task of testing Hanoi's air defense system for the first time were the pilots of the Thailand-based 355th and 388th Tactical Fighter Wings. After in-flight refueling from orbiting KC-135 tankers, the fighter-bombers roared across the North Vietnamese countryside at 300 feet—the eight planes from the 388th striking first from the south, the larger contingent from the 355th skirting the end of a promontory that came to be called Thud Ridge and attacking from the north. Within minutes enormous columns of thick black smoke fueled by boiling red flames towered 35,000 feet into the air.

Along with Navy pilots who simultaneously hit sites near Haiphong, the opening raid of the new campaign destroyed an estimated 60 percent of North Vietnam's POL supplies with the loss of only a single aircraft. Encouraged by the results, Washington gave the go-ahead for a full-scale effort. While additional strikes were made against the remaining fixed POL sites, Air Force planes blasted rail lines north of Hanoi linking the capital to China, then launched a separate campaign against infiltration routes and targets within fifty kilometers of the DMZ. Before its termination in September, the new U.S. air offensive reached a rate of 12,000 sorties a month, more than four times the rate of activity at the beginning of the year.

The air campaign against North Vietnam continued to escalate in 1967. Unprecedented resupply activity by the Communists during Washington's third bombing pause in February induced Johnson to turn up the pressure, including aerial mine-laying operations in North Vietnamese river estuaries south of the twentieth parallel and strikes against manufacturing targets near Hanoi and Haiphong. On March 10 and 11, Air Force fighter-bombers hit the sprawling Thai Nguyen steel and chemical plant sixty kilometers north of Hanoi and the Canal Des Rapides railway and highway bridge just seven kilometers from the capital. Over the next eight weeks, USAF aircraft struck thermal power plants, ammunition dumps, cement factories, and airfields—all within the Hanoi-Haiphong restricted zone. In July, Johnson expanded the air offensive even further. The revised Rolling Thunder target list opened up nearly forty new bridges, by-passes, rail yards, and military storage areas, including the crucial Paul Doumer railway and highway bridge struck for the first time by Air Force warplanes on August 2.

Spans of the Paul Doumer Bridge, an important railway entrance into Hanoi, lie crumpled in the Red River in May 1968, ten months after the first strikes against it.

During the fall, F-105 Thunderchiefs hit virtually every military, industrial, and transportation target within sixteen kilometers of Hanoi in a concentrated effort to isolate the capital. By year's end, American air power had dropped 864,000 tons of bombs on North Vietnam since 1965, severely damaging much of that country's industrial and transportation network, taking a heavy toll of ammunition and petroleum supplies, and diverting several hundred thousand of its people and millions of dollars to repairing the damage and fighting off the aerial invaders. If Rolling Thunder garnered the largest share of public and official attention back home, however, it was only a part of the Air Force mission in Southeast Asia.

Battlefield Indochina

With the outbreak of the war in 1959, North Vietnam began transforming the eastern half of neutral Laos into a vast infiltration corridor to the southern battlefields. At the same time, Hanoi increased its support of the Communist Pathet Lao. The United States, in turn, provided arms and ammunition to the Laotian government, mounted covert CIA paramilitary operations throughout the country, and dispatched advisers to assist the Royal Laotian armed forces. Among those advisers was a contingent of USAF special air warfare commandos who secretly instructed Laotian pilots at Udorn Air Base in Thailand.

Neither the Laotians, however, nor Thai mercenaries operating under CIA and USAF control, were able to halt

the North Vietnamese, and by December 1964, President Johnson had approved a limited American bombing operation code-named Barrel Roll. Designed to harass Pathet Lao and North Vietnamese forces challenging loyalist units in the northeastern section of the country, Barrel Roll had little impact on the war in South Vietnam. Thus, in March 1965, Washington authorized a second air campaign—designated Steel Tiger—to strike Communist infiltration routes in the southern Laotian panhandle.

By day, F-100s and F-105s blasted bridges, fords, and roads while other Thunderchiefs stood on "strip alert" at one of several Thai air bases waiting for targets of opportunity. By night, B-57 bombers and AC-130 flareships, sometimes directed by South Vietnamese ground reconnaissance teams, conducted armed reconnaissance missions looking for trucks and troops moving down the trail. Despite poor weather, Steel Tiger was soon averaging more than 1,000 sorties a month. But with the coming of the dry season at the end of the year, even this was not enough to cope with the increased rate of enemy infiltration.

The answer was Tiger Hound, a systematic air campaign against highways, truck parks, bridges, buildings, and antiaircraft artillery using Navy, Army, and Marine aircraft to augment the Air Force. The multifaceted operation included RF-101C and RF-4C reconnaissance jets equipped with infrared and side-looking radar, prop-driven O-1 Birddogs, and A-1E Skyraiders piloted by forward air controllers, eight modified World War II-vintage B-26 Invaders flown by the 609th Air Commando

Squadron out of Nakhon Phanom, Thailand, F-100 and F-105 fighter-bombers, B-57 bombers, UC-123 defoliation airplanes, AC-47 gunships, and C-130 flareships, all directed by airborne command and control aircraft. On December 11, 1965, B-52 bombers hit the Mu Gia Pass, the first of many B-52 strikes over Laos.

From January to May 1966, Tiger Hound attacks destroyed some 3,000 structures, 1,400 trucks, dozens of bridges, and more than 200 automatic weapon and anti-aircraft positions. The pace of operations dropped with the coming of the rainy season but gathered momentum again at the beginning of the new year. During the first four months of 1967, American pilots flew an average of 3,100 strike sorties a month in the Laotian panhandle, and by the end of the year the Air Force counted 1,718 B-52 sorties alone. Adding new weapons to its arsenal in Laos, such as the AC-119 gunship and a pair of specially equipped C-123s armed with BLU bomblet canisters, the Air Force kept constant and growing pressure on the major artery of Communist military infiltration.

Those North Vietnamese soldiers who survived the gauntlet of fire found the skies no more friendly at their destinations than they had during their journey. In March 1965, along with giving the go-ahead for the bombing of North Vietnam and stepped-up air operations in Laos,

President Johnson had lifted all restrictions on the use of U.S. aircraft for combat in South Vietnam. Over the next ten months men and planes poured into the country. To accommodate them, the U.S. constructed new airfields and made major improvements to existing facilities.

The machines that waged the in-country war included devastating modern aircraft, including the supersonic F-4 Phantom, which the Vietcong called "whispering death." Yet for sheer effectiveness, nothing could match the propellor-driven A-1 Skyraiders flown by the 1st and 602d Air Commando Squadrons. These rugged and reliable aircraft armed with four 20mm cannons and carrying bomb loads up to 8,000 pounds were capable of remaining on station far longer than the jets and proved virtually impervious to small-arms fire. The Skyraiders were particularly well suited to the frequent close air support missions that provided troops on the ground with the firepower needed to advance against entrenched enemy positions or to extricate themselves from ambushes. The greatest number of combat air operations in the South, however, were preplanned strikes against guerrilla strongholds and supply routes. As the war went on, aerial defoliation missions—code-named Operation Ranch Hand and conducted by C-123s spraying herbicides such as Agent Orange—increased dramatically. So, too, did the devastating Arc Light strikes conducted by the B-52 Stratofortresses of the 2d and 320th Bombardment Wings based at Anderson Air Force Base on Guam.

During 1965 this formidable arsenal was frequently the difference between survival and defeat. In June, Air Force Skyraiders, B-57s, and F-100s flew over 600 sorties in defense of the besieged Special Forces camp at Dong Xoai, 140 kilometers north of Saigon. When the Communists launched a similar attack against the Plei Me Special Forces camp in October, USAF pilots dropped more than 1.5 million pounds of bombs on the attackers. The battle for Plei Me turned out to be merely the prelude to a larger VC operation in the Ia Drang Valley in November, forestalled by the Army's 1st Cavalry Division (Airmobile) and by a massive air assault, including USAF fighter-bombers, flare ships, and B-52s employed for the first time in direct support of ground troops.

As MACV sought to take the war to the enemy in 1966, the Air Force increased its fighting capacity in South Vietnam. By the end of the year, there were twenty-eight tactical fighter squadrons in country that could mount as many as 300 preplanned interdiction and combat sorties a day, or, if necessary, be diverted to air support for ground troops. Another forty aircraft remained available as the first response to emergency calls for close air support of engaged troops. Improvements in forward air controller reconnaissance tactics and the routine employment of USAF fixed-wing gunships for night hamlet defense increased the effectiveness of American air power, as did the introduction of the Combat Skyspot bombing system,

which enabled ground radar controllers to direct B-52s to their targets even during bad weather.

In the major battles of 1967, the reliance of U.S. and South Vietnamese ground troops on American air power became greater than ever. During Operations Cedar Falls and Junction City at the beginning of the year, the Air Force flew over 6,000 sorties, including nearly 230 by B-52s. In addition, USAF pilots ferried thousands of soldiers into action—including flying the only U.S. combat parachute assault of the Vietnam War—and airlifted tens of thousands of tons of supplies to the men in the field. Moreover, the vast majority of enemy deaths during these two operations were the result of air strikes, a fact gratefully acknowledged by the commander of the Army's 1st Infantry Division: "We find the enemy, we fix the enemy, air destroys the enemy." That same pattern brought victory in November when allied forces, backed by more than 2,400 tactical and B-52 strikes, left 1,600 enemy dead at the battle of Dak To.

The limitations of air power

Air Force pride at the outcome of Dak To was tempered by the accidental bombing of an American position during the battle and by growing questions over the effectiveness of air operations in bringing the war to an end. For all the statistical success the Air Force claimed—for all the bridges brought down and trucks destroyed, for all the sorties flown and bomb tonnages dropped—after nearly three years of war it was becoming clear that there were obvious limitations to what the Air Force could accomplish in both North and South Vietnam. Some of those limitations were of nature's making: mountainous terrain, triple-canopy jungle, and thick monsoon weather that made flying a risky business for months at a time. But most of the problems encountered by the Air Force in Southeast Asia were manmade, beginning with those the Americans brought with them.

First of all, the U.S. military was trying with only partial success to adapt aircraft designed primarily for strategic nuclear warfare to the vastly different demands of a limited political conflict. Unwilling to expose expensive B-52s to North Vietnamese defenses, for example, the Pentagon used many of the strategic bombers for close air support in the South, albeit successfully. Meanwhile, tactical fighter-bomber pilots trained to support ground troops had to relearn how to drop their bombs on "hard" targets—buildings, bridges, rail lines—in the North. This general problem was compounded by the sensitivity of Washington to real or imagined political liabilities in Peking and Moscow, the tight rein the White House kept on the bombing campaigns, and the enormously complicated chains of command that resulted. Even worse, from the pilots' point of view, were the "prohibited zones" and restrictive rules of engagement that diminished the effectiveness and some-

The Long Blue Line

At the height of the Vietnam War more than 61,000 U.S. Air Force personnel called Southeast Asia their temporary home. Only a small percentage, however, were directly involved with combat operations. The vast majority played supporting roles and took on dozens of jobs essential to the maintenance and defense of America's air armada: building the runways and hangars, staffing the mess halls and control towers, servicing the sophisticated aircraft and exotic arsenals, or rescuing a downed flier in enemy territory. Behind the men whose feats garnered the lion's share of public attention was a long line of Air Force blue that stretched back to the United States.

The bombs dropped over Southeast Asia began their journey at Hill Air Force Base in Utah, where ordnance was stockpiled for the war. From there, it was shipped to the Philippines and finally to major airfields throughout the war zone. At U-Tapao, Thailand, for example, munitions experts from the 635th Munitions Maintenance Squadron assembled the component parts, then turned them over to the crews of the 4258th Squadron, who loaded the deadly cargo—an average of 3,000 bombs per day—into the base's thirty B-52s. Before any bombs were loaded, however, each plane was meticulously checked by aircraft crews working around the clock to ensure that aircraft flew trouble-free. As one crew chief noted, "We take care of them just as if they were the airplane taking us home."

The parts they needed were delivered by the Military Airlift Command (MAC), which maintained a continuous flow of personnel and supplies from the U.S. to Southeast Asia. In addition, the MAC flew thousands of tactical sorties to move equipment and troops within the war zone. First relying on C-124 Globemasters and C-133 Cargomasters, the Air Force later introduced the larger and more powerful C-141 Starlifter and C-5 Galaxy. Responsibility for tactical airlifts within South Vietnam belonged to the 834th Air Division, which by 1968 comprised some 7,500 men and 250 aircraft. Transport crews often flew dangerous missions under enemy fire, delivering supplies and picking up wounded at remote outposts.

To do so they had to dodge a bewildering variety of U.S. aircraft that flooded the skies over Southeast Asia. Reconnaissance jets, electronic countermeasures aircraft, and airborne command posts all provided crucial support for combat missions. Giant KC-135 Stratotankers served as flying gas stations for combat aircraft, pumping up to 1,000 gallons of fuel per minute into the thirsty planes. Often coming to the aid of aircraft critically low on fuel and in danger of crashing, KC-135 crews drew the appreciation and respect of combat pilots throughout the force.

With more than 53,000 air traffic movements in South Vietnam every day—takeoffs, landings, and major flight pattern changes—air traffic control was critical. At the two major air traffic control centers in Tan Son Nhut and Da Nang, as well as in smaller centers throughout the country, the 1964th Communications Group helped maintain order in the crowded skies over South Vietnam while the Thai-based 1974th Communications Group monitored air missions throughout Thailand, Laos, and North Vietnam. Monitoring their ground-controlled approach (GCA) or radar approach control (RAPCON) units, controllers worked grueling hours providing crucial flight information to pilots, often talking pilots down to safe landings in dangerous weather conditions. If a plane went down, controllers were responsible for pinpointing the area for rescue teams. In 1968 alone, controllers were credited with saving the lives of 660 crewmen and passengers.

Once a plane went down, it was the job of the USAF's 3d Aerospace Rescue and Recovery Group to coordinate search-and-rescue (SAR) missions. Stationed at bases throughout South Vietnam and Thailand, elements of the 3d ARRG initially relied on the enormous HH-3 Jolly Green Giant rescue helicopters. In 1967 the larger and more powerful HH-53 Super Jolly Green Giants were introduced.

Together with a squadron of A-1 Skyraiders stationed in Thailand, SAR helicopter crews staged thousands of rescue missions not only in South Vietnam but also deep in Laos and North Vietnam, in some cases risking their lives to snatch downed airmen from within miles of Hanoi. Many rescue operations were completed in less than an hour; others lasted two or three days. Throughout the course of the war SAR missions brought back 80 percent of all U.S. aviators shot down over North Vietnam and Laos who successfully ejected from their aircraft and contacted friendly forces with their survival radios. In all, between 1964 and 1973 search-and-rescue crews were credited with saving the lives of 3,883 men—nearly half of them U.S. airmen.

Like aircraft mechanics and tanker pilots, transport crews and ordnance specialists, search-and-recue was a vital part of the Air Force mission in Southeast Asia. Although American combat pilots received most of the public credit, without the support from thousands of USAF personnel behind the scenes, they would never have gotten their birds off the ground.

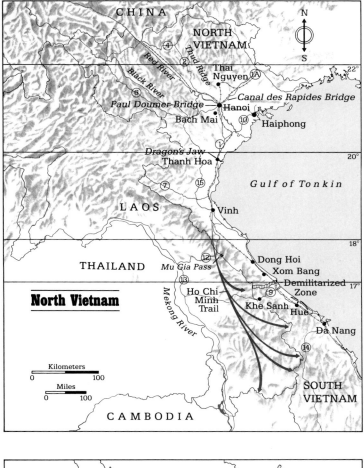

North Vietnam

U.S. Air Force Bases

times increased the danger of their missions. As the war went on a host of other problems dogged the fliers, including equipment and ammunition deficiencies, mismatched ordnance, pilot shortages, and interservice rivalries.

The biggest problem, however, was the enemy. In the South the Vietcong fought air power with camouflage, underground storage areas, dispersal of troops, an efficient early warning system, and, after their first brushes with American firepower, a strategy that avoided major engagements. Many of the same techniques were used by the enemy north of the DMZ. To minimize the impact of U.S. air superiority, Hanoi ordered factories taken apart and reestablished away from urban centers, sometimes underground; petroleum stores distributed around the country; truck convoys divided into small groups that traveled at night along unmarked roads; camouflaged way stations; and sunken concrete bridges difficult to make out from the air. To repair the damage done by the constant air strikes, North Vietnam mobilized an army of civilian workers armed with picks and shovels who rebuilt bridges and reconstructed roads almost as fast as the airmen could destroy them. And to make America pay a heavy price for its air offensive, the North Vietnamese covered their country with one of the most sophisticated air defense systems the world had ever seen.

That system, provided nearly in its entirety by the Soviets, was divided into three parts. The most important was an array of antiaircraft guns, from 37MM and 57MM able to fire up to 18,000 feet in the air to long-range 85MM and 100MM radar-directed guns capable of shooting down an aircraft at altitudes up to 45,000 feet. Starting with less than 1,500 at the beginning of 1965, a year later there were more than 5,000, and the numbers kept climbing. Less troublesome at first were the fifty-three Korean War-vintage MiG-15s and 17s that constituted the North Vietnamese Air Force. The addition of more advanced MiG-21s carrying infrared-homing air-to-air missiles in mid-1966, and the penetration of American aircraft into the Hanoi area in early 1967, precipitated an escalating series of aerial battles and the loss of several dozen U.S. aircraft before the remaining enemy planes were driven over the border into China. Long before that, American airmen had to contend with Russian-built SA-2 surface-to-air missiles (SAMs) that could blast a plane out of the sky 60,000 feet above the earth. Like the MiGs, these "flying telephone poles" were dangerous less on their own account than because the measures necessary to avoid them—that is, flying at low altitudes—made American pilots more vulnerable to enemy aircraft and AAA fire. Indeed, this multiplicity of threats forced such wide-ranging countermeasures—fighter escorts, orbiting electronic reconnaissance aircraft, early warning radar planes, and special "Wild Weasel" SAM-suppression aircraft among others—that the cost of air operations over North Vietnam rose out of all proportion to the damage being inflicted.

Serious doubts about the bombing campaign first surfaced in the wake of the 1966 POL campaign. Despite the almost total destruction of North Vietnam's centralized petroleum storage facilities, there was no evidence of shortages because back-up POL sites had been scattered around the country. In fact, concluded an independent panel of civilian scientists commissioned by Defense Secretary McNamara, Rolling Thunder operations in general had "had no measurable direct effect" on Hanoi's ability to support the war "nor shaken her resolve to do so." Five months later the CIA reported that the cost of the air war had risen from $460 million in 1965 to $1.2 billion in 1966 without a corresponding increase in results. Where it had once cost $6.60 to inflict a dollar's worth of damage on North Vietnam, it now cost $9.60. Moreover, noted the intelligence agency, there was no evidence that the bombing had materially reduced the flow of men and supplies to the South. As many as 80 percent of the infiltrators got through, and those who did fail to complete the journey were more often victims of accident and disease than of American bombs.

Once a staunch advocate of air power, McNamara became convinced that the bombing campaign against the North had failed to deflect Hanoi from its course. In May 1967 he submitted to the president a plan for a de-escalation of the air war. Military leaders, outraged at McNamara's defection, argued heatedly during hearings before the Senate Armed Services Committee in August that the bombing had reduced infiltration, pointing to the marked increase in traffic down the Ho Chi Minh Trail during periodic bombing pauses. If the air campaign had fallen short of its goals, they asserted, it was because of a needlessly restrictive bombing strategy controlled by Washington. Lift the prohibition on targets within the Hanoi and Haiphong prohibited zones, they said, cease civilian meddling in operational matters, and air power could be a decisive factor in ending the war. Even as the argument raged in Washington, however, Hanoi was busy with its own plans for ending the war.

Turning point

During the first weeks of 1968 two full North Vietnamese divisions—some 20,000 men—maneuvered into position around the small Marine combat base of Khe Sanh at the western end of the DMZ. On the morning of January 21 a ferocious barrage of enemy mortars, rockets, and artillery shells slammed into the base. The attack signaled the beginning of a siege that would last seventy-seven days and afford the Air Force an opportunity to display what unhampered air power could achieve.

Left. *An Air Force RF–4C Phantom on a reconnaissance mission twelve kilometers south of Dong Hoi avoids tracers fired from North Vietnamese antiaircraft guns, July 1966.*

With enemy artillery making landing risky, an Air Force C–130 transport plane parachutes supplies to the besieged Marine outpost at Khe Sanh in March 1968.

Two key elements to the survival of the base were Marine cargo helicopters and the planes of the 834th Air Wing. Battling low cloud ceilings, heavy air traffic, and enemy artillery zeroed in on Khe Sanh's single runway, C-130s ran the gauntlet a dozen times a day. When the risk to the giant transports became too great, smaller C-123K Providers and C-7A Caribous took over the dangerous landings while the C-130s shifted to parachute drops and experimental low-level delivery systems. By the end of the siege, this aerial life line had delivered a staggering 15,000 tons of supplies to Khe Sanh's defenders.

While the Marines hung on, the North Vietnamese endured constant bombardment from hundreds of USAF and Marine aircraft in an unprecedented air offensive code-named Operation Niagara. On an average day 450 tactical fighters, B-52s, reconnaissance jets, and FACs jockeyed for space under the direction of ground-based radar, USAF Combat Skyspot aerial radar ships, and C-130 airborne command control centers. At night, AC-47 gunships blasted enemy positions with their batteries of miniguns. Given the responsibility for coordinating this flying armada, 7th Air Force commander General William W. "Spike" Momyer requested complete authority over all available air assets. The "single air manager" concept had been hotly debated in the past and continued to be resisted by the Marines. When Westmoreland insisted, however, the Joint Chiefs endorsed the plan, and for the first time in the war all American air operations were placed under a single centralized control.

Throughout the siege, a torrent of destruction cascaded

from the bomb bays of American B-52s. A "cell" of three Stratofortresses from bases in Guam, Okinawa, or U Tapao, Thailand, arrived over the battlefield every ninety minutes. They concentrated initially on enemy staging, assembly, and storage areas in the outlying hills, each cell hammering a target "box" two kilometers square. When the North Vietnamese moved their bunkers and trenches close to the base, the bombers executed precision strikes within 1,000 meters of Marine positions. The 60,000 tons of high explosives delivered by the B-52s reduced the jungle around Khe Sanh to a blasted desert of splintered trees and monstrous craters. The effect of the Arc Light strikes on the enemy could be even more shattering: one deserter reported that three-quarters of an entire regiment had been wiped out in a single raid. Although there was good reason to question the accuracy of MACV's enemy casualty reports—official estimates ranged from 9,800 to 13,000 KIA—General Westmoreland, for one, had no doubt Khe Sanh had cost the North Vietnamese dearly. "Without question, the amount of firepower put on that piece of real estate exceeded anything that had ever been seen before in history by any foe. The enemy was hurt," declared the American commander, "and the thing that broke his back was the fire of the B-52s."

The level of air power maintained in support of the Marines was all the more remarkable in light of the demands placed upon the 7th Air Force by the stunning enemy offensive that erupted across South Vietnam nine days after the siege of Khe Sanh began, the storied Tet offensive. Under the cover of the new year holiday, the Communists launched attacks against thirty-six provincial capitals, five major cities, twenty-three airfields, and numerous district capitals, gaining sufficient footholds in several places that ground troops alone could not dislodge them. In Saigon and Hue, the Air Force used high explosives and napalm to drive the Communists from their entrenched positions. Outside the cities, air crews pounded enemy storage areas and troop concentrations without letup, keeping reinforcements from entering urban areas while providing continuous close air support for units engaged with Vietcong and NVA forces.

At each point of attack the Communists were thrown back with heavy casualties. Nonetheless, the ferocity of the Tet offensive, the level of destruction and loss of civilian life provoked public outcry among Americans back home. When the Joint Chiefs of Staff recommended the deployment of 200,000 more troops and an escalation of the bombing campaign against the North, a chorus of dissent that included former hawks within the administration persuaded the president to alter course.

On March 21 Johnson announced a halt to the bombing of North Vietnam above the twentieth parallel. Declaring he would not run for reelection, he called upon Hanoi to enter into negotiations to end the war. To the surprise of many, the Communists agreed to talk, and preliminary discussions began immediately. During the summer, while the Air Force intensified its interdiction strikes in the area immediately north of the DMZ, American and North Vietnamese representatives reached agreement on the details of the proposed peace conference. On October 31, the president ordered the end of all air, naval, and artillery bombardment of North Vietnam. Four days later Richard Nixon was elected president, inheriting the burden of U.S. policy in Vietnam.

Nixon arrived at the White House with a public mandate for ending the war and a "secret plan" to do so. First, he would accelerate the Vietnamization of the war, turning the fighting over to the South Vietnamese, in conjunction with a steady withdrawal of American troops. Second, he would place renewed emphasis on a negotiated settlement, playing upon Sino-Soviet rivalries and Moscow's desire for detente with the West. Finally, he would increase military pressure against Hanoi to convince the North Vietnamese of U.S. resolve. Because of domestic pressures for a rapid disengagement of American ground forces, Nixon turned to air power, and particularly the U.S. Air Force, as his primary weapon.

Unwilling for political reasons to resume the bombing of North Vietnam, Nixon adopted instead a plan put forward by the new MACV commander, General Creighton W. Abrams, for a short duration, concentrated B-52 raid on the suspected site of the Communist military headquarters for South Vietnam (COSVN), just across the border in Cambodia. When Communist forces launched a nationwide offensive in late February 1969, Nixon gave the Air Force the go-ahead. Over the next fourteen months, B-52s flew 4,308 sorties, dropping 120,000 tons of bombs on the Cambodian border region in a series of highly secret missions called Lunch, Dinner, Snack, Supper, and Dessert and known collectively as Operation Menu.

Despite the bombing, the Communist presence in Cambodia steadily expanded, leading to the overthrow of the neutralist Sihanouk government by more conservative forces in March 1970. To forestall a military collapse of the new, pro-Western regime, Nixon approved stepped-up air raids code-named Operation Patio and authorized a full-scale invasion across the border. During the two-month "incursion," the Air Force mounted numerous tactical sorties and hundreds of B-52 strikes in support of the ground forces, plus twenty-one operations, collectively known as Commando Vault, during which crewmen rolled 15,000-pound bombs out the rear cargo doors of C-130s to obliterate enemy positions or to create helicopter landing zones in the dense jungle.

After the withdrawal of American troops from Cambodia in late June, Air Force tactical air strikes code-named Operation Freedom Deal continued to pound supply lines along the border, then crossed the Mekong River to provide close air support for Cambodian army troops fighting the North Vietnamese and their Khmer Rouge allies. In all, between July 1970 and February 1971, the 7th Air Force flew 8,000 sorties in Cambodia, a full 15 percent of all American combat sorties flown in Southeast Asia.

In Laos, too, the first years of the Nixon administration saw a marked intensification of air activity, in part because of the president's determination to show Hanoi he meant business, in part because of the end of bombing missions over neighboring North Vietnam. The suspension of Rolling Thunder operations led to an immediate increase in the rate of infiltration down the Ho Chi Minh Trail. It also left hundreds of U.S. aircraft "sitting around with nothing to do," as one official put it. When U.S. air commanders pushed for a stepped-up interdiction campaign in Laos, they found a willing ear at the White House.

The Commando Hunt operations that began in November 1968 put Marine, Navy, and Air Force planes into the skies over Laos in unprecedented numbers. By October 1969, American aircraft were flying 400 sorties a day in Laos compared with 300 per day over North Vietnam at the height of Rolling Thunder. Bomb damage assessment statistics rose accordingly. The Air Force claimed 12,368 trucks destroyed during 1970, an increase of nearly 70 percent over 1968, and while both pilots and Congressional critics expressed skepticism at these figures, some experts estimated that no more than a third of the supplies that entered the Ho Chi Minh Trail ever reached South Vietnam. Unfortunately, concluded Pentagon analysts, the materiel flowing down the trail represented at most only about 15 percent of Communist supply requirements in South Vietnam.

Meanwhile, the Air Force was waging a different kind of war in northern Laos. There, beginning in early 1969, Operation Barrel Roll had evolved into a campaign of direct air support for loyalist ground forces threatened with defeat by a combined Pathet Lao-North Vietnamese offensive. Unlike the high-powered jets of the Commando Hunt operations, the majority of Barrel Roll sorties were flown in A-1 Skyraiders and T-28 Nomads by pilots from the 633d Special Operations Wing based at Nakhon Phanom. Flying over rough terrain, often in poor weather and with little navigational help from ground radar, the airmen averaged 300 sorties a month during 1969. When the Communist campaign resumed at the end of the year, Washington authorized the use of B-52s in Barrel Roll operations.

Almost inevitably, the growing air war in the rest of Southeast Asia after 1968 eventually spilled over into North Vietnam. Photo reconnaissance flights above the DMZ had been guaranteed safe passage under agreements made in Paris between Washington and Hanoi. When one of the unarmed U.S. jets was attacked in February 1970, President Nixon ordered "protective reaction" strikes against the responsible enemy gun sites. The new policy gradually escalated into a separate bombing campaign. During 1970, American aircraft flew more than sixty protective reaction strikes, a number that nearly doubled the follow-

ing year as the expanding Communist air defense system began harassing U.S. air operations over the Ho Chi Minh Trail. Stung by the loss of ten American aircraft and thirteen crewmen during the last three weeks of 1971, 7th Air Force commander General John D. Lavelle secretly ordered preemptive strikes against North Vietnamese targets. For exceeding his authority, Lavelle was removed from command. None could deny, however, that the continuing Communist buildup posed an ominous threat to South Vietnam—now relying more than ever on the protection afforded by American air power.

Full circle

Shortly after assuming office in January 1969, President Nixon declared his intention to end the American combat role in Southeast Asia by strengthening South Vietnam's ability to defend itself. During a trip to Saigon in March, Secretary of Defense Melvin R. Laird ordered an accelerated program of Vietnamization. Two months later, after a meeting with President Nguyen Van Thieu on Midway Island, Nixon announced plans to begin the withdrawal of U.S. troops. With American ground units beginning the process of disengagement, the U.S. Air Force became the primary guarantor of South Vietnamese independence.

An Air Force F–4E Phantom pulls away after dropping its ordnance on a target inside Cambodia in May 1970 during the two-month incursion by U.S. ground troops.

Fortunately for South Vietnam, the USAF had never been better equipped to meet its responsibilities. At the beginning of 1969, Air Force personnel stationed in South Vietnam and Thailand totaled nearly 55,000 men and women. Together they maintained and flew more than 700 fighter and strike aircraft—some armed with the latest in radar-guided bomb delivery systems—plus hundreds more support aircraft, including such new additions to the Air Force inventory as the OV-10 Bronco, a turboprop reconnaissance and observation plane capable of carrying bombs as well as marker rockets. The ability of Air Force pilots to locate the enemy was further enhanced by a variety of sophisticated sensors, including hand-held starlight scopes, which magnified existing light for night observation; infrared detectors able to pinpoint heat sources as small as a campfire; and such strange devices as the "people sniffer," which reacted chemically to the scent of the human body.

Such exotic equipment was not mere window-dressing, for the enemy had become more elusive than ever. Still recovering from losses suffered during the 1968 offensive, the Communists returned to a protracted war strategy emphasizing hit-and-run guerrilla tactics. The American way of war in Vietnam was also changing. Concentrating on the security of populated areas and the protection of military installations, MACV generally abandoned large-scale search-and-destroy sweeps in favor of numerous small-unit patrols. As a result, direct close air support missions dropped sharply, while "spoiling operations" designed to keep the enemy at arms' length increased. Such missions were well suited to B-52s, which during 1969 flew as many as 1,800 sorties a month against suspected enemy base areas, supply caches, and troop concentrations. In addition, both SAC bombers and tactical air provided much-needed support for remote Army fire support bases under enemy attack and for a growing number of ARVN offensive operations.

Like South Vietnam's ground troops, the Vietnamese air force was preparing to take on a much greater share of the war. Beginning in 1969, U.S. Air Force advisers oversaw a rapid buildup and modernization program that by mid-1970 had increased VNAF personnel from 29,000 to 35,000 and enlarged South Vietnam's aerial arsenal from 428 to over 700 aircraft. Along with expansion came modernization and instruction. Between 1968 and 1970, F-5 and A-37 jet fighters, plus AC-47, AC-119, and AC-130 gunships, were added to the VNAF inventory. Some Vietnamese pilots and mechanics received on-the-job training in the new aircraft from their USAF counterparts. Others traveled to U.S. Air Force bases in the United States. By 1971 the

A Vietnamese girl looks over the damage at Hon Gai, North Vietnam, in September 1972. Located fifty kilometers northeast of Haiphong, Hon Gai's military and industrial installations became a frequent target for USAF aircraft in Operation Linebacker I.

VNAF—now grown to nine tactical wings and some 40,000 officers and enlisted men—was flying more sorties in South Vietnam than all American air units combined.

Nonetheless, Saigon remained seriously dependent upon American air power, a fact made graphically apparent in February 1971 when South Vietnamese troops were routed with heavy losses during an incursion into southern Laos. Only mammoth support by U.S. fighter-bombers and B-52s—9,000 sorties delivering more than 50,000 tons of ordnance—prevented total disaster. In the aftermath of the ARVN debacle, American aircraft resumed interdiction strikes along the Ho Chi Minh Trail, but after two years of gradual cutbacks the momentum of withdrawal had caught up with the Air Force. By December 1971, less than 300 attack aircraft and less than 29,000 personnel remained in South Vietnam.

The Air Force attempted to bridge the gap between its continuing responsibilities and diminishing numbers of men and machines by relying on technology: advanced AC-119G Shadow, AC-119K Stinger, and AC-130 Spectre gunships; "Black Crow" ignition detectors, which could pick up static from gasoline engines as far as ten miles away; and the 20,000 acoustic and seismic sensors seeded along the Ho Chi Minh Trail since late 1967 as part of an interdiction operation called Igloo White. There was considerable doubt about the value of the sensor system, however, and in any case it was no substitute for pilots and planes should the North Vietnamese mount a new offensive. That grim prospect became all too real during the first weeks of 1972 when Task Force Alpha technicians monitoring the sensors from their computerized center at Nakhon Phanom recorded a major increase in enemy traffic moving south.

Linebacker

Spearheaded by tanks and mobile armor units, 40,000 North Vietnamese regulars poured across the DMZ on March 30, 1972, and advanced on the provincial capital of Quang Tri City. Despite ample warning, U.S. military officials were unprepared for the massive invasion. At the time of the North Vietnamese assault, the Air Force had only eighty-eight combat aircraft left in South Vietnam. Poor weather and heavy fire from enemy antiaircraft guns and mobile SAM sites initially neutralized what American air power there was in country as well as the Thailand-based fighter-bombers and B-52s diverted to Da Nang and Bien Hoa. By the second week of April, when the weather finally began to clear, the North Vietnamese had opened up two more fronts—one in the central highlands near Kontum and the other around An Loc northwest of Saigon. Although U.S. pilots were soon flying more than 500 sorties a day, it was not enough. More aircraft were desperately needed, and more aircraft is what the Air Force delivered.

Beginning with the 35th Tactical Fighter Squadron from Kunsan, Korea, the Air Force poured 700 planes and 70,000 men into the war zone. There they found a conventional, mechanized enemy force vulnerable to air attack and pounded it into submission. Between May 1 and June 30, USAF B-52s, fighter-bombers, and gunships flew 18,000 combat sorties, frequently against formidable antiaircraft fire, with the loss of only twenty-nine planes. The aerial onslaught stopped the North Vietnamese invaders, and by the beginning of July the ARVN had taken the offensive. Richard Nixon had not waited that long. On May 10, while the battle for South Vietnam was still in the balance, the president unilaterally suspended the ongoing Paris peace talks and authorized the resumption of full-scale bombing against North Vietnam. The operation was code-named Linebacker. The target for the first strike was the frequently hit, never destroyed, Paul Doumer Bridge.

On the morning of the tenth, thirty-two F-4 Phantoms from the 8th Tactical Fighter Wing based at Ubon, Thailand, rocketed untouched through heavy antiaircraft fire and an estimated 160 SAM missiles to destroy completely one span of the redoubtable bridge and badly damage several others. The following day, four more Phantoms dropped the remaining three spans, putting the bridge out of action for good.

The initial Linebacker raids were indicative of what was to come. Over the next eight weeks, Air Force and Navy fighter-bombers carried out strikes against targets from one end of the country to the other: fuel dumps, warehouses, marshaling yards, rolling stock, trucks, petroleum pipelines, and power plants. While the Navy mined Haiphong Harbor, the Air Force blasted SAM missile sites near the DMZ and bridges along the northeast rail lines to China. By the end of June, nearly 40 percent of existing POL stores had been destroyed. The raids crippled North Vietnam's transportation network and cut off supplies from its Communist allies.

Analyzing the effects of the renewed air campaign over the North, Major General Robert N. Ginsburgh suggested that Linebacker "had a greater impact in its first four months of operation than Rolling Thunder had in 3-1/2 years." The reasons why were not far to seek. Chief among them was the development of laser-guided and electro-optically guided bombs, also known as "smart" bombs. Powerful, extremely accurate, they were easily demolishing targets that had resisted tons of traditional "dumb" bombs. Another important factor was the continued development of electronic countermeasure equipment such as radar homing and warning (RHAW) gear and specialized ECM aircraft filled with radar detection and jamming devices. Linebacker also saw the revival of "chaff," strips of metal foil or metalized fiber glass that masked incoming bombers from enemy radar.

A third element was a general improvement in air-to-air combat tactics and refinements in early warning radar systems. In June, North Vietnamese pilots shot down more

U.S. aircraft than they lost themselves. By August, however, the Air Force's kill ratio had improved markedly, a development underlined on August 28 when Captain Richard S. "Steve" Ritchie downed his fifth MiG to become the first Air Force ace of the Vietnam War. Finally, Linebacker was conducted with fewer restrictions and less civilian control than previous bombing campaigns. Because there was no longer the same concern over Soviet or Chinese reaction, Nixon could leave the tactics, timing, and strength of each mission to his commanders, reducing the predictability and enhancing the intensity of attacks.

With its offensive in the South rolling backward and American bombs continuing to devastate the North, Hanoi opted for negotiations. The stalled peace talks resumed in Paris on July 19. By October the negotiations had progressed to the point where a provisional accord appeared imminent. On the twenty-third, as a gesture of good faith and with an eye to the national elections now only two weeks away, President Nixon ordered the bombing halted. "Peace," Secretary of State Henry Kissinger told reporters three days later, "is at hand."

But peace in Vietnam was like a mirage receding before the negotiators, even as they reached out to grasp it. Unable to nail down final terms, the two sides wrangled over who had promised what to whom until at last on December 13 the talks collapsed. The following day President Nixon demanded that Hanoi return to the negotiating table within seventy-two hours. When no reply was forthcoming, Nixon ordered another mining of Haiphong Harbor and a resumption of the bombing. But this time, there would be no target restrictions imposed by Washington. This time, B-52s would be sent over the heavily defended heartland of North Vietnam. This time, read the directive issued by the JCS informing field commanders of Operation Linebacker II, there would be "maximum effort, repeat maximum effort" to compel Hanoi to yield.

On the night of December 18, 1972, one-hundred twenty-nine B-52s struck five targets in and around Hanoi in the largest heavy bomber operation since World War II. Flying ahead were radar-jamming, missile suppression, and chaff planes. Along the way they were met by KC-135 refueling tankers. Accompanying the B-52s when they neared their targets were Phantoms flying anti-MiG escort, and behind them waited search and rescue teams to pick up any airmen unlucky enough to need their help. As the first bombers reached the outskirts of the North Vietnamese capital, the red flames of SAM rocket engines, fired in salvos of three or more at a time, lit up the sky in front of them. Over 200 of the missiles were launched that night, but only three of the B-52s were lost. The rest delivered their heavy loads on power plants, docks, communication facilities, POL stores, and transportation targets. By the time the last wave of bombers returned to base, the aircraft scheduled for the following day's mission were already warming up their engines.

Although the tactics and plan of attack for the second strike were virtually identical to the initial assault, the results were even better. But by the third night the North Vietnamese gunners were waiting for the Americans. Six of the multimillion-dollar aircraft were shot down in flames by surface-to-air missiles, provoking a wave of criticism from officials in Washington and air crews who saw in the predictability of the attack patterns a recipe for disaster. While SAC commanders tried to figure out a solution, Washington ordered the raids continued. For the next four nights the B-52s concentrated on SAM sites while F-111s—the newest and most sophisticated warplane in the Air Force arsenal—pounded MiG airfields ahead of the bombers. During the day, Air Force, Navy, and Marine aircraft struck bridges, railroad yards, and spur lines.

After a thirty-six-hour Christmas cease-fire, the attack resumed. This time, however, ten waves of B-52s—120 bombers in all—converged from seven different directions in a simultaneous assault designed to overwhelm the North Vietnamese air defenses. Two of the bombers were brought down, but the remaining B-52s obliterated their targets with 4,000 tons of high explosives. Bombs hitting one major petroleum storage area set off thirty large secondary explosions, the concussions ripping apart two warehouses and sending geysers of flame shooting into the night sky. At Bach Mai airfield, the attack destroyed thirty-one buildings.

The magnitude of the destruction and in particular the razing of a portion of the Bach Mai hospital sparked charges of "terror bombing." That the raids did result in civilian deaths there can be no doubt, some due to accident or miscalculation, others the inevitable result of proximity to military targets. Yet given the enormous weight of bombs that were dropped, the total of 1,624 civilian casualties reported by the North Vietnamese was surprisingly low—indeed, several magnitudes removed from what was experienced in comparable operations during World War II—and wholly insufficient to sustain charges of deliberate attack on the civilian population.

For their part, the North Vietnamese defended themselves ferociously, hurling everything they had into the sky in a vain attempt to stop the onslaught. On the twenty-seventh, the B-52s were met with barrage firings of SAM missiles that brought down two more of the bombers, but it was their last gasp. By the twenty-eighth, the North Vietnamese had exhausted their supply of 1,000 SAMs, leaving the Stratofortresses free to deliver their bomb loads unmolested. Far below the American aircraft lay the ruins of 1,600 military structures and 372 pieces of rolling stock, blasted airfields, rail lines cut to pieces, storage stockpiles scattered, and missile launchers destroyed. An estimated 80 percent of North Vietnam's electrical power production capacity had ceased to exist along with more than a quarter of its POL stores. Also left behind were the remains of fifteen bombers, all victims of SAM missiles, and eleven tactical aircraft; thirty-three air crewmen taken prisoner, four who died in crash landings; and twenty-nine reported missing. On December 29, Linebacker II came to an end. The following day, President Nixon announced that Hanoi had agreed to return to the negotiating table.

After eight long years of conflict, the talks, which resumed shortly after the New Year, moved swiftly to their culmination. On January 23, Henry Kissinger and Le Duc Tho initialed a formal cease-fire agreement. Under its provisions, Hanoi undertook to repatriate the 653 prisoners of war, including 325 members of the U.S. Air Force, held by the Communists. B-52s would continue to fly missions over Laos until April 17 and over Cambodia until August 15, but with the release of the final prisoner of war contingent on March 29, 1973, the American war in Vietnam came to an end.

In statements to the press, the administration strongly implied that the bombing had forced Hanoi back to the table. In fact, the North Vietnamese maintained throughout Linebacker II that they would return to the talks only when the bombing ceased. Moreover, the provisions of the cease-fire agreement achieved in January represented if

anything a net loss for the United States from what had already been agreed to in October.

The controversy over the role that bombing played in 1972 suggests the ambiguous legacy of air power in the Vietnam War. The Air Force argued from the beginning that if its pilots had been allowed to operate without restrictions they could have forced Hanoi to sue for peace. It was an assertion that underestimated the determination of the North Vietnamese and overlooked the fact that air power alone had never won a war. If the offensive capabilities of American air power in Vietnam remain subject to debate, however, what is indisputable is its vital role as a defensive weapon. Not only in South Vietnam but also in Laos and Cambodia, American air power, and in particular the United States Air Force, prevented the Communists from achieving victory. This was as true in 1972 as it had been in 1968 and 1965. Only when that weapon was finally withdrawn did North Vietnam triumph.

Lt. Col. Robert L. Strim, a POW since October 1967, is greeted by his family at Travis Air Force Base, California, on March 17, 1973, three days after his release.

Field Dress

MACV Adviser, 1965

In Vietnam, field uniforms were often as distinct as the individuals who wore them. By the middle of the war, many of the regulations that applied to dress had either been lifted by commanders or ignored by the troops themselves. Yet standards still existed and each unit chose its own uniforms and accouterments to suit its style and the kind of battle its men faced. These pages show the field dress worn by typical soldiers, sailors, airmen, and Marines of the major units profiled in this volume as well as each unit's shoulder patch insignia.

Shown on this page is a MACV adviser from the Vietnamese Ranger Training Center in Duc My. The insignia on his right sleeve shows that he formerly served with the Green Berets. He also wears combat infantryman and master parachutist badges (left breast). He is wearing the Rangers' insignia on his beret and using a second Ranger unit symbol as his shirt pocket tab. Metal ARVN captain's rank appears on both his coat and his beret; his right collar bears U.S. captain's bars and his left, the infantry insignia. MACV insignia and ranger tab are on his left sleeve. Above his privately purchased leather "jump" boots are an early style hot-weather coat and trousers. The harness contains a .45-caliber pistol, below which is a privately purchased knife. Opposite the knife on his pistol belt is a compass pouch.

Illustration by Donna J. Neary

1st Aviation Brigade

Door Gunner, 1968

This helicopter door gunner sits behind his 7.62MM M60 machine gun, which is mounted beside the UH-1D Huey's open cargo compartment. The decal on his flyer's glass outer shell, crash-type helmet indicates that he is a member of the "Starblazers," the 61st Aviation Company (Assault Helicopter), a separate unit within the brigade. The emblem's design features a gold shooting star, representing gunship swiftness, circling a pair of dice showing "six" and "one," the unit number

and a sign for luck. Opposite the decal is an American flag.

His nylon hot-weather shirt and trousers, nylon gloves, and leather combat boots are all designed to resist burning at the high temperatures generated by his gun, enemy rockets, or engine malfunctions or explosions. While many soldiers of that time wore lighter tropical combat boots, the brigade directed its men not to wear them because they melted in fires, resulting in severe burns or even in am-

putation. His left sleeve carries a locally produced 1st Aviation Brigade patch. He also wears a protective flak vest and carries an Air Force-issue survival knife.

Illustration by Donna J. Neary

101st Airborne Division (Airmobile)

Radio Telephone Operator, 1969

Pausing to transmit on his radio handset, this 101st Airborne Division radio telephone operator wears hot-weather jungle fatigues and tropical boots. Under his open coat is a tricot sleeping shirt, or jungle sweater, a common combination in Vietnam's mountainous regions. The coat's lower sleeves have been cut off to make it more comfortable. He carries the AN/PRC-25 radio set with its AT-892 "short" antenna extended. Covered with plastic to keep out moisture, the radio, with attached smoke grenades and plastic-covered spare batteries, is mounted on a lightweight rucksack frame. The longer AT-271A antenna—utilized for communications over greater distances or in thick jungle—is collapsed on the rucksack, which also carries two polyethylene one-quart canteens. He is armed with an M16 rifle and carries extra magazines in the cloth ammunition bandoleer he is wearing around his waist. His helmet graffiti is typical of GIs in Vietnam.

Illustration by Donna J. Neary

44

1st Cavalry Division (Airmobile)

Aero Rifle Scout, 1966

An aero rifle platoon scout of the 1st Squadron, 9th Cavalry, 1st Cavalry Division (Airmobile), hacks out a hastily cleared helicopter landing zone in 1966. The reconnaissance trooper is using an M1942 machete to chop undergrowth while holding his M16 rifle behind him. He has added burlap strips to his helmet to break its outline and has tucked a spare rifle magazine under his elastic camouflage helmet band. He wears the hot-weather coat and trouser jungle fatigue combination, with subdued 1st Cav shoulder sleeve insignia. The triangular bandage is worn as a scarf to wipe away perspiration and dirt. His field combat gear is typical of Vietnam-era U.S. infantrymen. Items include two first-aid packets attached to the shoulder pads of his cotton-webbing field-pack suspenders and three small-arms ammunition pouches attached to his pistol belt. Two fragmentation hand grenades are secured to the pouches.

Illustration by Donna J. Neary

7th Air Force

F-4 Phantom Pilot, 1970-1971

This Air Force captain's flight clothing and equipment are typical of those worn by Vietnam-era air crewmen. Over flame-retarding nomex fabric coveralls, he wears a survival vest and antigravity cut-away trousers. The vest pockets contain survival gear, including a radio, insect repellent, a compass, flares, a mirror for signaling rescuers, a first aid kit, a butane lighter, and a fishing net in case the crewman is downed in the ocean. In addition to the .38-caliber revolver he wears on his waist belt, he carries a second pistol in the vest (under his left arm, not visible here) along with ammunition. The "G-suit" trousers, which connect to the aircraft by the tube on his left, contain air bladders that fill automatically when the pilot is subjected to centrifugal forces. Pressure from the bladders prevents blood from pooling in the lower half of the body, which otherwise might cause the pilot to black out. Often, a crewman carried a knife on his lower leg. This pilot's G-suit pocket contains maps. He also wears a torso harness (visible over his shoulders) that attaches to the aircraft's seat, which contains his parachute. His inflatable life preserver (not visible) is attached to the harness.

Illustration by Donna J. Neary

U.S. Naval Forces, Vietnam
River Patrol Force

Gunner's Mate, 1968

Part of the brown water navy, the U.S. Navy River Patrol Force policed the larger streams and rivers of the Mekong Delta. Its purpose was to prevent the Communist guerrillas from infiltrating via inland waterways.

Here, a gunner's mate 2d class of the River Patrol Force grasps his .50-caliber machine gun aboard a river patrol boat (PBR) in the Mekong River Delta. Over his standard-issue fatigues he wears a flak jacket, which would not stop a bullet but could protect him from shrapnel. His helmet is also standard issue. His footware (not visible) is the green leather, canvas, and nylon tropical boot; it replaced the all-leather combat boot that exacerbated "immersion foot," a common affliction for Americans operating in Vietnam's wet regions. In his pockets the gunner's mate carries standard accouterments: cigarettes, a lighter, money, the P38 C-ration can opener along with a few "C-rats," toilet paper, and a variety of other personal items.

Illustration by Donna J. Neary

3d Marine Division

Rifleman, 1965

The first Marines to arrive in Vietnam made use of equipment and clothing more typical of their predecessors of the previous decade than the men who fought later in Vietnam. For example, this rifleman carries the Korean War-era 7.62MM M14 rifle, which some Marines used throughout the war instead of the new M16. Over his shoulders he carries pouches used exclusively by Marines for M14 ammunition. In addition he wears all-leather boots, which were soon to be found unsuitable for use in tropical climes.

His clothing is the standard olive green Marine Corps utilities, or fatigues. The letters USMC are barely visible on his left shirt pocket, as is the Marine eagle, globe, and anchor insignia. On each collar point appears his lance corporal rank designation, a metal pin showing a single chevron above crossed rifles. He wears a utility cap with the Marine Corps insignia stenciled on the front. In addition to his canteen he is carrying a bayonet and scabbard for the rifle and a nylon poncho, all of which are slung on his left side or behind him and are not visible.

Illustration by Donna J. Neary

1st Marine Division

Rifleman, 1969

By 1969, the Marines had updated both their appearance and their equipment. As displayed by this rifleman, they wore lightweight jungle utilities with large pockets. (This Marine has discarded his shirt and wears only an undershirt.) He wears the tropical boots designed specifically for use in Vietnam and carries a 5.56mm M16 rifle. His headgear is the M1

helmet with an Army-style reversible cover. By USMC directive, the cover bears his name and service number. Often, latter-day Marines wore fully camouflaged outfits, although this rifleman has opted for standard olive drab.

He wears a flak vest used exclusively by Marines. Eyelets, to which he can attach his equipment, are riveted along the

bottom edge. Below his vest this Marine carries two square pouches filled with M16 ammunition, a pair of grenades, a knife, two canteens (one just underneath his left arm, the other not visible on his right side), and a jungle first aid kit (also on his right and not visible). Slung across his shoulder are pouches containing additional rifle magazines.

Illustration by Donna J. Neary

The War Along the DMZ

It would take them to places called Helicopter Valley
and Mutter's Ridge, to Hill 881 and the Rockpile. But
for the men of the 3d Marine Division the war began
on a fine sandy beach five kilometers north of Da
Nang amid flowers and speeches and pretty Vietnamese girls giggling a welcome. At 9:03 A.M. on
March 8, 1965, the first wave of Battalion Landing
Team 3/9 leapt from an amphibian tractor and
splashed ashore. Within forty-five minutes the Marines were driving down Highway 1 toward the Da
Nang air base. There they were joined by the 1st
Battalion, 3d Marines, airlifted from Okinawa on
C-130 transports that dived toward the tarmac to
avoid Vietcong sniper fire. Together, the two battalions and a Marine helicopter squadron comprised
the 9th Marine Expeditionary Brigade. The first U.S.
ground combat units committed to Vietnam, their
arrival reflected growing concern in Washington
over a rapidly deteriorating situation.

Despite a decade of American economic aid and
military assistance, South Vietnam in spring 1965

Major General Lewis W. Walt, commander of the 3d Marine Division from 1965 to 1966, addresses his troops near the village of Lo My in 1965.

trembled on the brink of destruction—the government wracked by political upheavals, the army barely able to defend itself against Vietcong Main Force units threatening to cut the country in half. The deployment of U.S. troops to ports and airfields along the northern coast would release ARVN units for more aggressive operations and create American "enclaves" from which the war could be waged in the event of a total South Vietnamese military collapse. For the moment, however, the Marines sent to Da Nang had a more limited assignment: "To occupy and defend critical terrain features in order to secure the airfield and, as directed, communications facilities, U.S. supporting installations, port facilities, landing beaches and other U.S. installations against attack. The U.S. Marine forces will not, repeat will not, engage in day to day actions against the Vietcong."

Yet once begun, the Marine buildup proceeded rapidly. On April 10, the 2d Battalion, 3d Marines, arrived at Da

Preceding page. *Troops of the 2d Battalion, 5th Marines, 3d Marine Division, patrol territory just south of the Demilitarized Zone during Operation Prairie in October 1966.*

52

Nang fresh from training exercises in Thailand. Four days later, the 3d Battalion, 4th Marines, established a second enclave at Phu Bai, an electronic spy station and communications facility just outside of Hue. On May 6, the rest of the 4th Marines came ashore at Chu Lai, about 100 kilometers south of Da Nang. They immediately began construction of a 4,000-foot aluminum mat runway to take the pressure off the overloaded facilities at Da Nang where the 3d Division command group had just settled. Reflecting the expansion of Marine strength in Vietnam and to avoid unpleasant associations with the French colonial past, the "expeditionary" brigade was replaced by the III Marine Amphibious Force (III MAF). On June 4, Major General Lewis W. Walt arrived to take charge of both III MAF and the 3d Division.

The change of command ceremonies took place in the Da Nang officers mess because the carefully proscribed American military role in Vietnam still precluded the outdoor display of U.S. national colors. It was a prohibition rapidly losing any relation to reality, however. Already by the first week of June, the Marines had suffered over 200 casualties in skirmishes with the Vietcong, including twenty-nine killed in action (KIA).

Almost from the moment they arrived on Vietnamese soil the men of the 3d Division had chafed at the restrictions placed upon them. Confined to a narrow defensive perimeter surrounding their bases, they walked the wire through choking dust under a blazing sun waiting for the Vietcong to take the initiative. "This was never going to work," argued General Victor Krulack, commander of Fleet Marine Force, Pacific. Not only was it dangerous to allow the enemy to operate freely in the areas surrounding American installations, but U.S. troops "were not going to win any counter insurgency battles sitting in foxholes around a runway."

Following high-level conferences in Washington and Honolulu in early April, U.S. authorities approved "a change of mission" that projected the Marines into a mobile counterinsurgency role in the vicinity of their enclaves. Over the next two months, III MAF steadily expanded the area actively patrolled by Marine squads from less than ten to several hundred square kilometers. At first, contact with the enemy was light, the Vietcong carefully avoiding sustained combat. But as the Marines ventured farther and farther into insurgent territory, a major encounter became inevitable. In the wake of a July 1 Vietcong sapper attack on the Da Nang air base, General Walt was given authority to "seek out and destroy major Vietcong units, bases and other facilities." The result was Operation Starlite, the first regimental-sized U.S. battle since the Korean War.

On August 15, a Vietcong deserter revealed a major enemy buildup along the coast twenty kilometers southeast of Chu Lai. After three days of intensive planning, elements of the 3d and 4th Marines fell on the 1st Vietcong

3d Marine Division

Arrived Vietnam: May 1965   **Departed Vietnam:** November 1969

Unit Headquarters

Da Nang *May 1965–Oct. 1966*	Phu Bai *Oct. 1966–Jan. 1968*	Dong Ha *Jan. 1968–Nov. 1969*

Commanding Officers

Maj. Gen. William R. Collins *May 1965* Maj. Gen. Lewis W. Walt *June 1965* Maj. Gen. Wood B. Kyle *March 1966*	Maj. Gen. Bruno A. Hochmuth *March 1967* Maj. Gen. Rathvon McC. Tompkins *Nov. 1967*	Maj. Gen. Raymond G. Davis *May 1968* Maj. Gen. William K. Jones *April 1969*

Major Subordinate Units*

3d Marines (1/3, 2/3, 3/3) 4th Marines (1/4, 2/4, 3/4)	9th Marines (1/9, 2/9, 3/9) 26th Marines (1/26, 2/26, 3/26)	12th Marines (Artillery) (1/12, 2/12, 3/12, 4/12, 1/13, 2/13)
13,065 KIA	88,633 WIA	27 Medals of Honor

These figures reflect total Marine Corps casualties for the Vietnam War. The USMC does not keep casualty figures for individual divisions.

*Marine divisions are organized by regiment, and each regiment has its own numerical designation. In USMC nomenclature the word *regiment* is not used, thus the 3d Marines always refer to the regiment, not the division. The 3d Marine Division is always referred to by its full title.

Regiment in a multipronged land, air, and sea assault under the operational control of the 1st Division's newly arrived 7th Marines. Dug into entrenched positions, the surprised enemy troops fought back furiously, killing 46 Marines and wounding 204 more. But the VC were no match for the Americans' mobility and firepower. Vertical envelopment and aggressive infantry tactics trapped the Vietcong against the sea, where Marine air and naval gunfire tore them to pieces. During the first two days of the operation the insurgents lost nearly 1,000 men*, the battered survivors fleeing from the coastal plain where up until now they had found ready sanctuary.

In Starlite, Piranha, and other operations during the latter part of 1965, the Marines demonstrated to the Vietcong the futility of engaging in standup battles and the danger of remaining in the populated area along the coast. Their efforts pushed the VC west into the mountain valleys where they remained for the time being, avoiding major engagements. Meanwhile, with the enemy Main Force units held at arms' length, the Marines turned their attention to the VC guerrilla and the sea of people in which he lived.

Hearts and minds

The Marine coastal enclaves in central I Corps were surrounded by hundreds of villages, each of them serving as potential staging areas for Communist guerrillas whose political apparatus had long dominated the region. Security alone dictated that III MAF gain some measure of tactical control over the rural population. But General Walt was also convinced that the key to the war was the people—their allegiance and support. For both reasons the Marines very quickly found themselves deeply involved in "the pacification business."

Their first efforts were northwest of Da Nang, where the 3d Marines attempted to secure the Cu De River valley, and south along the coast toward Hoi An, where the 9th Marines operated. In each case the guerrillas reacted sharply to the American intrusion, fighting back with snipers, booby traps, and ambushes. But the Marines persisted, clearing the hamlets, establishing some measure of security from renewed Communist attack, encouraging the reintroduction of government control. Simultaneously, they initiated a coordinated program of self-help, medical assistance, and community development they called civic action.

In villages visited by Marine patrols, this effort might include the distribution of food, clothing, soap, and other relief supplies. Particularly effective were MEDCAP teams led by Navy corpsmen who treated the villagers, dispensed medicine, and trained local volunteers in rudimentary health care practices. In those areas actually occupied by Marine units, they helped to erect schools, dig wells, repair bridges, construct granaries, rebuild marketplaces, and stock experimental pig farms. The money to pay for all this came from the Marines themselves and from a civic action fund supported by Marine reservists in the United States.

Beyond these expanding "people-to-people" activities, the Marines employed a variety of innovative military and political techniques in their efforts to root out the Communist infrastructure in the villages. "Golden Fleece" operations were designed to protect hamlet rice harvests from Vietcong tax collectors. Marine infantry units patrolling the rice fields during the weeks of harvest not only reduced

---

* Note: Throughout this book, Communist KIA figures are based on the controversial official body count, a method subject to human error and, at times, exaggeration. Comparable figures for enemy wounded are generally not available.

A wary Marine passes frightened Vietnamese children during a sweep through a fortified enemy village south of Da Nang in October 1965.

mutual apprehensions between the farmers and the Americans but also effectively denied Main Force VC units of desperately needed rice. In "County Fair" operations, U.S. troops cordoned off entire hamlets and provided food, medical care, and entertainment to the villagers while local officials and police identified and interrogated VC suspects. Most innovative of all were Combined Action Platoons. Pairing a Marine squad with a Popular Forces platoon made up of local South Vietnamese villagers, the program enhanced security at the most basic level of society while at the same time training the local militiamen to defend their own homes.

By the spring of 1966, the 3d Marine Division had made significant progress in securing the 150-kilometer-long coastal plain stretching south from Phu Bai through Da Nang, Hoi An, Tam Ky, and Chu Lai (the latter turned over to the 1st Marine Division in March), a crucial strip of territory containing more than half the population of I Corps. Yet their efforts were constantly undermined by the inability of the South Vietnamese to provide more than sporadic rural security. Moreover, the Marines were beginning to realize that neither their compassion, ingenuity,

nor muscle could overcome the political instability of the Saigon government or the strategic decisions of the American military command.

The removal of popular I Corps commander Major General Nguyen Chanh Thi on March 10 set off riotous anti-government civil disorders in Hue and Da Nang amid threats of mutiny by the highly regarded 1st ARVN Division. Over the next three months the Marines were caught squarely in the middle of violent confrontations between rival South Vietnamese forces that several times found the Americans facing down the gun barrels of their erstwhile allies. Although the turmoil eventually subsided, the political crisis diverted the Marines' attention and paralyzed the South Vietnamese government's effort throughout I Corps, reversing the momentum of the pacification program and allowing the Vietcong to regain control over some of the villages so painfully cleared during the previous year.

Meanwhile, a long-standing dispute between III MAF and MACV was reaching a climax. Shaped by the realities of the tactical situation in which they found themselves, and by their conviction that the war against the Communists in Vietnam was fundamentally political, the Marines had fashioned their own approach to war. They constructed a "spreading inkblot" strategy that called for relatively small-scale clear-and-hold operations directed primarily against the VC cadres and guerrillas of the coastal plain. On the other hand, MACV commander General William Westmoreland favored large-scale search-and-destroy operations against the enemy's Main Force units located deep in their mountain base areas. From Westmoreland's point of view, to concentrate on the time-consuming counterinsurgency war allowed the enemy to expand Main Force units with impunity. To the Marines, however, there was no purpose in giving battle in the mountains when most of the population lived along the coast. "Our effort belonged where the people were, *not* where they weren't," argued Marine Corps Commandant General Wallace M. Greene, Jr. "I shared these thoughts with Westmoreland frequently, but made no progress in persuading him."

For a time, Marine Commander Gen. Walt was able to deal with pressure from MACV for more aggressive action against enemy Main Force units. He adopted what he called a "balanced strategy" of counterguerrilla, pacification, and search-and-destroy operations, the latter entrusted to ad hoc task forces created whenever larger enemy units could be definitely located and fixed. But time was rapidly running out. During the first few months of 1966, there were growing indications that the NVA was preparing for a major offensive along South Vietnam's northern border. When Marine reconnaissance patrols discovered elements of the 324B NVA Division crossing the demilitarized zone into Quang Tri Province, the debate between MACV and the Marines came to an abrupt end. Ordered north at the beginning of July to halt the incursion, the men of the 3d Division left their pacification programs behind. Where they were going there would not be enough time for winning hearts and minds.

The war along the DMZ

The NVA invasion across the DMZ changed forever the face of war in South Vietnam. Spearheaded by the 2/4 and the 3/4 Marines, eventually six Marine and five ARVN battalions under the operational command of Task Force Delta struck back in Operation Hastings, attacking north and west from their forward base at Dong Ha toward Cam Lo, Helicopter Valley, and a 700-foot pinnacle called the Rockpile. The operation began on July 15. For three weeks, more than 8,000 Marines and 3,000 South Vietnamese soldiers fought a ferocious battle against as many as 12,000 enemy troops in the largest operation of the war to that date. By August 3, when Hastings officially came to an end, the 324B Division had been sent reeling back across the DMZ with more than 800 dead.

After only a few weeks of recovery, however, the NVA resumed the attack, met this time by Operation Prairie. Throughout September and October, Marine units utilizing helicopter assaults, naval gunfire, tanks, air support, and artillery fire took on well-prepared North Vietnamese strongpoints. The violent clashes raged back and forth

along the DMZ from Mutter's Ridge to the mouth of the Cua Viet River. Prairie was to continue into January 1967, ultimately claiming more than 1,300 enemy KIA. But the commitment to defend the northern border had been a costly one for the Marines as well: 365 had been killed and 1,662 wounded in the bloody fighting.

Although the enemy incursions were beaten back, it had become clear by the fall that the North Vietnamese would not be contained along the DMZ without a major, ongoing commitment of U.S. forces. In October, 3d Division commander Major General Wood B. Kyle moved his headquarters from Da Nang to Phu Bai, establishing an advance command post at Dong Ha. As 1967 began, Kyle had his 3d and 9th Marines defending the DMZ, while his third regiment, the 4th Marines, covered the western approaches to Hue. By March, when Kyle turned over command to Major General Bruno A. Hochmuth, the full dimensions of the task that faced the division in northern I Corps had become only too apparent.

Stretching 100 kilometers from the Gulf of Tonkin to the Laotian border, once past the sand dunes and rice fields along the coast, the countryside was dominated by foot-

A view from "The Rockpile." The oft-contested 700-foot-high promontory stood above NVA invasion routes along the Cam Lo River nine kilometers south of the DMZ.

Operation Prairie was a fierce, bloody contest along the DMZ that left its scars on both the men who fought it and the rugged hills over which it raged. Here, during the two-day fight for Hill 484 in October 1966, one of the operation's key battles, Marines march through the rubble of the hilltop (right), while others fire on the NVA defenders (below left). Nearby, a wounded Marine (below right) is helped to an evacuation helicopter.

hills and peaks of the Annamite Mountains, their steep slopes, thickly covered by dense jungle growth, rising as high as 8,000 feet above sea level. It was a furnace of heat and dust from May through September. But during the winter monsoon temperatures plunged fifty degrees in torrential downpours producing flash floods and dense overcast so low that air operations had to be severely curtailed. Roads were few and primitive, the heavily used Cua Viet River an easy target for Communist interdiction. Air supply depended on the vagaries of the weather.

Marine commanders found it difficult enough just to keep the men they had fully equipped, yet they desperately needed more men. The manpower shortage forced the Corps to reduce recruit training schedules and make use of the draft. Even so, throughout 1966 infantry companies were regularly taking the field with less than 120 officers and men, about three-quarters of normal strength. Equally serious, the need for new officers stripped Marine NCO ranks of some of the Corps' most experienced small-unit leaders. In a war often fought by small units and in which corporals and sergeants bore the burden of command to a greater degree than ever before, it was an ominous development.

While Marine manpower in northern I Corps was stretched to the limit, the NVA nearly doubled their forces in the region during the last six months of 1966. Moreover, the enemy the Marines encountered along the DMZ was not the Vietcong guerrilla of the villages but fresh North Vietnamese regulars organized into battalions, regiments, and divisions. "We found them well equipped, well trained, and aggressive to the point of fanaticism," reported Gen. Walt. "They fought bravely and they fought well, and very few of them surrendered." Establishing secure rear bases in Laos and North Vietnam, they used the DMZ north of the Ben Hai River as a giant staging ground and supply cache. From there they attacked the Americans at times and places of their own choosing protected by the U.S. prohibition against ground attacks across South Vietnam's borders.

Combined with its manpower problems, the nonincursion policy condemned the Marines to a static war of attrition that they waged from a series of combat bases bristling with barbed wire and artillery strung out between Route 9 and the DMZ. Dong Ha, Gio Linh, Con Thien, Cam Lo, Camp Carroll, the Rockpile, Ca Lu, Khe Sanh—names synonymous with rain, mud, danger, and frustration—became at once both home and hell to the men of the 3d Division. Cast in an unaccustomed and unwanted defensive role, during 1967 and early 1968 the Marines engaged in a numbing succession of battles. Shaped largely by NVA initiatives, the fighting surged back and forth across northern Quang Tri Province like a great wave, beginning and ending on the narrow mountain plateau of Khe Sanh.

Since September 1966, this small western outpost and its modest airstrip had been guarded on a rotating basis by

individual Marine rifle companies. They sent out daily reconnaissance patrols through the rain and fog that clung to the steep hills guarding the northwest approaches to the base. Although evidence of NVA activity steadily increased during the early months of 1967, the enemy remained elusive. Then, on April 24, while scouting Hill 861, a squad from Company B, 9th Marines, was cut to pieces in an ambush that quickly engulfed the entire company. By that evening, the sudden, furious firefight had cost the Marines thirteen dead and seventeen wounded. It had also revealed the presence of the 325C NVA Division, which was heavily entrenched in the surrounding hills and poised to overrun the ill-defended combat base.

The 2d and 3d Battalions, 3d Marines, and Companies E, K, and M, 9th Marines, came to the base's relief in the next three days. They were able to extricate the survivors of Company B from their pinned-down position, but initial attempts to take Hill 861 were repulsed with heavy casualties. Pulling the infantry back, Marine air and artillery supported by the Army's 175MM guns at Camp Carroll bombarded the hill for two days, blasting away foliage with high explosives, then scorching the cratered peaks with napalm. When the ground troops resumed the assault on April 28, they found the enemy bunkers abandoned.

On the following day, the 3/3 advanced toward Hill 881S while screaming F-4 Phantom, A-4 Skyhawk, and F-8 Crusader jet aircraft hammered the hilltop with a half-million pounds of bombs. At 8:00 on the morning of the thirtieth, as the last rounds of the preparation fires whistled above, Company M began the assault. Scrambling up the tangled slopes, the lead platoons reached the summit by 10:30. Suddenly, automatic weapons fire poured into the Marines from concealed bunkers, which apparently had been strong enough to withstand the aerial bombardment. Diving for cover they could hear the North Vietnamese shouting in English: "Put on your helmets, Marines, we are coming after you!" Mortars and grenades crashed into the trapped men even as helicopter gunships and attack aircraft riddled enemy positions as close as fifty meters away. It was five long hours before what was left of Company M was able to withdraw from the hill. They came out with more than 100 wounded. Left behind, in violation of Marine Corps tradition, were 43 dead.

All of May 1 was devoted to a relentless bombardment of both Hill 881S and 881N, including 166 air sorties and nearly 1,500 rounds of artillery. Meanwhile, B-52s sealed off the Laotian border with scores of 1,000-pound bombs. By the afternoon of May 2, Companies K and M, 9th Marines, had secured Hill 881S and recovered the American dead. They encountered only scattered sniper fire on their way to the top, their climb impeded mainly by shell craters, fallen trees, and the shattered remains of 200 enemy bunkers.

While poncho-shrouded bodies were carried off Hill 881S, the 2d Battalion was working its way up the final enemy strongpoint, Hill 881N, under sporadic automatic weapons and mortar fire. Company E had almost gained the top of the peak when a violent rainstorm broke up the advance and forced the battalion to pull back for the night. Shortly before dawn, screaming enemy soldiers, some wearing uniforms stripped from dead Marines, burst through the battalion's perimeter and fell upon the outnumbered Americans. With the help of artillery, gunships, jets, and the recoilless rifles of the 3d Battalion on 881S, the Marines finally broke the attack. During the next two days, the 2d Battalion tightened the ring around 881N while artillery and air pulverized the summit. On May 5, after twelve days of continuous battle, the mud-smeared Marines regained the last of the Khe Sanh hills.

A triumph of air and ground coordination, the first battle of Khe Sanh drove the 325C NVA Division back across the DMZ with an estimated 1,000 dead and several thousand more wounded. But the cost of stopping the Communist effort had not been light: 580 U.S. casualties, including 155 KIA. Moreover, neither the horrendous enemy losses at Khe Sanh, nor similar casualties suffered during Operation Hickory—a lightning-fast American strike into the DMZ during late May—seemed to have anything more than a temporary effect. By early summer the North Vietnamese had simply shifted their attention seventy kilometers east to a flat, hot, scrubby piedmont bounded by the American combat bases at Cam Lo, Dong Ha, Gio Linh, and Con Thien—a place the Marines had nicknamed Leatherneck Square.

Buffalo

During much of 1967, Leatherneck Square was the preserve of the 9th Marines, who operated out of a series of strongpoints along the "one-zero line"—so named for the military grid line running from Cam Lo to Con Thien. Engaged in continuous day and night patrolling, frequent company- and battalion-size attacks, and occasional multibattalion sweeps, the Marines were also burdened with the construction of a 600-meter-wide barrier across the northern side of the square. This project, popularly known as "McNamara's Line" after its chief proponent, Defense Secretary Robert McNamara, was the first stage of an anti-infiltration "fence" designed to stretch across Vietnam and into Laos. It had been envisioned as a swath of bulldozed land strewn with mines, electronic sensors, and physical obstacles, all watched over from a series of heavily fortified strongpoints. Almost from the beginning of construction in April, both the barrier and its western terminus, Con Thien, acted as a magnet for NVA artillery, rockets, and ground attacks that steadily mounted in intensity through the month of June.

Responding to that pressure, Companies A and B, 9th Marines (the same Company B mauled at Khe Sanh six

While one rifleman tries to help a wounded buddy, other members of the 2/3 Marines assault Hill 881N during the first battle of Khe Sanh in the spring of 1967.

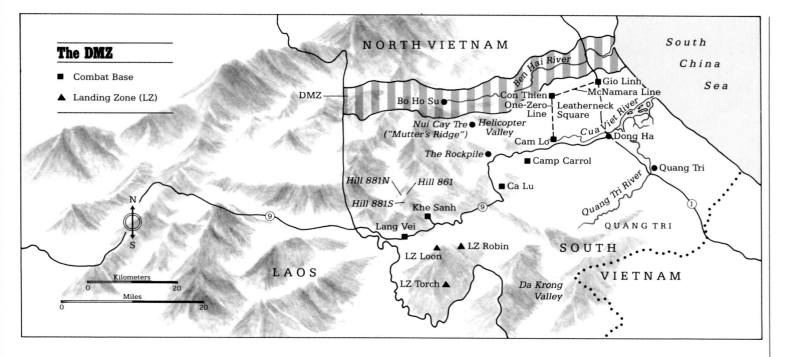

Map labels: NORTH VIETNAM · South China Sea · Ben Hai River · DMZ · Bo Ho Su · Gio Linh · McNamara Line · Con Thien · One-Zero Line · Leatherneck Square · Nui Cay Tre ("Mutter's Ridge") · Helicopter Valley · Cam Lo · Cua Viet River · Dong Ha · The Rockpile · Camp Carrol · Quang Tri · Hill 881N · Hill 861 · Ca Lu · Hill 881S · Khe Sanh · 9 · Quang Tri River · QUANG TRI · Lang Vei · LZ Robin · SOUTH · LZ Loon · VIETNAM · LZ Torch · Da Krong Valley · LAOS · N S · Kilometers 0 20 · Miles 0 20 · 9

weeks earlier), set out from Con Thien on Sunday morning, July 2, kicking off a search-and-destroy operation code-named Buffalo. They had marched barely four kilometers north up the hedgerow-lined Route 561 when the lead elements of Company B encountered enemy sniper fire. As the remainder of the company maneuvered to outflank the snipers, the road erupted in a furious barrage of mortar and artillery fire. Company A, attempting to come to the rescue, was driven back by intense small arms fire. The "snipers" were in fact two battalions of the 90th NVA Regiment, which systematically destroyed Company B.

Flame throwers drove the Marines into the open where they were cut down by automatic weapons and from massed artillery inside the DMZ. Within minutes of the ambush the company commander was dead, the 3d Platoon wiped out. Radio contact between the remaining platoons had been lost. Trying desperately to consolidate their position, the Marines inched back down the road, propping up the wounded so they could fire their weapons at the hundreds of enemy soldiers who steadily closed in. Only the sudden arrival of air support—including napalm dropped within twenty yards of friendly positions—prevented total catastrophe. The air strikes temporarily disrupted the enemy assault, allowing the 1st and 2d platoons to link up. After several hours a USMC tank and infantry relief force crashed through the North Vietnamese ring, guns blazing. "Sir," reported Staff Sergeant Leon R. Burns to the incredulous commander of the rescue column, "this *is* the company, or what's left of it." Out of 300 men, only 27 walked out of the ambush, one of the worst battle disasters the Marines suffered during the Vietnam War.

By the time the shaken survivors reached Con Thien, the remainder of the 1st Battalion, plus the entire 3d Battalion, were already in the field, joined on the following day by

the 1st Battalion, 3d Marines. For twelve hours on July 3 Marine air and artillery, plus the eight-inch guns of the 7th Fleet, mounted a continuous bombardment of suspected enemy positions in preparation for a counterattack on the fourth. But the NVA had added some new weapons of its own to the battlefield equation including large-caliber, long-range artillery, high-quality bazookas and rockets, and Russian surface-to-air (SAM) missiles. Almost as soon as it began, the Independence Day attack encountered heavy resistance and by dusk had ground to a halt.

As had been the case at Khe Sanh, however, the enormously powerful combination of American supporting arms was more than the North Vietnamese could long withstand. During July 5 and 6, artillery and tactical air struck again and again at large concentrations of enemy troops with devastating results. On the night of the sixth the NVA attempted to overwhelm the 3/9 and 1/3 with a massed regimental assault preceded by a thunderous bombardment of more than 1,500 rounds of artillery fire. For six hours the two sides traded blows, waves of attacking North Vietnamese hurling grenades and fuzed blocks of TNT into Marine positions, the Marines countering with flareships, attack aircraft, helicopter gunships, naval gunfire, and a storm of artillery. The next morning, the Communists began to withdraw back across the DMZ. Stretched out for thousands of yards in front of the American perimeter were more than 800 enemy dead.

By the time Buffalo was concluded on July 14, the Marines had lost a total of 159 dead to the enemy's 1,290 KIA. Yet within a month, the North Vietnamese returned to the attack, now committed to the elimination of Con Thien. During late August and early September, the NVA stepped up rocket and artillery strikes on Marine installations across the eastern half of the DMZ, including a ferocious

Con Thien

In Vietnamese it meant "Hill of Angels." For the men of the 3/9 Marines it was more like hell. During September and October 1967 the combat base at Con Thien—a blasted plateau of red mud, sodden trenches, barbed wire, and sandbags—endured daily bombardments from up to 1,200 rounds of NVA mortar, rocket, and artillery fire. The ceaseless pounding deafened ears and shattered nerves. It also took a steady toll of casualties, leaving the survivors looking, in their own words, like "the walking dead."

Left. *A Marine dives for cover after enemy fire hit the company radioman.* Below. *Flack–jacketed riflemen hug the ground during an NVA mortar attack.* Right. *Shells fired by an 81mm mortar team keep the enemy at bay. Following page. "Sir, this is the company, or what's left of it." An M48 Patton tank carries the bodies of some of the men of Company B, 9th Marines, ambushed north of Con Thien on July 2, 1967.*

bombardment of Dong Ha that damaged seventeen helicopters and set fire to the base's ammunition and fuel dumps. This was no more than a prelude, however, to the intense shelling directed at Con Thien during September, when the attempt to overwhelm the small outpost reached its climax. Over the course of one week, from September 20 to 26, Con Thien absorbed 3,077 rounds of artillery, rocket, and mortar fire. On September 25 alone, the Marines counted over 1,200 incoming rounds.

For the men of the 3/9 garrisoned at Con Thien during this onslaught, the "deep hole" became a constant preoccupation. In addition to the artillery barrages, there were also recoilless rifle fire and RPG sniping to contend with. Sappers armed with satchel charges and bangalore torpedoes, real probes, and simulated ground assaults also left everyone's nerves on edge. To make matters worse, heavy, unseasonable rains flooded trench lines, collapsed bunkers, and washed out all land lines of communication.

The weather was an even greater source of misery outside the perimeter where four more Marine battalions—the 2/4, 3/4, 2/9, and the 3/26—roamed the surrounding terrain trying to keep the enemy at arm's length. Artillery, attack aircraft, and B-52s hammered at the NVA in what the official Marine history calls "one of the greatest concentrations of firepower in support of a single division in the history of the Vietnam war." At the same time the grunts met the enemy on the ground in sharp firefights and violent battles including an assault on the 3/26 by an entire North Vietnamese regiment. Absorbing fearful casualties, the NVA were never able to mass sufficient forces for an all-out attack, and by the end of September the shelling began to taper off. On October 4, MACV headquarters announced that the "siege" of Con Thien was over and the enemy was in retreat. He had suffered, declared General Westmoreland, a "crushing defeat," losing over 2,000 men.

Turning point

At a ceremony at Da Nang on November 1, Vice President Hubert H. Humphrey presented the Presidential Unit Citation to the 3d Division for "extraordinary heroism and outstanding performance of duty." The award was richly merited. In the course of more than a dozen major operations during 1967—Prairie, Beacon Hill, Hickory, Cimarron, Crocket, Ardmore, Buffalo, Kingfisher, Bastion Hill, Fremont, and the recently initiated Kentucky, Lancaster, and Scotland—the men of the 3d Division took on North Vietnamese regulars in a savage conventional war under the most difficult conditions. Fighting with skill and gallantry and backed up by a devastating array of supporting arms, they had halted the NVA offensive across the DMZ, inflicted staggering casualties on the enemy, and completed the first section of the McNamara Line.

For all that had been accomplished along the DMZ, however, there was also cause for concern as 1967 drew to a close. Construction of the anti-infiltration barrier had seriously drained III MAF manpower and logistical resources. A continuing shortage of officers, inexperienced NCOs, and nagging problems with the M16 rifle, which had an alrming tendency to jam, and the CH-46 helicopter hurt the division's combat capacity even as the North Vietnamese funneled more men onto the battlefield. And despite the number of enemy killed—estimates ranged from 18,000 to 25,000—by year's end the ratio of American and South Vietnamese to Communist forces in the region had dropped to less than 4 to 1, the worst in Vietnam. Even more troubling, the marked improvement in NVA weapons had reduced the ratio of enemy to American dead. "It isn't great sport any more," complained one Marine back for his second tour. "You know, a 7 to 1 ratio of Communist casualties to the U.S.'s. It's now about 3 to 1, in some places 2 to 1, and even occasionally 1 to 1."

Victory was being purchased at an ever-greater cost. During 1967 there were 30,000 Marine casualties in I Corps including nearly 3,500 dead. Some questioned whether victory was being achieved at all, whether the Marines had simply been lured to the border to bleed. "We were pitting American bodies against North Vietnamese bodies in a backcountry war of attrition," General Krulak would later write, "while the enemy was free to make political speeches in the hamlets and villages" along the coast. "In the end, in terms of doing what we came to Vietnam to do, the costly, blood-sapping, grinding battles were blows in the air." For Krulak, and others who shared his viewpoint, nothing so exemplified both the power of American arms and the futility of American strategy as the second battle of Khe Sanh.

While enemy activity in the eastern demilitarized zone diminished after the September battles around Con Thien, it flared again to the west where the 1st and 3d battalions of the 26th Marines, deployed to Vietnam in several increments during the previous year, now maintained an uneasy vigil over Khe Sanh. In late December, American intelligence identified two NVA divisions closing in on the undermanned base. Gen. Westmoreland, who prized Khe Sanh as a crucial monitoring station of enemy infiltration and the eventual jumping-off point for potential ground operations to cut the Ho Chi Minh Trail, seized on the opportunity to pin this large enemy force in place and destroy it. Less enthusiastic about Khe Sanh's strategic value and suspecting the NVA was trying to draw troops away from the coast, the Marine command nevertheless promised to hold the base. On January 20, 1968, ten days before the Communists launched their Tet offensive, a sharp firefight in the hills to the north signaled the opening of the long siege.

For the next seventy-seven days, the 6,000 men at Khe Sanh, now including all three battalions of the 26th Marines (normally a regiment in the 5th Marine Division), the 1st Battalion, 9th Marines, and an ARVN Ranger battalion,

endured incessant bombardment, pouring rain, mud, stink, rats, and the constant fear of a massed ground attack. On February 6, the NVA did overrun the nearby Special Forces camp at Lang Vei, and several significant assaults were made against the hills north of the main base. But Khe Sanh itself was never more than probed by enemy ground forces, something Westmoreland attributed to the manmade firestorm created by U.S.-supporting arms. One hundred thousand tons of bombs and 200,000 rounds of artillery and mortar fire pulverized NVA positions and prevented the concentration of forces necessary to mount a major attack.

By the time a combined Army-Marine relief force linked up with the embattled garrison on April 6, MACV estimated that 10,000 enemy troops had been killed at Khe Sanh. By comparison, 205 defenders died during the siege with about 800 more seriously wounded. This stark contrast was hailed as a vindication of the decision to defend Khe Sanh in the first place. Others saw in all the suffering and sacrifice little that brought the U.S. closer to victory in Vietnam. "They tied us down, they diverted us from the people, they exacted an impressive penalty in men, time, and materiel while they proceeded with their Tet strategy," argued Krulak. "Their only investment was blood, to which they assigned a low importance. And when it was over nothing had changed—nothing." In that the general was wrong. Overwhelming victory or costly mistake, Khe Sanh marked a decisive turning point in the war along the DMZ for the men of the 3d Division.

New strategy, new tactics

In the aftermath of the Tet offensive, events in Washington and Vietnam produced a fundamental change of direction that moved the Marines into a new phase of combat. President Johnson's decision to halt the bombing of North Vietnam, the beginning of negotiations with the Communists, the rejection of Gen. Westmoreland's request for substantial reinforcements, and Westmoreland's replacement as COMUSMACV by General Creighton W. Abrams meant an end to escalation and a shift away from the strategy of attrition. Abrams reduced the emphasis on big-unit, search-and-destroy operations, concentrating instead on preemptive raids against Communist base camps and supply depots. With his concurrence, the Marines abandoned Khe Sanh and suspended further work on the McNamara Line. Freed to a substantial degree from the defense of fixed positions, the 3d Division and its new commander, Major General Raymond G. Davis, immediately assumed a more aggressive approach.

For Davis the key was mobility, and he set out to

A CH-46 Sea Knight crashes during a July 1966 assault into the Song Ngan Valley. Problems with this transport helicopter hampered Marine operations early in the war.

reshape the division to that central requirement: eliminating unessential combat bases and strongpoints, defending those that remained with reinforced companies rather than battalions, creating a mobile strike force out of the newly released troops, regaining unit integrity by returning scattered battalions to the operational control of their regiments, expanding reconnaissance and intelligence efforts, and providing the division with an airmobile capacity heretofore available only to such Army units as the 1st Air Cavalry and the 101st Airborne. Davis had the good fortune to arrive in Vietnam just when the long-standing shortage of Marine helicopters was finally overcome. With rebuilt CH-46s and growing numbers of CH-53s, he launched a series of swift, punishing operations against the NVA.

His first target was the newly infiltrated 308th NVA Division, whose 88th and 102d Regiments were harassing convoys along Route 9 and constructing a road across the trackless mountain jungles south of Khe Sanh. Under the control of Brigadier General Carl W. Hoffman, the operation was a two-phase assault code-named Robin North, Robin South. On June 2, elements of the 1st and 4th Marines flew by helicopter into Landing Zones Robin and Loon, which had been blasted out of the jungle canopy in the middle of the enemy's area of operations. The 1st Marines attacked northward toward blocking positions established by the 2d Battalion, 3d Marines, along Route 9. Meanwhile the 4th Marines launched a series of battalion-size forays to the south toward LZ Torch, occupied by the 3d Battalion, 9th Marines, only two kilometers from the Laotian border.

The NVA reacted violently to the abrupt invasion of what had been for years their private domain, challenging the Marines in a succession of fierce engagements that drew American blood but failed to halt the devastating raids. In a rapid sequence of assault and maneuver, the 4th Marines slashed through the rugged border area killing 725 enemy troops, destroying whole sections of the new road, and capturing large amounts of equipment and supplies, including rice, weapons, ammunition, explosives, engineering tools, trucks, and a large Russian mobile machine shop. After two weeks in combat, the battered 308th was on its way back north for refitting.

What Davis had done in the Robin action was to adapt classic Marine amphibious doctrine to the problem of combat in the mountainous jungles of northern I Corps. The objectives were individual "islands" of enemy strength in areas inaccessible by overland means. The jump-off points were dry land "beachheads" called fire support bases to which the assault force was carried by helicopter instead of landing craft. These temporary mountaintop strongpoints were blasted out of the jungle with air-delivered high explosives and napalm. They provided overlapping "artillery fans" under which entire battalions, resupplied wholly by helicopter, methodically searched the area of operations for Communist soldiers, equipment, and supplies. As the ground troops reached the edge of their artillery protection, new fire support bases were rapidly constructed, permitting still deeper penetration of the operational area. In this manner even the most impenetrable terrain could be interlaced with a pattern of LZs and artillery bases from which powerful ground assaults were launched against the enemy and his well-defended logistical system.

These techniques were further refined during a three-regiment combined operation west of Con Thien in July and, even more spectacularly, a month later when the 320th NVA Division attempted to penetrate the DMZ as part of a nationwide offensive. Alerted by a North Vietnamese prisoner to the impending attack, the 3d and 9th Marines intercepted three enemy regiments north and west of Camp Carroll. This provoked heavy fighting that surged along Mutter's Ridge and into Helicopter Valley. For more than two months the battle raged across the southern demilitarized zone, the Marines leapfrogging battalion-sized units progressively farther north into new fire support bases constructed atop key terrain features. Their avenues of retreat blocked, the NVA regiments disintegrated into small groups, many of which were trapped by superior American forces and annihilated. Meanwhile, U.S. units, now including elements of the 4th and 26th Marines, swept through the southern DMZ destroying infiltration facilities and uncovering huge stockpiles of food, munitions, weapons, and rockets. By late October, as the last American units left the DMZ, the 320th Division had lost nearly 1,600 KIA at a cost to the Marines of 182 men dead and wounded.

Between April and October 1968, the 3d Marine Division had decimated three North Vietnamese Army divisions, the 304th, 308th, and 320th, and driven their remnants from South Vietnamese soil. What six months earlier had been one of the most contested regions of the country was now one of the most secure. While the enemy licked his wounds and the monsoon rains made extended operations difficult, the Marines conducted a vigorous pacification drive along Route 9 from Camp Carroll to Dong Ha. But Davis had no intention of allowing the NVA to regain the initiative in Quang Tri Province. On January 20, 1969, the 3d Division returned to the attack with Operation Dewey Canyon.

Aimed at a major enemy logistical complex in the Da Krong Valley along the Laotian border, the operation projected the 9th Marines fifty kilometers from the nearest U.S. base into some of the most difficult terrain in I Corps. For seven weeks the Marines battled foul weather conditions and tenacious defenders, conducting search-and-destroy missions including a secret incursion into Laos. The men combined the high-mobility tactics refined during the previous months with a conventional "regiment-in-the attack" overland infantry assault for the final drive. In the end, they bettered the casualty ratios achieved the previous fall

Stingray

During their first two years in Vietnam, the Marines looked for a way to fight an enemy who often seemed both invisible and everywhere. They deployed multi-battalion search-and-destroy missions, mounted cordon operations, and built a network of strong points across the country. Finally, they adopted the tactics of the enemy in what came to be called Stingray patrols. Employing small, five-man teams of specially selected men, the Marines could go out at night and fight the way the Vietcong did. The Marines could become guerrillas.

"When we first started going out small at night, guys from regular units told us the Vietcong would just eat us up," said one rifleman. "I can remember sitting in muck up to my neck being eaten alive instead by mosquitoes, but afraid to move because I had been told the Vietcong were everywhere." But the teams did get results, and as the Marines gained confidence in the new technique they found there was no need for an elite force—the average rifleman could do the job well.

For a handful of men to leave a fortified base and plunge into no man's land took courage. But the Marines soon learned they were safer on a Stingray patrol than they were on a battalion sweep. "You'll stay alive," officers preached, "even if the work is hairier." They also discovered that man for man they were six times deadlier as members of a strike team than as part of a larger operation.

By 1968, when Stingray operations were declassified and expanded, the patrols became routine. That year, more than 1,600 teams entered enemy territory within the 3d Marine Division's area of responsibility. That meant that roughly twenty teams were patrolling at any given time. On a typical day, four made contact with enemy soldiers.

Escorted by a search-and-rescue ship and two Huey gunships, a Stingray team ferried in a CH–34 or CH–46 helicopter to a predetermined landing zone. This was dangerous. Moments after scrambling off the transport helicopter, the team set up a perimeter and poised for combat. The gunships remained buzzing overhead, ready to intervene. If the enemy did not attack the landing, the aircraft departed for base, leaving the Marines behind.

Then it was time to stalk the Vietcong. From concealed positions, the Marines sometimes heard the chopping of wood. At night, they watched lanterns bobbing across the valley floor. It could be eerie, but the Marines felt some reassurance knowing that they were always within the range of friendly artillery emplacements.

When the patrol stumbled upon small groups of enemy guerrillas, the men relied on surprise and their M16s to settle the engagement. But when the patrol found a larger enemy unit, it called in the supporting arms that made it so formidable, even against a sizable enemy force. Fixing the enemy position on his map, the artillery spotter radioed in a strike. As soon as the distant battery found the range, the patrol members abandoned their position, leaving Claymore mines to cover their withdrawal. If the enemy pursued, they risked ambush.

The early successes of Stingray patrols inevitably produced countermeasures from the VC and the NVA. They learned to refrain from attacking newly arrived Marine patrols. Instead, they waited until the delivery aircraft departed and they could concentrate fire on the isolated team. When the enemy's battle plans required moving soldiers in force, advance patrols combed the route like destroyers around a convoy, screening the main body and trying to root out any Marine patrols they found along the way.

If, according to statistics, a Stingray patrol was relatively safe, it still ran the risk of being wiped out. Indeed, when the enemy caught hold of a Stingray patrol, they could reinforce until the Marines were hopelessly overwhelmed. Yet the American "guerrillas" had resources their pajama-clad counterparts could never muster. A single call of distress sent artillerymen a horizon away slamming shells into the breeches of their big guns. At airstrips along the coast, jet fighters scrambled into the sky. Gunships sprayed the jungle around the trapped Marines while choppers swirled overhead, waiting for the chance to fly the Marines out. Meanwhile, a reaction force boarded transport helicopters and prepared to come to the rescue if extraction proved impossible.

The patrols, of course, could not seize and hold terrain or fight a decisive battle. But by the end of 1968, the Marines realized that their growing reliance on stealth rather than massed force, on Stingray patrols rather than battalion operations, was producing results.

A lower casualty rate was an immediate benefit (and served one of Washington's political priorities). The strike teams also covered more terrain with less manpower, and at a lower cost. The combination of elusiveness and firepower meant that Communist units could not enjoy the comfort of relaxing. And, to the extent that Stingray patrols forced countertactics upon the enemy, they diverted strength from offensive operations. Moreover, if the patrols were deployed and debriefed shrewdly, the data they brought in could reveal patterns of enemy activity, improving the ability of the Marines to deal more decisive blows.

The Marines who conducted Stingray patrols were guerrillas with a punch. Few in number and operating in enemy territory, they moved by stealth, attacked by surprise, and withdrew unseen. Relying primarily on foot power and eyesight to find the enemy, they did the job with a combination of individual cunning and the awesome force of American supporting arms. It was, thought some Marine commanders, the best way to fight this kind of war.

February 1969. A heavily laden platoon of the 2/9 Marines crosses a stream during Operation Dewey Canyon, a major foray along the Laotian border southwest of Khe Sanh.

against the 320th NVA Division and uncovered some of the largest caches of ammunition and supplies captured during the war.

Tactically sophisticated and enormously successful, Dewey Canyon would be the high-water mark for the 3d Division. The day the operation began, Richard Nixon took the oath of office as president, promising not victory but peace. While the 9th Marines were still slogging through the sodden jungle, MACV formulated a new campaign plan emphasizing Vietnamization, pacification, and the security of the cities. By the time Dewey Canyon came to a close on March 18, rumors of withdrawal had already begun to circulate. "I felt, and I think that most Marines felt that the time had come to get out of Vietnam," remembered Marine Corps Commandant General Leonard F. Chapman. The post-Tet counterattack had run its course. The new reality was disengagement.

MACV's 1969 campaign plan reflected not only General Abrams's appraisal of the military situation on the ground but even more the pressure he was receiving from Washington to reduce American casualties. "The realities of the American political situation indicate a need to consider time limitations in developing a strategy to 'win,'" conceded Abrams. "Time then is running out." Time also had become a preoccupation of Hanoi's. Still recovering from the losses suffered during Tet, and convinced that American public opinion would force Nixon to withdraw, the North Vietnamese retreated to a defensive strategy of protracted war. The result was a significant reduction in the level of fighting throughout Vietnam, including northern I Corps. The NVA continued to lob rockets and mortars into night defensive positions and landing zones, but most of the Marines' confrontations along the DMZ now consisted of brief clashes with small groups of enemy soldiers.

If the intensity of combat had declined, however, the mission of the 3d Division remained the same: to halt North Vietnamese incursions through the demilitarized zone and to preempt Communist offensives by attacks against NVA staging bases along the Laotian border. In both of these roles the 9th Marines remained the most active of the division's units.

Three weeks after the end of Dewey Canyon, a reconstructed 308th NVA Division sent its 36th Regiment across the DMZ west of Con Thien. Dispatched to blunt the enemy probe, the 9th made only sporadic contact until April 21 when the Marines ran into entrenched enemy positions between Cam Lo and the Rockpile. Soon after the continuing fighting was formalized as Operation Virginia Ridge, however, the 9th passed control on to the 3d Marines and headed back to the Da Krong Valley as part of Operation Apache Snow. The southern phase of that action, conducted by a brigade of the 101st Airborne Division, encountered harsh resistance culminating in the battle for Hamburger Hill. But the extensive reconnaissance patrols mounted by the Marines discovered little in the way of enemy troops or supplies. By early June the 2d and 3d battalions had been committed to a new operation, Cameron Falls, against elements of the resurgent 304th NVA Division in the old Robin operational area, while the 1st Battalion teamed up with the Army's 1st Brigade, 5th Infantry Division (Mechanized), in Operation Utah Mesa near Khe Sanh.

Over the course of a month and a half both operations together netted a little over 400 enemy KIA, a far cry from the soaring casualty figures of a year earlier. With Communist military activity steadily diminishing and Washington intent on turning the war over to the Vietnamese as quickly as possible, President Nixon announced on June 10 the start of U.S. troop withdrawals. First in, the 3d Marine Division would be among the first out. Twenty-five thousand American servicemen were scheduled to leave by the end of August, including the 9th Marines. On June 23 the 1st Battalion fired its last shot and came in from the field to join its sister battalions at Vandegrift Combat Base. By August, the 9th Marines had redeployed to Camp Courtney, Okinawa. The following month the entire 3d Division received orders to commence stand-down operations in preparation for departure from Southeast Asia.

Since mid-July when Virginia Ridge ended, the 3d Marines had been patrolling the area between Con Thien and the Rockpile as part of Operation Idaho Canyon. Ironically, on September 17, the day after the stand-down orders reached division headquarters, the Marines found themselves engaged in one of the most violent encounters of the summer, a six-hour battle north of the Rockpile in which twenty-five Marines and forty-eight North Vietnamese soldiers were killed. Although all combat operations ceased for the division a week later, it was a bitter reminder of what the war had cost and how far away peace remained.

For more than four years the men and officers of the 3d Marine Division had waged war against guerrilla insurgents and the regular troops of the North Vietnamese Army. They had taken on enemy squads in coastal hamlets and slugged it out with enemy divisions on the shell-blasted hills of the demilitarized zone. They had answered political terror with pacification and protected South Vietnam's northern frontier with firepower. Now it was time to go "home," the 4th Marines and division headquarters to join the 9th on Okinawa, the 3d Marines bound for Camp Pendleton, California. By the end of November the last units were gone. For the men of the 3d Marine Division, the Vietnam War was over.

Yet the war went on—along the DMZ, where a battered but unbroken enemy waited for the rest of the Americans to be withdrawn, in the mountain valleys west of Hue, where thousands of NVA conscripts replenished the stocks of ammunition and supplies the Marines had so laboriously destroyed, and to the south, among the crowded villages of Quang Nam Province. There the 1st Marine Division waged its own special war, one no less costly, against an opponent no less determined, in places called An Hoa and Que Son and the Arizona Territory and Charley Ridge.

Men of the 3d Marine Division land at San Diego on October 27, 1969, as part of the first withdrawal of American troops from Vietnam.

1st MAW

Along with the deployment of two divisions—the 1st and 3d—the Marine Corps committed a large share of its air power to the war in Vietnam. At the height of the conflict, one–half of the Corps' aircraft were in South Vietnam, flying missions day and night throughout the Indochina Peninsula as the 1st Marine Aircraft Wing (1st MAW).

The 1st MAW established its headquarters at Da Nang during the start of the U.S. troop buildup in 1965. After taking command of all Marine aircraft in Vietnam, some of which had been there since 1962, the 1st MAW confronted a lack of aviation facilities in South Vietnam. To complement the jet–capable air base at Da Nang—the only one in I Corps—Navy Seabees and Marines constructed in a matter of weeks a short airfield for tactical support (SATS) at Chu Lai, fitted with an aluminum–plank runway, an aircraft catapult, and arresting gear. For the wing's helicopters, they built major bases at Phu Bai, at Ky Ha, near Chu Lai, and on Marble Mountain, near Da Nang, along with numerous outlying fields capable of handling helicopters and KC–130 transport planes. With bases in place, the wing grew quickly to include six Marine Air Groups (MAGs), three with helicopters (MAGs 16, 36, and 39) and three with fixed–wing craft (MAGs 11, 12, and 13). Each group contained approximately seventy–five aircraft.

Normally an air wing supports one division, but by the spring of 1966 the 1st MAW had to meet the needs of the 1st and 3d Marine divisions, both now fully deployed to South Vietnam. This large mission and the wing's abrupt deployment to Southeast Asia stretched Marine aviation

As smoke billows from an F–4 Phantom strike, Marines in Operation Union II rush one of their wounded to an evacuation helicopter.

Top. *Soldiers from Marine Aircraft Group 12 reload an A–4E Skyhawk with 250–pound bombs and 20MM cannon rounds in June 1967.* Above. *Lance Corporal Vincent Pisco and Private First Class Norman Pearson raise the landing gear on an F–4B Phantom at the Chu Lai air base on November 8, 1966. Marine mechanics routinely checked all aircraft parts for wear and tear.*

resources to the limit. Along with inadequate numbers of armaments and ground crews, the Corps found itself lacking approximately 1,000 pilots if it were to ensure sufficient skill levels and an equitable rotation of pilots in and out of Vietnam. It was a problem the Corps could never fully solve. The Marines sent some pilots to the Army for helicopter training and others to the Air Force for fixed–wing training but still had to operate with fewer pilots than they needed, relying on the aviators' courage and endurance.

The aircraft of the 1st MAW flew a variety of missions in Indochina. F–4 Phantoms and A–4 Skyhawks flew strategic bombing runs against selected targets in North Vietnam and along Communist supply routes in Laos. With the introduction of the A–6A Intruder in late 1966, the Marines had the finest all–weather bomber available. They employed it as far north as Haiphong and Hanoi. The EA–6B, an A–6 equipped with radar–jamming equipment, became in 1969 one of the U.S. military's primary

electronic warfare aircraft and flew in support of Air Force and Navy as well as Marine strikes. It replaced the outmoded EF–10B, which arrived in–country with one of the 1st Marine squadrons deployed to Vietnam. During the opening phases of the air war against North Vietnam, heavy, slow "Willie the Whale," as pilots nicknamed the Korean–War–vintage EF–10, had been the only electronic warfare jet available in America's arsenal in Southeast Asia.

The primary mission of the 1st Marine Aircraft Wing was to provide air support for the Marine divisions in I Corps. Marine jets prepared the way for ground operations by clearing forward areas with napalm and bombs. Others escorted transport and supply craft. When ground units ran into particularly tough resistance, Marine Phantoms and Sky-hawks—some of which were on "hot pad alert" at Chu Lai—responded quickly, striking enemy base areas and troops. Later, as U.S. Army and other allied units moved into I Corps, Marine jets supported

Top. *Marine F–4B Phantoms await their turn on the flight line at Da Nang Air Base in January 1966.* Above. *The 650–foot nylon tape of Chu Lai Air Station's mobile arresting gear (MOREST) brings a Marine A–4 Skyhawk to an abrupt halt after a mission in December 1966. MOREST teams stood on twenty–four–hour alert to help Marine jets land in emergencies or bad weather.*

An A–6A Intruder is loaded with 500–lb. bombs in August 1967. Introduced in late 1966, the high–tech, all–weather bomber proved powerful and versatile, flying missions over Laos and North Vietnam as well as supporting combat troops in the South.

their operations as well. By the end of the war, many Marine jet squadrons had flown staggering numbers of missions. Squadron 311 alone conducted 50,000 combat sorties.

The 1st MAW also made the most of its three helicopter groups. The transport helicopters—the UH–34s and the CH–37s, later replaced by the CH–46 Sea Knights and CH–53 Sea Stallions—carried everything from troops and supplies to heavy artillery. On at least one occasion, they even transported elephants as part of village relocation operations. In 1968, Marine helicopters transported an average of more than 50,000 men and 6,000 tons of cargo per month. The armed helicopters of the UH–1 Huey series and later the AH–1G Cobras were invaluable, being more available and maneuverable than jets. They were used as gunships, for command and control and administrative duties, for aerial reconnaissance, and as platforms for searchlights and sensors.

An F–4B Phantom pulls away after striking a Vietcong staging area near Da Nang in May 1967. Right. Sorely needed replacement pilots arrive at Da Nang Air Base.

Left. *In March 1971, a Marine Huey gunship fires on the enemy southwest of Marble Mountain.*
Above. *Lieutenant Colonel McDonald D. Tweed of Medium Helicopter Squadron 361 prepares his men to pick up the 3d Battalion, 5th Marines, during Operation Colorado on July 4, 1966.*

Every Marine helicopter in the air could also be called upon to evacuate casualties, perhaps the most hazardous mission of all. In 1968, Marine helicopters evacuated 67,000 people during some 42,000 sorties.

Most Marine ground operations required air support, and many fully utilized the 1st MAW's capabilities. During the siege of Khe Sanh in 1968, for example, the 1st MAW resupplied hill outposts through a coordinated operation called "Super Gaggle." A single mission used a tactical air coordinator (TAC) and KC–130 tankers from Da Nang, A–4s from Chu Lai, UH–1E gunships from Quang Tri, and CH–46s from Dong Ha. Rendezvousing above the assigned outposts, each aircraft performed its mission under the direction of the TAC. First, Skyhawks hit the surrounding area with napalm, rockets, and smoke. Then, CH–46s lowered their loads, while Hueys hovered nearby to protect the other helicopters and to pick up any downed crewmen.

Above. *UH-34 transport helicopters take off after landing Marine riflemen in April 1966.*

Within five minutes, the transport heli-copters deposited the supplies and headed home. The jets, in the meantime, hooked up with KC–130 tankers, refueled, and returned to base.

As in past conflicts, the Marines strug-gled with the Air Force over control of Marine aviation assets. While the Ma-rines argued that full authority should remain with III MAF so that Marine air power could ensure timely support to Ma-rine ground units, the Air Force believed that during wartime, a single manager, in this case the commanding general of the 7th Air Force, should control all air operations.

After three years of bickering, the issue came to a head in 1968, when General Westmoreland, frustrated by the lack of air coordination during the Tet offensive, ordered the 7th Air Force to direct all air operations. Despite vehement Marine protests, single management became a reality on March 10, with the Marines henceforth having to inform the Air Force of their daily fixed–wing capabilities. (They maintained control over their heli-copters.) Both services, however, at-tempted to make the system work, and, in the end, MACV received better air sup-port while the Marine Corps lost none of its capability to protect its own troops.

After thousands of missions, units from the 1st MAW began departing Vietnam in 1969. The wing itself left on April 14, 1971. Only a handful of Marine aviation units from MAGs 12 and 15 remained on duty in Indochina and helped to block the North Vietnamese Easter offensive of 1972 and hit enemy positions throughout Indochina until January 1973. Marine helicopters performed their last mission in South Viet-nam on the eve of the government's de-feat, evacuating over 2,000 people from Saigon in April 1975. In all, the 1st MAW lost 252 helicopters in combat and 173 fixed–wing aircraft. Two Marines of the 1st MAW distinguished themselves by re-ceiving the Medal of Honor.

Wounded near Dong Ha in December 1967, a Marine is helped by two comrades toward a multipurpose UH–1E Huey.

The Village War

In early November 1965, Secretary of Defense Robert S. McNamara prepared for President Lyndon Johnson a memorandum reassessing the situation in Vietnam eight months after the commitment of U.S. ground forces. Although the initial troop deployments had blunted the Communist military offensive and prevented a collapse of the Saigon government, wrote McNamara, victory was nowhere in sight. Three weeks later the secretary's warnings were reinforced by General William Westmoreland, who reported that despite the American buildup Communist forces in South Vietnam had more than doubled, including the addition of at least six and possibly nine regiments of the North Vietnamese Army. To meet this challenge, Westmoreland asked for 150,000 additional men. After a hurried visit to Saigon at the end of the month, McNamara recommended to the president that Westmoreland's request be granted. Among the units slated for the Phase II deployments was the 1st Marine Division. Its mission: to take on the war in southern I Corps.

In a ceremony at Da Nang, a joint honor guard marks the arrival of the 1st Marine Division in Vietnam on March 29, 1966. The division opened its command post at Chu Lai, along the coast 65 kilometers south of Da Nang.

Unlike the 3d Division, which was fully committed three months after the first battalion landing team came ashore, the 1st Marine Division trickled into South Vietnam over the course of a year. In fact, some elements of the division were already in Vietnam at the time of the November decisions. Two battalions of the 7th Marines had made separate landings at Qui Nhon in July to provide temporary security for an Army airfield and logistics base, then joined an artillery battalion from the 11th Marines at Chu Lai in August. That same month the 1st Battalion, 1st Marines, came ashore at Da Nang, followed in November by the 2d Battalion at Phu Bai. During the first three months of 1966, the remainder of the 1st Marines and all three battalions of the 5th Marines arrived in country. In March,

Major General Lewis J. Fields opened the division command post at Chu Lai, and by June the 17,000 men of the 1st Marine Division were firmly ensconced in the Chu Lai area. Well before then, however, the division had met the enemy in battle. Somehow it never seemed to take Marines very long to go to war.

First blood

Only four days after Colonel Oscar F. Peatross brought the 7th Marines' headquarters ashore at Chu Lai on August 14, 1965, the regiment was committed to combat as part of Operation Starlite. Deployed from offshore at the critical moment of the battle, elements of the 3d Battalion braved intense enemy fire in an attempt to come to the relief of a stranded supply column. Although losing four of their own, the 1st and 3d Battalions accounted for fifty-four Vietcong KIA over the next six days of sporadic fighting through the fortified hamlets of the Van Tuong Peninsula—getting an early taste of what the war was all about and winning a Navy Unit Commendation in the process.

Following the beating they received during Starlite, Vietcong Main Force units abandoned the coastal plain in

Preceding page. In February 1970, men of the 1st Battalion, 7th Marines, battle the enemy on Charley Ridge, a launching site for enemy rockets aimed at nearby Da Nang.

1st Marine Division

Arrived Vietnam: March 1966	**Departed Vietnam:** April 1971	

Unit Headquarters

Chu Lai *March 1966–Nov. 1966*	Da Nang *Nov. 1966–April 1971*	

Commanding Officers

Maj. Gen. Lewis J. Fields *Aug. 1965*	Maj. Gen. Carl A. Youngdale *June 1968*	Maj. Gen. Edwin B. Wheeler *Dec. 1969*
Maj. Gen. Herman Nickerson, Jr. *Oct. 1966*	Maj. Gen. Ormond R. Simpson *Dec. 1968*	Maj. Gen. Charles F. Widdecke *April 1970*
Maj. Gen. Donn J. Robertson *June 1967*		

Major Subordinate Units

1st Marines (1/1, 2/1, 3/1)	7th Marines (1/7, 2/7, 3/7)	11th Marines (Artillery)
5th Marines (1/5, 2/5, 3/5)	27th Marines (1/27, 2/27, 3/27)	(1/11, 2/11, 3/11, 4/11)

13,065 KIA	88,663 WIA	24 Medals of Honor

These figures reflect total Marine Corps casualties for the Vietnam War. The USMC does not keep casualty figures for individual divisions.

---

favor of the mountain valleys to the west, where for more than a month they assiduously avoided the Marines. Although III MAF increased the number of battalion-size operations against VC Main Force elements, the enemy refused to give battle. With the coming of the monsoon season in October, however, the insurgents launched a new offensive featuring sapper and mortar attacks against U.S. installations and operations against ARVN units. The main targets of the monsoon attacks were isolated district capitals and market towns garrisoned by local militia units. Overwhelming these scattered outposts, then ambushing the South Vietnamese forces that came to the rescue, the VC sought to grind the ARVN down before the continuing American buildup tipped the military balance in the government's favor.

On the night of October 27, VC raiders attacked airfields at China Beach, east of Da Nang, and at Chu Lai, destroying 26 aircraft, killing 2 Americans, and injuring nearly 100 more. Three weeks later, with the monsoon rains now averaging an inch a day, the refitted 1st Vietcong Regiment overran the district capital of Hiep Duc, the western gateway to the heavily populated, strategically vital Que Son Valley. Two battalions of the 5th ARVN Regiment recaptured Hiep Duc the following day after fierce fighting, but because of a shortage of troops they had to abandon it almost immediately. The ARVN withdrawal encouraged the VC, now reinforced with North Vietnamese heavy weapons units, to continue to move eastward into the Que Son Valley. When enemy pressure mounted on government garrisons at Viet An and Que Son during the first week of December, the Marines launched Operation Harvest Moon with the double objective of relieving the embattled outposts and trapping the 1st Vietcong Regiment between the two pincers of a combined South Vietnamese and American assault.

The operation kicked off on the morning of December 8 when units of the 56th ARVN Regiment and the 11th Vietnamese Ranger Battalion marched into the valley from the east. Anticipating no resistance until the following day, the South Vietnamese troops were unprepared for a sudden ambush by a full regiment of enemy soldiers. "They attacked in a mass and hit us from all sides," remembered an American adviser with the ARVN force. "People were dropping around us right and left." Within fifteen minutes the Ranger battalion had lost nearly one third of its men, including the battalion commander, who was wounded. Marine air support and the commitment of an additional ARVN unit temporarily drove the attackers off. But next morning the VC struck again, this time killing a battalion commander and sending the South Vietnamese reeling backwards.

It was now that the Marines entered the battle, the 2d Battalion, 7th Marines, and 3d Battalion, 3d Marines, flying by helicopter to landing zones on either side of the beleaguered ARVN. The 2/7 landed without incident, but the 3/3 ran into a substantial enemy force almost immediately. The ensuing firefight raged into the early evening before the VC broke contact. When the 2d Battalion, 1st Marines, attempted to close an avenue of escape to the south on the following day, they too were met with machine-gun, mortar, and small arms fire that left twenty Marines dead and eighty wounded by the time men from the 2/7 came to the rescue. The three battalions spent December 11 consolidating their positions only to discover that the enemy had vanished, presumably into the Phuoc Ha Valley, a Communist base area ten kilometers to the southeast. For the next three days the 3/3 and 2/1 scoured the new objective behind four B-52 strikes, the first delivered in direct support of Marine operations. The two battalions discovered large amounts of enemy supplies and equipment but not the 1st VC Regiment.

As the 3/3 and 2/1 began to leave the valley on December 16, Lieutenant Colonel Leon N. Utter's 2/7 Battalion searched the Khang River to the south with equal lack of

success. In fact, the Marines were having more trouble with the weather than the enemy. The incessant rain dogged every step, turning the ground into a quagmire and forcing the evacuation of a steady stream of men incapacitated by crippling immersion foot. Turning east toward Tam Ky on December 18, the battalion was moving in a column formation along a narrow road through hedgerow-bordered rice fields when they ran into the 80th VC Battalion at the village of Ky Phu.

Allowing the lead company to pass through the town unmolested, the Vietcong drew a second company to the south with sniper fire before the main enemy body opened fire on Company H&S still west of the village. Within minutes the Marines were surrounded. Firing, ducking, splashing through two feet of water and mud, their rifles soon fouled, leaving many men with only their .45-caliber pistols to fight back. "Six this is Five," radioed the company commander to Colonel Utter. "The enemy is on all sides and closing in. Our rifles aren't functioning. We're pretty well pinned down right now and it's getting hotter. Can you help us? Over." While Utter marshaled reinforcements and directed artillery fire to within a few meters of the embattled company, the commander of Company H&S plowed back and forth across the rice field shouting encouragement, carrying wounded, and firing his pistol until he grabbed an M79 grenade launcher from the hands of another Marine and blasted twenty-two successive rounds at the VC. The disgruntled Marine finally turned to his platoon commander and asked, "Sir, is it all right if *I* fire a couple of rounds from *my* weapon?"

By nightfall the fighting was over. The 80th VC Battalion left 105 bodies littering the battlefield, more than half killed by artillery fire. The 2/7 lost 11 men, with 71 more wounded. In all, Operation Harvest Moon accounted for 407 enemy KIA at a cost of 45 Marine dead and over 200 wounded. Although the Marines and South Vietnamese had uncovered a significant number of weapons and supplies, the main VC force had escaped. Bloody but inconclusive, Harvest Moon demonstrated what the Marines could do to the enemy when the latter stood still and how difficult he was to find when he did not.

Utah

For more than a month after the conclusion of Harvest Moon, the level of combat in I Corps remained low thanks to the observance of truces at Christmas and Tet, the celebration of the lunar new year. At the end of January, however, the Communists shelled the airfields at Da Nang and Marble Mountain with 120MM mortars. Only the second time such heavy-caliber weapons had been encountered

Men of the 1st Battalion, 7th Marines, assemble in a rice field on the Batangan Peninsula for one of ten battalion-size operations conducted between April and July 1966.

As a fellow Marine watches for VC, a grenadier from Company F, 2d Battalion, 7th Marines, fires an M79 grenade launcher on the first day of Operation Utah, March 4, 1966.

by the Marines, the attacks marked a new round of fighting that steadily drew more 1st Division units into the war: Operations Desoto and Double Eagle in Quang Ngai Province; Operation Stone south of Da Nang; Operation New York on the Phu Thu Peninsula northeast of Phu Bai; and, perhaps the most violent of them all, Operation Utah.

Increasing sightings of North Vietnamese units during the first three months of the year had produced little in the way of solid contact. In the elaborately designed Operation Double Eagle, for instance, four separate Marine battalions spent nearly three weeks fruitlessly searching the border of Quang Ngai and Binh Dinh Province for the 325C NVA Division. Thus, when a regiment of the 2d NVA Division was located a few kilometers northwest of Quang Ngai City on March 3, III MAF immediately decided to mount a coordinated attack with the 2d ARVN Division. Through the day and on into the night, U.S. and South Vietnamese commanders mapped the details of the upcoming operation. Meanwhile, the Marines moved a howitzer battery into supporting range, and three Marine aircraft groups prepared for high-volume flight operations the next day. The Marines were so eager to fight that one officer characterized the battle plan as "nothing more than get on your horse and go."

Despite the speed with which the operation was launched and the intense aerial bombardment of the landing zone the next morning, the first waves of helicopters carrying the ARVN 1st Airborne Battalion were met by withering 12.7MM machine-gun fire that struck four ac-

companying gunships and brought down an F-4 fighter-bomber. The helicopter pilots reported that the LZ was one of the hottest they'd ever encountered. Then they climbed back into their ships and flew in a load of ARVN troops. By 10:40, with 400 South Vietnamese soldiers on the ground and moving against the enemy, the first elements of the 2d Battalion, 7th Marines, were dropping under heavy fire into a second landing zone nearby. Twelve of the thirty helicopters that began the lift that morning were knocked out of operation.

Although the 2/7 initially encountered only light resistance on the ground, the ARVN swiftly fell to a hot firefight and called for help. Advancing to the right of the South Vietnamese, the Marines ran into entrenched enemy positions from which poured small arms, automatic weapons, and mortar fire. For the next five hours the Marines traded blows with NVA troops in a vicious engagement at ranges as close as twenty-five meters. One badly shot-up platoon cut off from the rest of the battalion survived only with the aid of repeated air and artillery strikes called in closer to friendly troops than military wisdom deemed possible. By nightfall ammunition shortages, medical resupply, and casualty evacuation had become critical. Pulling back under cover of bombs, rockets, napalm, and strafing runs, the battalion finally disengaged from the enemy and set up night defensive positions.

Concluding that "we have a tiger by the tail," III MAF alerted additional units while Marine air pummeled the North Vietnamese. Artillery fire from Binh Son was so heavy—in one two-hour period hurling 1,900 rounds into suspected enemy positions—that two ammunition resupply truck convoys were sent from Chu Lai, the first time a Marine convoy had ventured from an enclave at night. When they reached their destination, the trucks were backed up to the gun positions, their ammunition unloaded one round at a time directly into the weapons chambers. Thanks to the heavy application of supporting arms and their own tenacity, both the Americans and the South Vietnamese held off furious NVA counterattacks during the night as they waited for daylight and reinforcements to arrive.

Brigadier General Jonas M. Platt, III MAF chief of staff, had already swung the Marine command into action, ordering the deployment of another 155MM battery to Binh Son, activating a task force to direct the expanding operation, establishing a command post on "Buddha Hill" some ten kilometers south of the embattled 2/7, and sending the 3d Battalion, 1st Marines, into blocking positions on high ground seven kilometers north of the main battle. At daybreak Platt ordered the 3/1 south to relieve pressure on a battalion of ARVN airborne soldiers. Meanwhile, 2d ARVN Division Commander Brigadier General Hoang Xuan Lam had positioned his 37th Ranger Battalion and the 1st Battalion, 5th ARVN Regiment, along a railroad line to the east and helilifted the 5th ARVN Airborne Battalion into the same landing zone used a day earlier by the 2/7. When General Platt inserted the 2d Battalion, 4th Marines, into the southern Utah area, the NVA were seemingly surrounded.

The 2/4 not only encountered heavy machine-gun fire at the landing zone that put several helicopters out of commission, it was almost immediately engaged by enemy ground forces from fortified positions in hamlets on either side of the LZ. Only after more than an hour of close combat was the battalion able to disengage and join the 2/7. To the north, the 3/1 had moved unhindered toward a linkup with the ARVN airborne battalion until brought to a sudden halt at the base of Hill 50. There a large NVA force shielded from sight by bamboo fences and hedgerows, entrenched in an elaborate network of tunnel-connected bunkers and spider traps, and protected by minefields and booby traps, waited for the Americans. It took three-and-a-half hours before the enemy was dislodged from his formidable defenses in bitter fighting that continued to swirl around the base of the hill for the rest of the afternoon.

With nightfall came a general disengagement of forces, except to the south where Company B of the 1st Battalion, 7th Marines, guarded a downed helicopter at the landing zone used by the 2/4 earlier in the day. Despite air strikes against enemy units steadily encircling the Marine position, pressure on the LZ mounted through the afternoon preventing ammunition resupply or medical evacuation. Three times during the night, several North Vietnamese companies supported by mortars and automatic weapons stormed the Marines' perimeter. Only with the help of repeated barrages of artillery and the courageous efforts of two helicopter crews who ignored intense antiaircraft fire to deliver desperately needed ammunition were the Marines able to repulse the determined attacks.

The assault on Company B marked the end of organized enemy resistance. When 3/1 and the two ARVN Airborne battalions moved forward on the morning of March 6 following an intensive two-and-a-half hour air and artillery bombardment, they found weapons, documents, equipment, and a well-developed tunnel complex, but no NVA. By the seventh, the Marines were on their way back to Chu Lai. Short and fierce, the battle had claimed an estimated 600 North Vietnamese dead—about a third of the enemy regiment's original strength—at a cost of over 500 friendly casualties including 98 Marines killed in action. "They're not supermen," observed one Marine of the northern regulars. "But they can fight."

His willingness and ability to fight was not the only thing the men of the 1st Marine Division had learned about the enemy from their first encounters with him. The Marines also discovered that he possessed considerable destructive capacity. A battalion of Main Force VC or NVA infantrymen carried weapons that were roughly comparable to those available to a Marine battalion, including such weapons as the Russian AK47 assault rifle, heavy machine guns and mortars, recoilless rifles, and the B40 rocket-propelled grenade—weapons that by 1966 were bringing total Marine casualties (although not deaths) closer to Communist losses and subjecting Marine aircraft to significant damage. If the Americans had the advantage of artillery, helicopter gunships, and tactical air strikes to call upon, the enemy had advantages of his own. Not the least of them was the special combat environment of southern I Corps.

The village war

Unlike the sparsely populated hills along the DMZ, the coastal zone from Da Nang to Chu Lai had a population density of 2,000 people per square mile. The vast majority were peasant farmers living in thatched-hut villages surrounded by hedgerows and crisscrossed by winding dirt paths. The war in these villages was an exhausting round of searches and sweeps by day and patrols and ambushes by night, a counterpoint of boredom and terror in which surprise was almost impossible to achieve against an enemy only rarely seen. It was a war of sporadic contact, more than half the American casualties caused by snipers, mines, and booby traps. It was a war of endless repetition, the same battles fought on the same bloody fields because the enemy could be kept from any given area only as long as the Marines remained there. Waged among civilian communities, it was a war in which the Americans' greatest asset—firepower—could not be fully brought to bear for fear of harming peasants who usually treated the Marines with indifference and sometimes conspired in their destruction. Most of all, it was a war on the enemy's own turf. Not only the guerrillas but also many of the Main Force Vietcong were native to the region, intimately acquainted with every tree line and field, practiced at concealment, and adept at escape.

In July 1966, the 1st and 2d Battalions, 1st Marines, and the 3d Battalion, 5th Marines, joined 3d Marine Division units in halting an NVA drive across South Vietnam's northern frontier as part of Operation Hastings. With the permanent deployment of the 3d Division to the northern two provinces in October, however, Major General Herman Nickerson, Jr., moved 1st Marine Division headquarters from Chu Lai into a bunkered command post on Division Ridge just west of Da Nang and assumed responsibility for Marine operations in Quang Nam, Quang Tin, and Quang Ngai provinces.

For the next fourteen months, the men of the 1st Marine Division guarded Da Nang from rocket attacks and staged a series of pacification operations along the coast. Much of this activity consisted of small unit operations. During the first three months of 1967, for example, the division conducted nearly 37,000 company-size operations, patrols, and ambushes in the Da Nang area alone. The most costly

Fighting the Elements

The 1st Marine Division had to cope not only with the enemy but also with terrain and weather that made military operations arduous. West of the shifting sands of the coast lay murky rice fields, and farther inland appeared the overgrown jungles of the Annamite Mountains. Each year in September, the northeast monsoon hit I Corps, shrouding the countryside in mist and fog until April and unleashing an average of 128 inches of rain per year, the heaviest rainfall in Vietnam.

Above. Men of Company F, 2d Battalion, 1st Marines, struggle to get an M274 Mechanical Mule—a half–ton light–weapons carrier—up a riverbank on Route 9 near Khe Sanh, April 1968. Left. Marines of the 2d Battalion, 7th Marines, crouch under their ponchos, waiting for a downpour to end during Operation Pitt in December 1967. Right. In the rain and mud, PFC James G. Kahabka of the 2d Battalion, 7th Marines, takes a break from Operation Meade River, November 1968.

fighting, however, was the result of assaults into Communist base areas in the mountain valleys to the west, harsh engagements against elements of the 1st Vietcong Regiment and the 2d NVA Division at places called An Hoa and Que Son, in operations like Calhoun and Essex and Swift and Union.

Union

Called variously Phuoc Valley or the Nui Loc Son Basin or the Que Son Valley, the heavily populated, rice-rich bowl lying along the southern boundary of Quang Nam Province was a strategically important region long dominated by the Communists. They mobilized its human and agricultural resources to maintain their military operations and used it as a convenient path to the coastal lowlands. It was an old battleground for the Marines as well, the site of Harvest Moon and of an August 1966 operation called Colorado. Following the conclusion of Colorado, elements of the 2d NVA Division returned to the valley in force. In January 1967, the Marines decided to do something about it, deploying Company F of the 2d Battalion, 1st Marines, to a small hill in the middle of the valley floor. From their

base the Marines initiated civic action efforts in nearby villages and gathered intelligence on enemy activities. Their primary mission, however, was to "create a situation"—to disturb the 2d Division enough to lure it into open battle. On April 21 the NVA took the bait.

Three days earlier Company F's commander, Captain Gene A. Deegan, had advised 1st Marine Division headquarters of apparent preparations for an enemy assault on his position. Determined to strike the first blow, headquarters prepared a battle plan and alerted a three-battalion reaction force, then ordered Captain Deegan to go out and find the NVA. Early on the morning of the twenty-first, Company F left its hilltop base and headed toward the village of Binh Son. As the Marines approached, they were met by automatic weapons and grenade fire. The initial skirmish left eighteen men wounded. Fourteen more were dead, including Private First Class Gary W. Martini of Lexington, Virginia, whose attempts to save two of his wounded comrades won him the Medal of Honor. Firing

South Vietnamese villagers are caught in the middle, as a Marine reconnaissance patrol reacts to Vietcong sniper fire during a mission in My Son village on April 25, 1965.

concentrated volleys from prepared positions within the village, the NVA pinned the entire company to the ground. When repeated artillery and air strikes failed to relieve the pressure on the Marines, the division air-assaulted two battalions into the fight.

The first to hit the ground were the men of the 3d Battalion, 1st Marines, who leaped from their helicopters into a spray of enemy bullets, then fought their way 1,500 meters toward the village where Captain Deegan, despite serious wounds, continued to direct his company until he was evacuated. Meanwhile, the 3d Battalion, 5th Marines, landing well east of the battlefield, pushed aside scattered resistance and linked up with the 3/1. During the evening the 1st Battalion, 1st Marines, flew in from Da Nang. By dawn on the twenty-second, all three infantry battalions were locked in battle. They received artillery support from Battery B, 1st Battalion, 11th Marines, which was lifted into Que Son Village some five kilometers to the north.

After driving the NVA from Binh Son, the Marines pushed them northward, while air and artillery strikes exacted a heavy toll of enemy casualties. The pursuit across the valley and into the surrounding mountains continued for nearly a week, the Marines destroying a number of small enemy units. In the process they uncovered several caches of equipment and supplies, including a regimental storage site containing recoilless rifle rounds, surgical kits, maps, shoes, and 8,000 uniforms. On April 27 a rifleman with the 3/5 tripped a string of land mines. The resulting explosions left one man killed and forty-three wounded. But by the end of the month enemy resistance had largely disappeared. The 1st Marines returned to the Da Nang TAOR, leaving the Que Son Valley for the moment in the hands of the 5th Marines.

Despite the temporary lull, intelligence reports indicated that major enemy forces were still in the area, and it soon became apparent that Operation Union was far from over. On May 3 a mortar attack wounded twenty-seven Marines. Three days later the 1/5 encountered increasing resistance while searching the northern side of the valley. Finally, on May 10, Company C had just begun moving up the southwestern slope of Hill 110 when an NVA battalion, dug in on an adjoining hill, opened fire. Operation Union, part two, was under way.

The Marines scrambled to the summit only to find themselves the targets of more NVA soldiers shooting from a sugar cane field on the far side of the hill. Two companies from the 1/3, operating farther north, responded to Company C's calls for help but were themselves chewed up by the enemy crossfire. Intense antiaircraft salvos aborted attempts at airborne relief, and when a forward air controller inadvertently placed his marker rockets into the middle of Company A of the 1/5, as it prepared to push through the enemy positions, streaking F-4 Phantoms strafed the Marines, killing 5 and wounding 24. Only after several hours of difficult maneuvering was the remainder of the 1/5 able to reach Company C's position. When they did, they let loose so many mortar rounds the tubes were "just about red hot," according to one officer. Working down from the top of the hill under the cover of this barrage, the riflemen forced the NVA to abandon their positions just as darkness began to fall. Once more punishing air and artillery strikes followed the North Vietnamese as they withdrew. The next morning, the Marines found 116 bodies left behind by the retreating enemy. Marine losses had also been high: 33 killed and 135 wounded in the daylong battle.

On May 12 the 1/3 reported for Special Landing Force duty (see sidebar, page 97), its place in the field taken by the 1st Battalion, 1st Marines. For the next three days the 1/1, along with two battalions of the 5th Marines, stayed in almost continual contact with enemy platoons and companies in the valley. Most costly to the NVA were Marine artillery missions and air strikes that harried their every attempt at escape. Mute testimony to the devastation caused by supporting arms were the 122 Communist bodies found on the thirteenth and the 68 dead enemy soldiers discovered on the fourteenth—almost all of them killed by bomb concussions or fragments.

The last major battle of the operation took place on May 15 when two companies of the 3/5 came upon another enemy bunker complex. While air and artillery pounded the fortifications, the Marines maneuvered into assault positions. The ensuing fight continued through the evening. Not until midnight were the riflemen able to subdue the last entrenchments. Two days later Operation Union came to an end. In almost a month of heavy combat against elements of the 2d NVA Division and the 3d VC Main Force Battalion, the Marines suffered 110 men killed, 2 missing in action, and 473 wounded. Enemy casualties, as usual, were even more severe: 865 confirmed KIA and another 777 "probable" battle deaths. In addition, the Marines captured 173 prisoners and picked up seventy weapons.

But for Colonel Kenneth J. Houghton, commander of the 5th Marines, favorable casualty ratios told only part of the story. Because of the beating received at the hands of the Americans, Houghton maintained in his after-action report, "the enemy loss in prestige in the eyes of the people is readily apparent. The psychological impact of Operation Union equaled or even exceeded the material damage to the Communist effort in this area." It would be some time, thought Houghton, before the enemy was able to regain influence in the Que Son Basin.

Battered but not beaten

Yet, enemy influence in the area was far from erased. Ten days after the conclusion of Operation Union, reports that two NVA regiments were moving back into the basin induced Operation Union II, which killed 701 enemy soldiers at a cost of another 110 Marine dead and won for the 5th Marines a Presidential Unit Citation. Despite the heavy losses suffered during the Union operations, however, the enemy continued to pump replacements into the Que Son region, provoking new attempts to keep them out. From June through September, the 1st and 5th Marines returned again and again to the area bounded by Hoi An, Tam Ky, and Hiep Duc in operations including Adair, Calhoun, Pike, Cochise, and Swift. Each enemy thrust into the region was repulsed with heavy Communist losses in men and materiel, but each time they kept coming back for more.

Nonetheless, there were tangible gains to be pointed to throughout the 1st Marine Division TAOR. An improving level of rural security could be seen in higher turnouts for local and national elections; terrorism had been reduced in the villages, including fewer attacks on government officials; and there was greater freedom of movement on rural roads. Although the diversion of troops to major operations had reduced Marine emphasis on population control and

---

Men of the 3d Battalion, 5th Marines, receive air support from an F-4 Phantom 17 kilometers northwest of Tam Ky during Operation Union in May 1967.

92

civic action initiatives, the Combined Action Platoon pacification program actually expanded during 1967, the number of platoons involved in the program increasing from fifty-seven to seventy-nine. The activities of these units helped regain the momentum the pacification program had lost during the troubles of 1966 and noticeably increased the difficulty faced by the Vietcong in recruiting new members.

From a strictly military point of view, the activation of the Army's Task Force Oregon in April and its assumption of responsibility for the Chu Lai TAOR created a much more acceptable troop density in the region. By the end of the year, Task Force Oregon (redesignated the Americal, or U.S. 23d Infantry Division, in September) was taking on the enemy in Quang Ngai and Quang Tin provinces, freeing the 1st Marines for Operations Medina and Osceola along the DMZ in October and November and allowing the 5th and 7th Marines to concentrate their efforts in Quang Nam Province.

At the same time, the heavy fighting of the summer left many villages severely damaged and whole areas devastated. As a result, the refugee population in I Corps almost doubled during the year. Artillery and rocket attacks against Da Nang and Marble Mountain in August and September demonstrated the continuing ability of the enemy to wreak havoc in the populated areas along the coast. And if they were battered, they were far from beaten, something apparent in December when Communist forces overran the District Headquarters at Binh Son, the site of the bloody firefight that began Operation Union eight months earlier. Even more ominous, as 1967 drew to a close, was mounting evidence of an impending enemy offensive of major proportions.

Tet

Between January 29 and 31, 1968, the Communist command hurled some 80,000 North Vietnamese soldiers and Vietcong guerrillas against 105 cities and towns throughout South Vietnam. In I Corps the enemy assault fell on Quang Tri City, Phu Loc, Hoi An, Tam Ky, and Quang Ngai City, while Phu Bai and Chu Lai suffered rocket attacks. The main urban targets of the offensive in the northern provinces, however, were the region's two largest cities: the former imperial capital at Hue and the sprawling port of Da Nang.

The enemy's try for Da Nang began just after three o'clock on the morning of January 30 when members of the NVA 402d Sapper Battalion struck the ARVN I Corps headquarters behind a booming volley of rockets and mortars. With the help of a nearby Marine Combined Action Platoon the headquarters staff managed to hold on until a hastily created relief force composed of South Vietnamese and Marine military police roared up from the airfield and threw the Communists back in a furious counterattack.

The mission of the infiltrators had been to disrupt command and control while the 2d NVA Division launched the main attack from south and west of the city. But reconnaissance units of the 1st Marine Division spotted the NVA columns as they left the protection of the foothills west of An Hoa. Slowed down by Marine air and artillery strikes, the enemy division was intercepted and driven back by the 3/5 and 2/3 Marines without ever reaching Da Nang.

The pattern was much the same in the rest of I Corps. Unlike other areas of the country, the offensive in the northern provinces found U.S. and South Vietnamese forces at great strength—approximately 250,000 troops—and prepared to respond quickly. While small groups of infiltrators were able to penetrate major population centers, and Communist rockets caused minor damage to ARVN and U.S. military installations, most of the major ground assaults lasted no more than a few days and failed miserably. By February 6 the enemy remained in force only at Hue. There, however, seven Communist battalions held the city so firmly it took a month of savage house-to-house fighting to win it back.

The battle for Hue began in the predawn darkness of January 31. As 122MM rockets shrieked down upon the unsuspecting city, NVA and Vietcong troops swept through Hue carrying out systematic assaults on more than 200 specific targets. By daylight the gold-starred, blue-and-red flag of the National Liberation Front flew above the city. The only remaining pockets of anti-Communist resistance were the ARVN 1st Division headquarters located within the Citadel on the north side of the Perfume River and the MACV compound on the southern bank. A bobtailed battalion made up of the command group and Company A of the 1st Battalion, 1st Marines; Company G of the 2d Battalion, 5th Marines; and a platoon of tanks fought their way into the city from Phu Bai. They encountered intense small arms and automatic weapons fire on the outskirts but reached the MACV compound by early afternoon. Over the next several days, the remainder of the 1/1 and 2/5 arrived in Hue as the Marines set about the grim task of clearing the enemy from the southern half of the city.

The Marines had seen nothing like it for nearly twenty years. With enemy troops contesting every building of every street, the counterattack began on February 1 and moved forward a few feet at a time. House by house, down alleyways cluttered with wreckage, facing machine guns and recoilless rifles, the Marines took six days to fight their way from the MACV compound to the provincial hospital— a distance of four blocks—at a cost of 150 casualties. To get there they had to deal not only with individual enemy squads but also well-manned, heavily fortified strongpoints. These defensive positions were usually three-story buildings surrounded by a stone fence strung with barbed wire. They were protected by snipers placed on the top floor and in other buildings along the route of advance. On the lower floors were more men with automatic weapons.

A network of spider holes circled the buildings, each manned by a soldier equipped with an AK47 rifle and a B40 rocket launcher. As one Marine put it, "You had to dig the rats from their holes." It was a brutal, bloody, frustrating business made worse by a misting drizzle that periodically turned into a cold, drenching rain. The accompanying overcast and fog limited visibility on the ground and made air operations almost impossible. "Seoul was tough," said a veteran of the Korean War and the last major city battle waged by the Corps, "but this—well, it's something else."

Accustomed to fighting their battles among the rice fields and tree lines of the countryside, the Marines had to learn the tactics of urban warfare. They did so in a hurry. They discovered that the 3.5-inch rocket launcher packed a much greater punch than the M72 light antitank weapon (LAW) and that CS (tear gas and smoke) grenades were invaluable in clearing out enemy bunkers. They found that aiming just below windows rather than through them created a useful "shrapnel effect" and that the dust and smoke generated by 106MM recoilless rifles could be used to cover street crossings under enemy fire. Most of all, they learned how to isolate each source of enemy resistance and destroy it. "Four men cover the exits of a building, two men rush the building with grenades, while two men cover them with rifle fire," explained Lieutenant Colonel Earnest C. Cheatham, commander of the 2/5. "We hope to kill them inside or flush them out for the four men watching the exits. Then, taking the next building, two other men rush the front. It sounds simple, but the timing has to be just as good as a football play."

At first, the fear of killing innocent civilians and a desire to minimize destruction in the city restricted the use of heavy supporting arms. But the enemy proved so difficult to root out with direct-fire weapons, such as recoilless rifles, tanks, mortars, tank guns, and rockets, that the prohibitions were soon lifted. Although poor weather still ruled out air strikes, beginning on February 5 artillery and naval gunfire were brought to bear, the warships of the Seventh Fleet hurling armor-piercing rounds twenty-three kilometers into NVA bunkers that had withstood everything else the Marines could muster. Even with the added firepower, it was not until February 10 that the area south of the river was declared secure. The following day the 1st Battalion, 5th Marines, joined ARVN forces in the fight for the north bank.

The assault against the main enemy stronghold within the Citadel proved even more savage than the battle for southern Hue. Supported by artillery, naval gunfire, Ontos recoilless rifle vehicles, and air strikes, flak-vested riflemen clawed their way forward through rain and fog from one doorway to the next, the enemy contesting every foot with machine guns, antitank rockets, mortars, and captured tanks. Constantly under fire, sleeping a few hours at a time, unrelieved by fresh troops, the men of the 1/5 took a fearful pounding. Nine days after they were thrown into

Battle for Hue

The battle to recapture Hue, the imperial capital, was one of the fiercest and bloodiest of the war. It took ARVN troops and two Marine battalions more than a month of exhausting building-to-building assaults to dislodge seven well-entrenched enemy battalions. When the fighting was over, the once beautiful capital lay in ruins.

Right. *A U.S. Marine, carrying an M79 grenade launcher, glances at the body of a Vietcong killed in street fighting in Hue on February 11, 1968.* Below. *Three Marines gaze warily out a window as they prepare to continue the battle.* Opposite. *U.S. Marines evacuate one of their wounded through the nearly leveled eastern wall of the Citadel on February 17.*

battle, the battalion's ten rifle platoons were commanded by three second lieutenants, one gunnery sergeant, two staff sergeants, two buck sergeants, and two senior corporals. Coated with dirt and numb with fatigue, the Marines pressed forward. On the twenty-first all organized resistance in their zone of action came to an end. Three days later, ARVN soldiers recaptured the Imperial Palace and raised the South Vietnamese flag over the walls of the Citadel. The battle of Hue, among the bloodiest and most destructive of the war, was over. Its end had not been cheaply gained. The Marines suffered 142 killed in the fighting, plus nearly 900 wounded. Yet the price of defeat was more terrible still. In the rubble that had once been the most beautiful city in all of Vietnam lay more than 5,000 enemy dead.

Counterattack

Despite their extraordinary losses during the Tet offensive—an estimated 40,000 NVA regulars and VC cadres in I Corps alone—the Communists still had ample capacity to do harm, a fact made manifest by a countrywide series of rocket attacks on May 5 during which the airfields at Da Nang, Marble Mountain, Quang Tri, and Chu Lai, the MACV compound at Hue, and the headquarters of the 101st Airborne Division were all hit. Nonetheless, the 1st Marine Division saw in the post-Tet landscape a golden opportunity to administer an even more severe beating to the already battered enemy. The chance to do so was enhanced by the arrival of the 27th Marines in February. But before a full-scale counteroffensive could be mounted, the tactical situation around the war-struck population centers had to be stabilized.

To keep the enemy away from Da Nang, the Marines mounted intensive patrols through the "rocket belt" surrounding the city and launched two mobile screening operations into the An Hoa Basin: Allen Brook, in which the 7th and newly arrived 27th Marines surprised the 36th and 38th NVA Regiments in the vicinity of Go Noi Island, and Mameluke Thrust, which sent the 7th Marines into "Happy Valley" north of An Hoa where the 31st NVA Regiment threatened the Thuong Duc Special Forces Camp. Despite these spoiling operations, VC sappers penetrated the southern outskirts of Da Nang on August 23, seizing one end of the vital Cam Le Bridge along Highway 1. After a short, hard fight, the combined efforts of the Marine 1st Military Police Battalion and Company A of the 1/27 drove the attackers from the bridge, while several kilometers to the south other elements of the 27th Marines joined ARVN Rangers in a savage mauling of the 38th NVA Regiment. During the remainder of the Marines' stay in Vietnam, the enemy never again attempted to enter Da Nang by force.

With the "protective shield of containment" firmly in place, the Marines turned their attention to the countryside, where pacification efforts had been severely disrupted by the Tet attacks. The beginning of the Paris peace negotiations in October only heightened pressure to bring as many villages as possible under Saigon control. Joining the South Vietnamese in an Accelerated Pacification Campaign throughout the country, the 1st Marine Division concentrated on civic action and an expanded CAP program, de-emphasizing search-and-destroy operations in favor of village cordons designed to promote area security. One of the most successful was Meade River, a ten-battalion cordon-and-search operation launched on November 20 fifteen kilometers south of Da Nang.

The target area, known by the Marines as "Dodge City," was a long-time VC stronghold. Within its forty square kilometers of rice fields and swampland honeycombed with camouflaged caves and tunnels lay eight villages, an estimated 100 members of the Vietcong infrastructure—tax collectors, recruiters, political agitators—and approximately 1,300 North Vietnamese soldiers. Among the attacking forces were elements of the 1st, 5th, 26th, and 27th Marines. In order for the operation to work, the cordon would have to appear virtually overnight. It happened even faster. In one of the largest helicopter assaults in Marine history, seventy-six choppers lifted 3,500 troops into forty-seven separate landing sites in just two hours. Truck convoys hauled more Marines, plus ARVN and Korean soldiers, into position. Before the enemy had a chance to escape, 7,000 allied troops had encircled them in a thirty-kilometer cordon so tightly held there was one man for every five meters of turf.

Once on the ground, the Marines evacuated 2,600 civilians to a joint U.S./ARVN interrogation center where they were screened, fed, given medical attention, and issued new identification cards. Among the evacuees, investigators discovered seventy-one Vietcong agents. During the three days devoted to this process, helicopters equipped with loudspeakers circled the objective area dropping leaflets and calling upon the enemy to "surrender or die." Then, with the hamlets emptied, the Marines began to close the trap.

Each day, the Marines searched out bunkers and tunnels. When strongpoints were discovered, the riflemen backed off and let artillery, naval gunfire, and air strikes do the job. Each night, Air Force C-47 "Spooky" gunships flew overhead, dropping flares that lit up the sky and occasionally unleashing miniguns firing 18,000 rounds per minute on enemy targets below. At first, small groups of guerrillas tried to break through the human barrier, only to be destroyed. But as the circle became smaller the Communists fought back with a ferocity born of desperation. Under the ceaseless hammering of American ordnance, the battlefield became one great scar of singed grass and gaping shell holes. Broken, unburied bodies of enemy soldiers littered the ground.

By December 10 the circle had shrunk to a boot print. Meticulously planned, systematically executed, Meade

The Amphibious Tradition

Since its establishment in 1775, the U.S. Marine Corps has maintained its tradition as an amphibious strike force. In fact, the Marines were the first American troops ashore in Vietnam precisely because they could be supplied over the beach at their "temporary" enclave at Da Nang. Yet, once committed, the Marines became engaged largely as infantrymen in a defensive land war.

The tradition of the Corps continued, however, in the form of the Special Landing Force—a rotating reserve battalion drawn from Marine units deployed to Vietnam and serving afloat with the Navy's Seventh Fleet.

Between 1965 and 1969 the Marines staged sixty-two SLF operations along the Vietnamese coast. Unlike the Corps' experience in the Pacific during World War II, the enemy rarely did more than harass the landing force. "There were no classic beach assaults," wrote one Marine histo-

A landing craft (LCU–1495) and other boats of the Special Landing Force prepare for an amphibious assault in September 1965 as part of Operation Dagger Thrust.

rian, "no great flaming battles fought at the water's edge."

More typical were repeated sweeps across Barrier Island and the Batangan Peninsula designed to disrupt seaborne infiltration from North Vietnam and to keep watch over a local population that gave the Vietcong much support. The SLF proved even more successful when used as a mobile reserve able to exploit opportunities created by in-country operations, a role assumed frequently by SLF battalions during the big battles along the DMZ in 1967 and 1968.

In all, SLF operations claimed more than 6,500 enemy killed, 483 prisoners taken, and nearly 800 weapons captured. Equally important, the landings provided a testing ground for amphibious doctrine in a combat environment, keeping alive and well the historical mission of the Corps.

River had destroyed an important Communist base area, along with hundreds of bunkers, tunnels, and other fortifications, at least temporarily eliminating a major infiltration route for enemy units headed toward Da Nang. Equally significant, the arrest of seventy-one Vietcong agents had crippled the local guerrilla apparatus. How fast the Communists would recover from these blows was a matter of speculation. What was more certain was the fate of the enemy soldiers who had fought the battle. More than 180 were captured, some incapacitated by wounds, others choosing surrender over death. But most of those caught in the trap had fought to the end, and 1,210 of them would never fight again.

Following up on the success of Meade River, the 1st Marine Division's Task Force Yankee—including the 5th Marines and two battalions of the 3d Marines—pushed beyond An Hoa into the rugged "Arizona Territory" and the high ground to the west and south, which harbored the enemy's Base Area 112. Using some of the same mobile firebase techniques the 3d Marine Division would employ with equal results in Operation Dewey Canyon, the Marines remained in the field for three-and-a-half-months,

killing over 1,800 enemy soldiers and capturing enormous stores of equipment and supplies. By driving the Communists from their long-time sanctuary, Operation Taylor Common also permitted the establishment of a secure line of supply from Da Nang to the expanding Marine base at An Hoa. This inland foray was matched along the coast in January 1969 by Operation Bold Mariner, which sent the 2d and 3d Battalions of the 26th Marines sweeping across the Batangan Peninsula south of Chu Lai in a successful search for local VC political cadres. Two months later, in Operation Oklahoma Hills, the 7th Marines destroyed a regimental-sized base camp behind Charlie Ridge on the northern side of the An Hoa Basin.

The post-Tet counteroffensive reached a climax in May when four Marine battalions joined South Vietnamese and Korean forces in Operation Pipestone Canyon. The objective of the operation was to rid Go Noi Island once and for all of the 36th NVA Regiment and render it uninhabitable as a future Communist base. Using a complex scheme of maneuver and fire support to isolate and destroy small groups of enemy soldiers, the combined force killed approximately 800 North Vietnamese soldiers during the first four weeks of the operation. But this time after the Americans left the field the enemy would not be able to reoccupy the labyrinth of tunnels, caves, and trenches that crisscrossed the region. Following behind the advancing Marines, gigantic Rome Plows supplied by a U.S. Army engineer company smashed through vegetation and churned up the land at a rate of 200 acres a day. By the time the operation came to an end, 6,750 acres had been razed and Go Noi Island was forever transformed.

When Pipestone Canyon moved south into the Dodge City area in July the Marines noted an unusual lack of enemy contact. After four years of steady escalation, the war was beginning to wind down. During the remainder of 1969, battalion-size operations steadily declined, and both Communist and Marine casualties dropped sharply. Instead of large-unit search-and-destroy maneuvers, III MAF began to rely on small "Stingray" reconnaissance teams supported by rifle platoons and helicopter gunships to locate and engage an increasingly elusive enemy. By fall, when the 3d Marine Division withdrew from Vietnam, the enemy in southern I Corps had largely reverted to guerrilla and terrorist operations. For the men of the 1st Marine Division, the war had entered its final phase.

The long good-bye

The period 1970 to 1971 was one of steady disengagement. The departure of the 3d Marine Division was followed by the subordination of III MAF to the Army-commanded XXIV Corps and the turnover of Marine operating areas north and south of Quang Nam Province to ARVN and U.S. Army units. Reflecting this changing state of affairs, the 1st Marine Division—now down to its three organic infantry regiments, the 1st, 5th, and 7th Marines, and its artillery regiment, the 11th Marines—moved back to Da Nang and the combat bases extending from that city into the An Hoa Basin. Although the enemy continued to make limited assaults against Marine targets, such as a sapper attack on FSB Ross in January 1970 that killed thirteen Americans, the Communists generally avoided large-scale engagements, contenting themselves with guerrilla activity along the coast. For the Americans, the twin objectives now were turning the war over to the Vietnamese and reducing U.S. casualties.

The Marines continued to de-emphasize battalion sweeps in favor of the small-unit "Pacifier package." Conducted largely by the 1st Battalion, 5th Marines, from its base on Division Ridge west of Da Nang, these quick-response helicopter operations of platoon or company size were used as often as six or seven times a week during 1970. Meanwhile, the Marines curtailed Special Landing Force operations, reduced artillery and air strikes, and redeployed most of III MAF's tanks and amtracs outside Vietnam. When they undertook large operations, such as the 7th Marines' thrust into Base Area 112 during Operation

Pickens Forest in July, little contact was made with enemy forces. Even more significant, a long-standing pattern had been reversed: now ARVN units were out in front with the Marines in a supporting role. On August 31, behind a thundering air and artillery barrage, the 7th Marines launched a final assault on the Que Son Valley in Operation Imperial Lake. A few weeks later the 7th went home to Camp Pendleton, California, and the 5th Marines took their place in the Que Son. Left alone to guard the Da Nang area, the 1st Marines fanned out over the zone formerly patrolled by the 5th. But most of the great combat base at An Hoa was razed and the remainder turned over to the ARVN.

Along with declining levels of combat and the beginning of troop withdrawals, the division experienced a marked reduction in casualties. Compared to 1,051 killed and 9,286 wounded during 1969, in 1970, 403 men were killed and 3,623 wounded. Despite these obvious indications of impending disengagement, or perhaps in part because of them, disturbing signs of turmoil and disintegration appeared among the Marines. Unauthorized absences, drug use, and barracks thefts increased. Racial tensions, including violent confrontations between white and black Marines, also mounted, along with "fraggings," attacks on unpopular officers and NCOs. The majority of such incidents took place in rear areas, which also witnessed an increase in crimes against Vietnamese civilians, but there were also indications of reduced enthusiasm and professionalism in the field.

With only two reinforced regiments left by the beginning of 1971, the 1st Marine Division found itself primarily involved with static security operations in the immediate vicinity of Da Nang. Patrols continued to prowl the "rocket belt" around the city, the men spurred on by the promise of a trip to Hong Kong or Bangkok for any Marine finding an enemy rocket, but the division's responsibilities were rapidly diminishing. Exemplifying this was the substitution of "tactical areas of interest" (TAOI) for "tactical areas of responsibility" (TAOR), the reduced range of Marine patrols, and the increasing number of South Vietnamese combat operations. In fact, the few months remaining to the division in Vietnam were largely spent turning over villages and installations to the ARVN and loading tons of equipment on Navy vessels for shipment to Okinawa or Japan.

In January, the 1st Marines put two battalions on Charlie Ridge in Operation Upshur Stream, an unsuccessful attempt to track down the enemy rocketeers who continued to shell the city. Contact was light, most of the friendly casualties the result of mines and booby traps. By the time the operation ended on March 29, the 5th Marines had left for home. In response to an NVA attack on the district headquarters at Duc Duc, the 1st Marines made one last raid west of An Hoa during the second week of April but found little for their trouble. On April 14, Major General

Charles F. Widdecke departed with the 1st Marine Division colors for Camp Pendleton, California. The 1st Marines remained in Vietnam for another month, the last battalion standing down on May 26.

After six years of combat, 160 named operations, and thousands of small-unit actions, the 1st Marine Division had completed one of the lengthiest combat tours for a unit of its size in American military history. Less than a year later, Marine pilots would return briefly to Vietnam to help stop the Communists' 1972 Easter offensive, but by the summer of 1971 all Marine ground operations had ended in what had become the longest, and in some ways the biggest, war in Marine Corps history. Overall, an estimated half a million Marines served in Vietnam during the course of the war. At its peak in 1968, III MAF had 87,755 Marines under its command—more than went ashore at Iwo Jima or Okinawa during World War II. Thirteen thousand and sixty-five Marines were killed in Vietnam (nearly 30 percent of all U.S. battle deaths) and 88,589 more were wounded. On the other side of the ledger, 86,535 enemy deaths were attributed to Marine actions.

The Marines had come to Vietnam to protect American installations and to assist the South Vietnamese in their struggle against Communist aggression. What they discovered was a bitter contest of surpassing complexity that defied solution, even at the cost of so many lives. When they left, the issue still remained very much in doubt. If this was a source of dismay for many who served, they knew also that they had done the job assigned to them with honor and distinction. Whatever judgment history might make on the wisdom of their enterprise, that much, at least, was beyond dispute.

After a five-hour march to Hill 190 northwest of Da Nang, men of the 1st Platoon, Company L, 3d Battalion, 26th Marines, rest along a stream in December 1969.

Dominion Over the Skies

It was January 31, 1968. Tet. At dawn, a helicopter gunship from the 174th Assault Helicopter Company took to the air near the city of Quang Ngai. At the edge of the city's airfield, the helicopter's pilot, Warrant Officer Michael Magno, and his aircraft commander, Warrant Officer Russell Doersam, sighted a battalion-sized force of uniformed men of the North Vietnamese Army. Suddenly, the enemy soldiers opened fire. "We had our windshield shot out before we even made our first pass," recalled crew chief Specialist 5 Ronald Conner of Silsbee, Texas. "It was still pretty dark and with all those tracers coming up at us, it looked like Christmas."

The gunship swooped low, strafing the enemy position as it flew by, then turned to make another pass. A second helicopter from the 174th soon joined them and then two more. Twice the helicopters fired their full loads of ammunition at the NVA forces. Each time they returned to their base only long enough to rearm and refuel before resuming their positions over the battlefield.

On March 10, 1963, Sp5 William Tankersley of the 45th Battalion, UH–1 Section, works on the main rotor hub of a UH–1B helicopter at the Port of Saigon.

At last the attackers withdrew from the airfield, but the pilots had little time to rest. Responding to a call from ARVN troops, they flew to the north side of the city where NVA forces had seized an ARVN training center. The North Vietnamese had already repulsed several ARVN assaults. The gunships, however, quickly routed the enemy. "The NVA started to break and run down the hill and out of the trenches," said door gunner Specialist 5 Harold Koster of Reading, Pennsylvania. "We kept making runs with the door guns until there were no more of them running."

As the day wore on, the helicopters crisscrossed the city, participating in a number of pitched battles. Each time, the arrival of the gunships turned the battle in favor of the defending forces. During a heated battle for possession of the city jail, the helicopters halted the enemy attack with a fusillade of more than forty 2.75-inch rockets, killing 50 NVA. By sunset, the combined ARVN and U.S. forces had

Preceding page. *The pilot of a UH–1 from the 1st Aviation Brigade guides his helicopter loaded with 25th Infantry Division troops into an LZ west of Saigon in 1969.*

secured the city. The gunships, despite suffering numerous hits, killed 238 NVA soldiers in a total of thirty-four hours of flight time. American advisers credited the helicopters with playing a key role in stopping the NVA attack and preventing them from taking control of the city.

The helicopters that fought at Quang Ngai belonged to the 1st Aviation Brigade. USARV had formed the brigade in March 1966. As the rapid growth of army aviation in Vietnam outstripped the ability of USARV's own small aviation staff to handle the mounting administrative and logistical needs of these far-flung units, the Army recognized the necessity of a countrywide command that would coordinate and support them. That command was the 1st Aviation Brigade. Although its inspiration may have been a bureaucratic necessity, to the supporters of army aviation, the formation of the brigade marked the passing of a significant milestone. After nearly twenty years, the Army once again had its own aviation command. Colonel R. Joseph Rogers, then an aviation adviser in I Corps, recalled, "Those of us who had spent a number of years in aviation were getting the opportunity to prove the concepts which had been developed during the preceding years."

By 1966, the helicopter and the concept of airmobility had firmly established themselves in Vietnam. These rotary-winged craft flew across the length and breadth of the country as U.S. commanders employed them in ever-increasing numbers for an ever-increasing variety of operations. Observers in Vietnam accurately dubbed it "the helicopter war," and the 1st Aviation Brigade with its more than 3,000 helicopters and over 14,000 pilots became one of the most important units in this new type of war.

Rebirth of the cavalry

Despite its preeminence in Vietnam, the helicopter and the concept of airmobility had not always received such widespread support. In the years following WW II, many within the Army adamantly opposed the idea of airmobility, deeming the helicopter too vulnerable and too expensive. They received support from the Air Force, which bridled at any apparent intrusion into "its" skies. Only the stubborn support of a small but committed group of officers kept the concept alive. Outspoken Army men such as Lieutenant General James M. Gavin, whose 1954 article "Cavalry, and I Don't Mean Horses" called for the development of tactics and battle hardware that would "give its soul back to the cavalry," refused to let the idea die.

In the years of the Eisenhower presidency, dominated by massive nuclear retaliation theories, the airmobility concept found little support at the top of the government. However, with the inauguration of President John F. Kennedy, that changed quickly. Kennedy and his advisers, in particular, Secretary of Defense McNamara, emphasized the development of conventional warfare and flexible response. Airmobility became an important option.

1st Aviation Brigade

Arrived Vietnam: May 25, 1966   **Departed Vietnam:** March 28, 1973

Unit Headquarters

Tan Son Nhut *May 1966–Dec. 1967*   Long Binh *Dec. 1967–Dec. 1972*   Tan Son Nhut *Dec. 1972–March 1973*

Commanding Officers

Brig. Gen. George P. Seneff *May 1966*	Brig. Gen. George W. Putnam, Jr *Jan. 1970*	Brig. Gen. Robert N. Mackinnon *Sep. 1971*
Maj. Gen. Robert R. Williams *Nov. 1967*	Brig. Gen. Jack W. Hemingway *Aug. 1970*	Brig. Gen. Jack V. Mackmull *Sep. 1972*
Brig. Gen. Allen M. Burdett, Jr. *April 1969*		

Major Subordinate Units

11th Aviation Group (227th; 228th; 229th)	17th Aviation Group (10th; 14th; 52d; 223d; 268th; 7th Squadron, 17th Cavalry)	164th Aviation Group (13th; 214th; 307th; 7th Squadron, 1st Cavalry)
12th Aviation Group (11th; 13th; 145th; 210th; 214th; 222d; 269th; 308th; 3d Squadron, 17th Cavalry)	160th Aviation Group (101st; 158th; 159th; 2d Squadron, 17th Cavalry)*	165th Aviation Group (replaced the 58th Aviation Battalion)
16th Aviation Group (14th; 212th)		

1,701 KIA (Casualty figures are "Vietnam Era.")	5,163 WIA	4 Medals of Honor

*160th Aviation Group was redesignated 101st Aviation Group on June 25, 1969, and made organic to the 101st Airborne Division (Airmobile).

In October 1961, McNamara initiated a study of Army aviation. The study revealed the staunch conservatism that had stifled the development of airmobility for more than a decade. On April 19, 1962, McNamara issued a memorandum to the secretary of the Army ordering a review of its aviation plans. "I shall be disappointed," he warned, "if the Army's reexamination merely produces logistically oriented recommendations to procure more of the same, rather than a plan for employment of fresh and perhaps unorthodox concepts which will give us a significant increase in mobility."

In response to McNamara's memorandum, the Army appointed a board, headed by Lieutenant General Hamilton H. Howze, to review Army aviation. The board delivered its report to McNamara on August 20. The primary tactical innovation proposed by the Howze Board was the establishment of an air assault division with its own organic aviation assets. However, the board also argued for the organization of an air cavalry brigade and pointed out the necessity of expanding all Army aviation personnel programs to make these proposals work. In particular, it argued for a major upgrading of the warrant officer program, which became the chief source of helicopter pilots.

The report concluded with an emphatic declaration of approval for the airmobile concept. "Adoption by the Army of the airmobile concept—however imperfectly it may be described and justified in this report—is necessary and desirable. In some respects the transition is inevitable, just as was that from animal mobility to motor."

The Howze Board paved the way for the reemergence of Army aviation, in eclipse since the transformation of the Army Air Corps into the Air Force in 1947. Initially, its proposal for an air assault division took shape as the 11th Air Assault Division, which engaged in several very suc-cessful tests in the United States before deployment to Vietnam in 1965 as the 1st Cavalry Division (Airmobile). Less directly, but just as surely, the Howze Board also helped lay the groundwork for the establishment of the 1st Aviation Brigade. It not only opened the eyes of many Army leaders to the possibilities of the airmobile concept but also initiated the expansion of army aviation that culminated in the formation of the brigade.

Onto the battlefield

While in the U.S. the Howze Board helped to open the minds of many officers to airmobility, in Vietnam, Army aviators had already begun proving the concept on the battlefield. Following the deployment of the first company-sized unit—the 57th Transportation Company, Light Helicopter—in December 1961, the Army steadily increased its aviation commitment, expanding its presence on the battlefield and gradually changing the face of the war.

With few precedents to follow and no tactical handbook to guide them, these early helicopter crews developed the new concept of airmobility through trial and error. In the beginning, they spent much time teaching the South Vietnamese soldiers how to enter and exit helicopters. They found their efforts further hampered by ARVN leaders who insisted upon using the helicopters primarily on large, ineffective operations that one senior U.S. adviser, Colonel William "Coalbin Willie" Wilson, described contemptuously as "rattle-assing around the country." However, working in conjunction with U.S. advisers and several more innovative ARVN leaders, these American crews soon developed much more sophisticated tactics.

They experimented with arming the helicopter, attaching M60 machine guns on movable door mounts manned

A CH–47 Chinook airlifts a sling–loaded artillery piece into a 4th Infantry Division firebase during the battle at Dak To in November 1967.

by separate door gunners and later adding various combinations of rocket and grenade launchers. They also abandoned the large, clumsy air assault tactics of the early years for a more precise and successful operation called the Eagle Flight. A typical Eagle Flight consisted of one command and control ship, seven troopships, and five helicopter gunships. This force, which was kept either on standby or airborne, could react quickly to a situation already developing on the ground or find and engage the enemy itself. It could also execute multiple assaults, landing and taking off several times a day until contact was made. The Eagle Flight remained an effective air assault operation for the duration of the war and enjoyed great popularity with U.S. infantry commanders.

Of equal importance, the Army also used this period to test a new generation of helicopters. In 1961 it put into service the new Bell UH-1B, followed soon after by the UH-1D. These helicopters, known as Hueys, soon became the workhorse of army aviation. With their very reliable turboshaft engines, these machines proved much more suited to the harsh operating environment in Vietnam than earlier piston-engined helicopters. They also silenced many critics who had declared helicopters too fragile to survive in a combat environment. Hueys regularly survived multiple hits from enemy fire, and although they required continuous and often expensive maintenance, neither the time nor the expense outweighed the benefits of these machines. The Army used them primarily as troop movers but also experimented in arming them for use as escort gunships, close air support, aerial reconnaissance, and medical evacuation.

The Army also deployed the new Boeing Vertol CH-47—the Chinook. This twin-bladed helicopter could lift up to thirty-three battle-equipped troops or nearly ten tons of cargo or sling-load heavy artillery. The Chinook and the Huey, noted Lieutenant General John J. Tolson, former commander of the Army Aviation School, allowed Army aviation "to take a large step forward at this time."

"Build, build, build"

Although Army aviation had expanded greatly by 1965, it still had to struggle to meet the sudden increase in demand for helicopters and aviation personnel when the U.S. government decided to escalate its involvement in Vietnam. "At that time it was build, build, build," recalled Colonel R. Joseph Rogers. "We were constantly opening new installations. Units which were here when the buildup started sponsored new units into the country. We procured real estate for them, we designed installations, we helped the units get on their feet."

Supply shortages plagued the incoming units. In December 1965, six weeks after its arrival in Vietnam, the 116th Aviation Company, due to supply shortages, could still only call upon one quarter of its UH-1Ds. Similarly, the 128th Aviation Company, which arrived in Vietnam on October 20, 1965, was still waiting for most of its equipment and all of its land vehicles to arrive at the docks in Saigon when it moved to its new base at Phu Loi. Furthermore, its new "base" consisted of an abandoned Japanese airfield surrounded by rice and peanut fields with one runway, undrinkable water, poor roads, and no electricity.

More pressing than the lack of supplies, the shortage of trained aviation personnel, both pilots and maintenance crews, threatened to cripple Army aviation efforts from the start. The official history of the 116th Aviation Company noted, "The experience level of the helicopter crew chiefs and mechanics on the UH-1 helicopter and T-53 turbine engine left much to be desired. Approximately 40 percent of the mechanics lacked practical experience on the helicopter and the engine." In addition to increasing its own training programs, the Army also sought to alleviate the shortage of skilled support personnel by employing trained civilians. By 1969, more than 2,000 civilian personnel augmented the Army's own corps of mechanics and skilled laborers. Despite these efforts, however, the shortage of qualified mechanics and laborers remained an ongoing problem for Army aviation in Vietnam.

The shortage of pilots appeared even more pressing. In January 1966, the Department of the Army informed MACV commander General William Westmoreland that all aviator resources had been exhausted. The Army predicted that by June it would need 14,300 pilots and would be able to muster only around 9,700. This deficit threatened to grow wider in 1967 as MACV estimated that the need for pilots would reach 21,500 while only 12,800 pilots would be ready for service.

To meet that demand, pilots regularly exceeded the number of flying hours considered safe. Most commonly flew over 100 hours a month and many averaged 120 or more. This greatly increased the chances of error from pilot fatigue. From May to July, the 1st Aviation recorded forty-four major accidents. This figure rose to fifty-seven during the following quarter. The vast majority of these accidents were the result of fatigued pilots.

To offset the pilot shortage, the Army instituted a number of measures. They informed aviators who had already served in Vietnam to expect no more than a one-year hiatus before returning to duty there. They also ordered many higher ranking officers into duty as pilots. Brigadier General George P. Seneff, the 1st Aviation Brigade's first commanding officer, observed, "Some of the companies that went over in the '66 time frame went over with 15 to 20 majors in them, just filling cockpit seats. A hell of a waste of skills." Finally, the Army siphoned off aviation strength from other parts of the world, stripping its European bases of all but 250 pilots and leaving only 34 in Korea. They even sought pilots from among the reserves, sending letters to more than 2,000 pilots asking them to volunteer. This effort, however, brought only sixty responses.

Of greater importance to those seeking a long-term solution to the problem, the Army expanded the size of the Army Aviation School at Fort Rucker, Alabama, to meet the growing need for aviators. In 1962, Fort Rucker produced 80 aviators per month. That figure increased to 120 per month in 1964, then to 410 in March 1965, and finally peaked at 610 per month in December 1966. More than 90 percent of the graduates shipped out directly to South Vietnam after completing the thirty-two week course.

A large number of these new aviators came from the Army's Warrant Officer Aviator Program. The majority of these men were young—most were barely twenty—and they had joined the Army with one aim—to fly. "I was dissatisfied with college," said twenty-year-old James Petteys of Shippensburg, Pennsylvania, adding simply, "I wanted to fly." Surprisingly, these young pilots performed

Soldiers of the 1st Infantry Division run through the wind and dust kicked up by helicopters waiting to carry them into battle in 1966. Behind them sits an Army O–1 Bird Dog observation plane.

admirably, equaling and, in many cases, soon surpassing the skill level of many older, more experienced pilots.

The rapid, haphazard deployment of U.S. forces resulted in a profusion of ad hoc operating procedures between aviation units and the ground units they supported. The lack of standardization made it difficult to shift the still limited aviation units around the country when necessary. In 1965, the Army formed the 12th Aviation Group to provide a central control unit and the next year added the 17th Aviation Group. "Once we got two aviation groups," explained Colonel R. Joseph Rogers, "it was necessary to form an aviation headquarters to supervise them and that's where the 1st Aviation Brigade came in."

Enter the 1st Aviation Brigade

The 1st Aviation Brigade assumed command of all the nondivisional Army aviation assets in Vietnam. (The helicopters and aviation personnel of the 1st Cavalry Division [Airmobile] remained under the command of that division.) However, the individual units operated under the control of the infantry units to which they were attached. This was an important aspect of the 1st Aviation Brigade. The Army recognized the need for centralizing its aviation assets. It did not have enough helicopters to support adequately every infantry unit at the required level and needed flexibility to be able to deploy its helicopters as needed. However, the Army also recognized the necessity of close relationships between the aviation units and the units they supported.

"Our companies lived with the brigades they supported," recalled Gen. Seneff.

This was the pattern on which we stationed elements of the Brigade. We tried to put one lift company with each infantry brigade, and one lift battalion headquarters with each infantry division. That battalion worked primarily with that division, and if they needed 20 helicopter companies for a given operation we would put them under the OPCON (operational control) of that battalion headquarters for that given operation. So while we had the capability of massing our air assets under a given ground element for a given operation, we were still able to maintain a very close personal relationship between the two chopper companies and the people that they worked for. They were under their OPCON at all times, and this is what made the difference.

Before this relationship could reach an optimum level of performance, however, the brigade needed to improve and standardize its own operations. "There was quite honestly, in some areas at least, a degree of laxness in aviation performance that left a lot to be desired," said Seneff. "In other words, people were not really getting with it, no busting their asses to get the job done. There were many problems of that sort that had to be sorted out, standardized, and developed."

A flamboyant but capable officer, Seneff had spent much of his earlier career as one of the maverick support-

ers of Army aviation. He had served in the important position of commander of the 11th Air Assault Division's aviation group during its test period. Once in Vietnam, he gathered about him many of the people who had worked with him on that project and instituted a number of important changes. Recognizing the need for stability, he insisted that his battalion commanders commit themselves to the brigade for at least a nine-month tour of duty as opposed to the six-month stints common to command positions in other units. He also established in-country training programs both for pilots and aviation support personnel. To offset the problem of pilot fatigue, he ordered that any pilot exceeding ninety hours per month be monitored closely by a flight surgeon. Finally, the general and his staff published a handbook outlining standard operating procedures for the brigade, and every month he gathered his battalion commanders together to "read them the riot act" and make sure these programs were proceeding successfully.

Although he could browbeat his own people into better performance, Seneff could not so easily educate infantry commanders in the intricacies of airmobile tactics. "The infantry elements coming in didn't know zilch about airmobility," Seneff complained. Furthermore, the infantry commanders were not always willing to change methods that had worked well for many years. "We did the best we could to try to sell people on things," Seneff recalled, "but we were completely at the mercy of the ground commanders in this. They could listen to us or not as they liked, but—people don't like to be told how to do their jobs." Eventu-

Training at Fort Rucker, Alabama. Below. Capt. Roy R. Steves receives instruction in December 1963 from SFC Vern L. Aurentz on a simulated instrument control panel for Army fixed-wing aircraft. Right. Helicopter pilots practice landings on the world's largest helicopter pad at Fort Rucker in January 1966.

ally, working in conjunction with the 1st Infantry Division and its commanding officer, Major General William E. DePuy, Seneff and his staff developed effective methods of support of infantry by an aviation unit that were incorporated in the brigade's handbook and disseminated throughout the country.

Throughout 1966 and into 1967, the brigade grew at an astounding rate. By the end of 1966 it numbered more than 14,000 soldiers. By the end of 1967, it had grown to more than 24,000. Eventually the brigade included more than 25,000 soldiers, nearly 3,200 helicopters, and over 650 fixed-wing aircraft divided among more than 100 aviation units scattered across Vietnam. In only one month during 1967, the brigade logged 83,288 flying hours (equal to nearly ten years), flew 218,408 sorties, airlifted 200,000 troops, killed 704 VC/NVA, and destroyed or damaged 584 enemy boats.

A second air force

Although many hailed the rapid development of Army aviation in Vietnam, others remained skeptical. Many Air Force leaders, who usually reacted strongly to any perceived infringement upon their territory, viewed the 1st Aviation Brigade as a second air force. In 1966, after a long squabble, the Army agreed to relinquish control of its C-7

An Army CV–2 Caribou flies over South Vietnam in September 1966, just months before the Army relinquished control of its Caribous to the Air Force.

Caribou transport aircraft to the Air Force, transferring control of its six Caribou companies in January 1967. In return, the Air Force acquiesced to the Army's control of helicopter operations in Vietnam.

An even more heated argument arose over the Army's development of an armed helicopter to provide close air support for ground troops. Tactical air support had traditionally fallen under the control of the Air Force. However, the Army argued that the Air Force's fixed-wing, tactical aircraft could not provide the type of close support needed in Vietnam where often less than fifty meters separated U.S. and enemy forces. They maintained that only the Army's new fleet of highly maneuverable, armed helicopters could adequately perform this job.

The French were the first to show the effectiveness of armed helicopters during its war in Algeria in the late 1950s. The U.S. also began experimenting with arming helicopters that decade when Colonel Jay D. Vanderpool of the Army Aviation School's Combat Development Office attached a machine gun to a helicopter. In Vietnam, the armed helicopter appeared in the early 1960s as the Huey gunship. Armed initially with only M60 machine guns, the Huey soon added a 40MM grenade launcher, 7.62MM door-mounted machine guns, and 2.75-inch rockets. With this formidable armament, the Huey provided close air support, accompanied air assaults and ground convoys, and performed a variety of aerial reconnaissance missions.

The Army took the helicopter gunship one step further when it introduced the Bell Cobra AH-1G helicopter in 1967. Whereas the Huey gunship had been an effective but nonetheless jury-rigged adaptation of what was essentially a troop carrier, the Cobra was designed specifically as an assault craft. This two-seat helicopter possessed a narrow profile (only three feet across), advanced weaponry (twin turret-mounted 7.62MM miniguns, 40MM grenade launcher, and 2.75-inch rockets), and increased speed and maneuverability (190 knots—50 knots faster than the fastest Huey model). The Cobra brought the helicopter gunship to a new level.

Despite its several advantages over the Huey, including its greater speed that allowed it to move faster than the troopships and increased firepower, many pilots felt the Cobra had one major drawback. Lacking the two door gunners of a Huey, the Cobra crew could not always identify when they were being fired upon or from what direction. This diminished considerably the craft's ability to survive in low-altitude combat and forced it to operate at a much higher level—1,500 feet or more. It also limited the Cobra's ability to locate and destroy targets. One air cavalry troop commander noted that in his command, door gunners accounted for two-thirds of the gunship kills. These problems were offset somewhat by the Cobra's improved stability and increased accuracy from higher altitudes, but it did force a change in tactics.

Supporters of both the Huey and the Cobra agreed that both ships provided better close air support than Air Force fighters. "The biggest limitation of the Air Force was that it doesn't have a weapon that is accurate enough and small enough to provide the real close air support that is sometimes necessary in Vietnam," observed one aerial weapons platoon leader. "Sometimes we had units that were in contact with enemy forces 20 to 25 meters away, and about the closest the Air Force can put any kind of ordnance in a good situation is about 50 meters." Another pilot noted that while it normally required thirty minutes for the Air Force to respond to a request, Army helicopters, operating under the command of the engaged infantry units, could respond within ten minutes. Furthermore, they could remain over the target area nearly three times longer.

Air assault

While the Air Force could debate the relative merits of the helicopter as an attack craft, it could not deny its effectiveness as a troop carrier. Able to deposit troops in even the most difficult, remote terrain, the helicopter allowed the

Army to cover a much larger area than ever before. For the infantry commander, it became a much-prized and highly favored asset. He could now place his troops almost exactly where he wanted them, when he wanted them there.

For the average infantryman, the air assault became a way of life. Although landings were often dangerous, most preferred flying over the jungle to walking through it. The brief ride in the wind-filled cabin gave a soldier a welcome respite from the oppressive heat. "Getting into a chopper and taking off is like walking into a big air conditioner," observed one soldier from the 25th Infantry Division.

Whether it was an air assault employing hundreds of aircraft, such as the airlift of troops during Operation Junction City in 1967, or an airlift of only a single ship, as became more common later in the war, the air assault required careful planning and coordination. The landing zone had to be scouted and photographed or, if one did not exist, blasted out of the jungle. Intelligence reports had to be consulted. The helicopter units had to coordinate with the infantry commanders while the gunships coordinated with local artillery units and the Air Force in preparing the landing zone with fire.

On his way to the LZ, the pilot flew at an altitude of 1,500 feet or more to protect his craft from enemy ground fire. As he approached the LZ, however, he descended quickly. Helicopter gunships preceded the troopship, running several strafing runs around the LZ before pulling back overhead where they flew in a daisy-chain figure, ready to react at the first sign of enemy resistance.

The pilot then directed his craft into the LZ along a narrow corridor marked on one side by air strikes from Air Force tactical fighter-bombers and on the other by last-minute artillery fire. It was at this point, just as it prepared to land, that the helicopter was most vulnerable. Hovering stationary for a few seconds, it waited until its cargo of infantrymen had piled out of the cabin before lifting off and flying back the same way it had come in.

The pilots worked hard to limit the time it took to deposit the soldiers on the ground and pull out. "We figure anything more than 15 seconds is too long for an insertion," said 1st Lieutenant Steve Hamilton of the 214th Combat Aviation Battalion. "The ships offer good targets to the enemy and the pilots know it." Even the fastest drop-off, however, did not guarantee safety.

The VC/NVA developed a number of tactics for attacking landing helicopters. Sometimes they booby-trapped the LZ, placing claymore mines in the trees around the landing zone with fuses to be tripped by the wash from the helicopter blades. In other cases they would attack ground troops, then set up an ambush for the helicopters that were sure to follow in support of the infantry. Three helicopters from the 361st Aviation Company suffered heavy damage from such an ambush when they responded to a call for help from the 23d AVRN Infantry Division near Phan Thiet in June 1968. On their second pass over the area, every

gunship in the team received heavy fire. Although all of the helicopters reached base safely, they realized that the VC had aligned their weapons with the sole purpose of attacking the helicopters.

Other pilots were not so lucky. On January 8, 1968, the 173d Assault Helicopter Company flew to deliver a blocking force of eighty infantrymen along the east bank of the Can Giuoc River, ten kilometers south of Saigon. Vietcong soldiers were trying to break contact with a unit from the 9th Infantry Division, and the infantry commander hoped to catch them with the blocking force.

Four helicopters from the 214th Aviation Battalion and ten from the 173d took to the air with full loads of troops. Their landing zone was a rice field about thirty or forty acres in size, encircled by heavy stands of palm and banana trees. Artillery had not prepped the LZ, and the Air Force had mistakenly placed its air strike beyond the river. The gunships had time for only a single strafing run before the first troop carrier hit the ground.

The first two helicopters landed uncontested, but when the third neared the LZ, heavy automatic weapons fire swept the open paddy. As the third helicopter hovered just above the ground, a rocket-propelled grenade (RPG) ripped into it. The blast shattered the Plexiglas windshield and blew off the right front door, knocking the pilot, Captain William F. Dismukes, unconscious and severely wounding the aircraft commander in the seat beside him.

When he revived, Dismukes found the engine still running and enemy fire ripping through the downed aircraft. He shut down the engine, and with the help of the crew chief, a specialist fourth class named Jarvis, he tried to pull the aircraft commander through the cabin and out the door. From the rear of the craft the helicopter's door gunner, Private First Class Gary Wetzel of Oak Creek, Wisconsin, splashed through the water-covered rice field to the other side of the cabin to aid them.

Just as Wetzel pulled open the door, however, two more RPGs slammed into the craft only inches away from him. The blast tore off his arm from the elbow down, ripped open his left leg from his thigh to his calf, and covered him with burning shrapnel. Dazed and bleeding, he pulled himself back up into the cockpit long enough to push the wounded aircraft commander out of his seat toward Dismukes. Then Wetzel fell back into the rice field.

At that moment, the enemy barrage suddenly increased in intensity, ripping into the exposed U.S. unit. Soon, every member of the assault force lay either wounded, dead, or pinned down by the heavy enemy fire. Of the six infantrymen in Wetzel's helicopter, one lay dead inside, two others had died within five feet of the craft, and the other three lay

---

Screened by smoke and artillery fire, a line of UH–1 Hueys descends into a landing zone in the Long Nguyen Forest sixty kilometers northwest of Saigon during Operation Manhattan on April 24, 1967.

wounded less than five meters away. Dismukes and Jarvis were also pinned down on the right side of the downed craft, wounded before they could reach a nearby dike.

Looking out from beneath the craft, Dismukes saw Wetzel begin to drag himself through the paddy. "I saw him start to crawl back toward his machinegun," he said. Turning, he saw the VC emerge from their bunkers. "They were forming an assault wave in the trees to sweep the LZ. There was almost no return fire from the LZ to stop them!"

Although bleeding profusely, Wetzel seized his M60 and with his remaining arm and hand began to return fire. The surprised VC halted and turned their weapons on Wetzel. With the enemy concentrating on the helicopter, the other U.S. soldiers seized the opportunity to take cover behind a nearby dike, dragging their wounded with them through the ankle-deep water. Wetzel, however, continued to fire and not only stopped the VC charge but also drove them back, destroying an enemy bunker before his gun jammed.

Dropping down from the helicopter, Wetzel fell unconscious, weakened by his loss of blood. Regaining consciousness soon after, he started to pull himself to safety. On the far side of the craft he came upon the crew chief, also badly wounded, trying to pull the aircraft commander to a dike several meters away. Wetzel came to his aid. En route he passed out once more, but finally they all reached the dike and safety.

Later that night, medevac ships located and carried the wounded soldiers to safety. Gary Wetzel, despite losing his arm, survived the fight. At the evacuation hospital, he met his pilot, Capt. Dismukes, and asked him if he thought his family would be proud of him. "I told him I was sure they would be," Dismukes said. On November 19, 1968, President Lyndon Johnson presented Wetzel with the Medal of Honor. Wetzel was the first member of the 1st Aviation Brigade to earn this distinction.

While the helicopter made possible the revolutionary development of the air assault, it also proved capable of performing a wide variety of other tasks. In particular, the helicopters were adept at one of the cavalry's traditional roles—reconnaissance and screening. Able to skim easily over the rugged landscape, terrain that would tire and break even the hardiest foot soldier, the aerial scout could search out the enemy in areas beyond the reach of infantry scouts. And he possessed the firepower to destroy him.

In 1967, several air cavalry squadrons were dispatched to Vietnam to concentrate exclusively on aerial reconnaissance and scouting: the 7th Squadron of the 1st Cavalry and the 3d and 7th Squadrons of the 17th Cavalry. (The 1st Squadron of the 9th Cavalry and the 2d Squadron of the 17th Cavalry were also deployed, but these served as organic units for the 1st Air Cavalry Division and the 101st Airborne Division respectively and not for the 1st Aviation Brigade.) These cavalry squadrons contained full complements of observation and attack helicopters as well as an aero-rifle platoon that commanders could insert on the

A hunter–killer team in action. With the target spotted by the hunter, a Light Observation Helicopter, or Loach (below), the killer, a Huey Cobra (above), swoops down on the enemy.

ground as reinforcements. Aerial reconnaissance, however, was not restricted solely to the cavalry squadrons as many of the helicopter companies already in Vietnam performed these operations on a regular basis.

In developing the art of aerial reconnaissance, the brigade made full use of its extensive arsenal of weapons and aircraft. The various aircraft employed on these missions included the several models of the Huey series; the OH-6A Cayuse, a light observation helicopter (LOH), commonly called a "Loach" by the soldiers; the Cobra; and the OH-58A Kiowa, another LOH. The Army also used two fixed-wing reconnaissance aircraft: the O-1 Bird Dog and the various models of the OV-1 Mohawk. Brigade units employed these aircraft in combinations as diverse as the craft themselves, dependent only upon availability and the imagination of unit leaders.

Generally, an aerial reconnaissance patrol consisted of a reconnaissance craft and an attack craft—a so-called Hunter-Killer team (also called a Pink team). The most common combination consisted of a Cobra gunship and an OH-6A Cayuse observation helicopter. While the Cobra hovered above at an altitude of 1,500 feet or more, the Cayuse skimmed across the treetops searching for the

enemy. If the Cayuse made contact, it summoned the Cobra, which swooped down on the target.

Initially, the VC/NVA soldiers fired upon helicopters immediately upon sighting them, thereby revealing their position. However, they soon learned to hold their fire once they recognized the helicopters' intent. To counter this, the LOH pilots resorted to tactics such as "reconnaissance by fire." By shooting into a suspected VC/NVA location, the pilots hoped to make the enemy soldiers believe that they had been spotted and return fire. As Warrant Officer Don Purser, an LOH pilot with C Troop, 7th Squadron, 17th Cavalry, explained, "We would go in 'hot,' start the shooting ourselves. Then they don't hesitate about throwing lead, and we can get a definite location on them."

It became a deadly game of hide-and-seek with the pilot of the observation craft, suspended only 100 feet or so above the ground, betting his team could kill the enemy before the enemy could kill them. The trial, as WO Wayne Forbes of Galveston, Texas, described it, was "to go in deep enough to get the enemy to commit himself by opening fire but not so deep that you can't get out."

"While the enemy is still hiding below, he has all the advantages over us," noted Captain Douglas M. Bohrisch, a scout platoon leader for B Troop, 3d Squadron, 17th Cavalry. "He knows pretty much where we are, what we're doing there and what we're capable of. We don't know how many of the enemy are there, how they are armed or even **if** they are down there."

As a matter of survival, scout pilots became excellent trackers, working in much the same capacity as Jim Bridger and William "Buffalo Bill" Cody had for the U.S. Army during the Indian Wars. Forbes maintained that he could tell how recently someone had passed by the state of his footprint. "If the print is indistinct, and the water in it is still muddy, you can tell that the guy was here recently. But if the print has eroded and the water is clear, then he went through some time ago."

Bring on the night

Although aerial reconnaissance proved effective during the day, at night it gave the Army an entirely new capability. The night had traditionally belonged to the VC and NVA. It was a time for them to attack, using the cover of darkness and their knowledge of the terrain to overcome America's superior firepower and support. U.S. military leaders recognized this fact, and they turned to Army aviation to help fight this war for the night.

In their earliest operations, dubbed Firefly missions, Army aviators simply mounted a cluster of seven landing lights from a C-130 transport plane in the door of a Huey. With these lights illuminating the ground below, the Huey searched through the night followed closely by a gunship just outside the light's halo. If it discovered any guerrilla activity, the lightship would hold its light on the enemy until the gunship could attack.

As the war progressed, however, the Army developed more and more advanced weaponry to pierce the darkness and find the enemy. Nighthawk teams employed a single UH-1H Huey armed with an infrared night observation device, a xenon searchlight, and a 7.62MM minigun. Operations given the code name Nighthunter did not use normal light at all, relying instead on sniper's starlight light amplification scopes to locate the enemy. Other detection systems included FLIR (forward looking infrared radar) and low-light-level television, an image amplification system similar to the starlight scope.

Perhaps the most advanced pairing of ships was the Snakehunt team. This coupled a Cobra gunship with the electronically advanced OV-1 Mohawk. Outfitted with either SLAR (side looking airborne radar) or IR (infrared sensing devices), the Mohawk scouted ahead for the enemy. When it detected activity, it dropped a flare to mark the spot for the Cobra, which dove down to attack. The

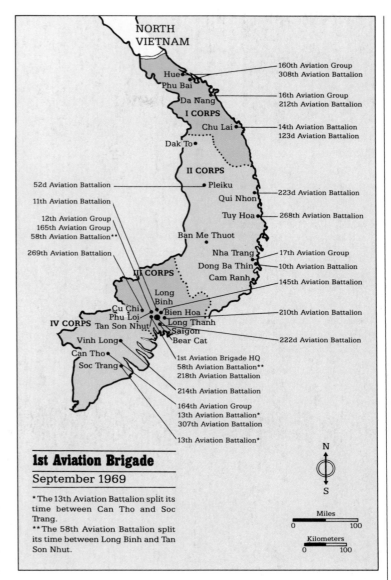

NORTH VIETNAM

- 160th Aviation Group
- 308th Aviation Battalion
- Hue
- Phu Bai
- 16th Aviation Group
- 212th Aviation Battalion
- Da Nang
- I CORPS
- Chu Lai — 14th Aviation Battalion / 123d Aviation Battalion
- Dak To
- II CORPS
- 52d Aviation Battalion — Pleiku
- 11th Aviation Battalion
- Qui Nhon — 223d Aviation Battalion
- 12th Aviation Group
- 165th Aviation Group
- 58th Aviation Battalion**
- Tuy Hoa — 268th Aviation Battalion
- Ban Me Thuot
- 269th Aviation Battalion
- Nha Trang — 17th Aviation Group
- Dong Ba Thin — 10th Aviation Battalion
- Cam Ranh — 145th Aviation Battalion
- III CORPS
- Long Binh
- Cu Chi
- Phu Loi
- Bien Hoa — 210th Aviation Battalion
- IV CORPS
- Tan Son Nhut
- Long Thanh
- Saigon
- Bear Cat — 222d Aviation Battalion
- Vinh Long
- Can Tho
- Soc Trang
- 1st Aviation Brigade HQ
- 58th Aviation Battalion**
- 218th Aviation Battalion
- 214th Aviation Battalion
- 164th Aviation Group
- 13th Aviation Battalion*
- 307th Aviation Battalion
- 13th Aviation Battalion*

1st Aviation Brigade
September 1969

* The 13th Aviation Battalion split its time between Can Tho and Soc Trang.
** The 58th Aviation Battalion split its time between Long Binh and Tan Son Nhut.

N
S

Miles
0   100

Kilometers
0   100

307th Combat Aviation Battalion employed the Snakehunt team extensively in Operation Delta Falcon from March to June 1968 with impressive results. A final tally for the three-month operation included 417 VC killed and 721 sampans either destroyed or damaged.

Despite the tremendously advanced technologies that the Army brought to its night operations, they were never entirely successful. The Mohawk, for example, while effective over flat, open marshland, produced disappointing results when used over the thickly canopied jungles and forests that covered much of Vietnam. Another of the Army's night operations, the insertion and extraction of long-range patrols, also suffered occasional problems. Although these patrols used radios, flares, and signal panels to guide the helicopters to their position, all too often the helicopters failed to locate them.

The pilots on these night operations also faced a number of problems not encountered during daylight operations. Flying through the darkness while focusing upon the intense brightness of the lights carried on Firefly missions often caused pilots to experience momentary vertigo. "Looking at the center of the moving light can cause target fixation," said Warrant Officer James J. Kaye, a member of a Firefly team for the 334th Armed Helicopter Company, "and when it happens you're in a vacuum." Warrant Officer Gary L. Lucas, also from the 334th, described the sensation "as like driving through a dense fog, eyes on the road, and you see two white lines. Your speedometer reads 80 and you're looking for ants."

Night reconnaissance pilots also had to contend with the increased possibility of harming civilians. On the night of February 28, 1967, pilots from the 336th Assault Helicopter Company operating out of Soc Trang received intelligence reports that a VC battalion would try to cross the Bassac River later that night. Around midnight, the helicopters spotted the VC massing in sampans to cross the river. After receiving clearance from MACV headquarters to fire, they made several runs on the sampans. The men aboard the small craft returned fire with heavy automatic weapons, but the helicopter crews destroyed several sampans before using up their ordnance.

The helicopters returned to base to rearm and refuel, and on returning to the battle site they spotted an estimated forty sampans about one kilometer south of the original battle heading away from the area. According to the unit history. "Anything moving on the canals after eleven o'clock was considered fair game." The helicopters opened fire and destroyed most of the sampans before

returning to base. A search of the area the next day revealed sixty-nine dead VC at the site of the first attack. At the second battle, however, they found no VC, only thirty-one dead civilians. Frightened by the earlier battle, civilians in the area had fled aboard their sampans. Tragically, they sailed in the direction of the returning helicopters, which mistook them for VC. The episode drew national headlines and censure from many in the U.S.

Dustoff

In addition to its use as a war machine, the helicopter also distinguished itself as a vehicle for saving lives. As a medical evacuation craft, the helicopter was responsible for saving thousands of lives in Vietnam.

During WW II, only 71 percent of Army casualties survived their wounds. In Korea, where the U.S. made limited use of the helicopter as an aerial ambulance, that figure increased to 74 percent. But in Vietnam, the percentage of survivors increased to 81 percent. This was particularly impressive considering that 20 percent of the wounded in Vietnam suffered serious multiple injuries compared to 2 percent in WW II and 3 percent in Korea. That so many more wounded men survived was in large part attributable to the speed with which the helicopter crews ferried the wounded to hospitals for treatment.

Pilots often boasted that a wounded soldier could be moved to a field hospital faster than he would be in the

UH–1D medical evacuation helicopters prepare to lift wounded soldiers from the 2d Battalion, 14th Infantry, 25th Infantry Division, out of an LZ on June 17, 1966. The helicopter's speed and the skill and daring of the pilots greatly increased a wounded soldier's chances of survival.

U.S. Depending upon the situation, medevacs could deliver a wounded soldier to a medical station within half an hour of being hit. And the pilots flew anywhere at any time to pick up the wounded. Warrant Officer Stephen B. Peth evacuated 242 wounded to hospitals over one four-day span. Another medevac pilot, Major Patrick H. Brady, evacuated 51 wounded during a single day's action, braving heavy enemy fire throughout and later received the Medal of Honor. At the peak of the war, medevac crews carried more than 22,000 wounded per month.

The medevac was often one of the most dangerous helicopter missions in Vietnam. Usually, they were forced to land in the midst of a battle, and the loading of wounded required them to remain on the ground much longer than a troop or supply ship. The enemy also singled out the helicopters as prime targets. Knowing that ground forces always called for both gunships and medevacs during a battle, they waited for the helicopters to arrive and then attacked.

On March 26, 1969, 1st Lieutenant William D. Bristow of the 14th Combat Aviation Battalion settled into a landing zone near the village of Tien Phouc to medevac a wounded soldier from the 23d Infantry Division. As the helicopter departed the landing zone, however, it began taking fire. Bristow's crew chief, Private First Class Robert Wilhelm, and his door gunner, Specialist 4 Boyd L. Kettle, responded to the enemy fire immediately with their door-mounted M60 machine guns. Bristow pushed his craft for more altitude. Suddenly, the helicopter lurched forward. They had been hit. Flames spread through the cabin. As Bristow dropped the burning craft into the nearest open area, his copilot, Warrant Officer Paul E. Lunt, issued a distress signal giving their sign and location.

Hitting the ground, the crew, carrying their medevac patient with them, abandoned the Huey just before its fuel cells exploded. Pulling away from the burning wreck, Bristow checked his situation. Stranded in hostile territory with darkness approaching, they had only one M16 rifle with thirty-five shells and a .38-caliber pistol with twenty rounds. He hoped someone had heard their distress call.

Only one-half hour after the crash, three Huey "slicks" and two gunships from the 176th Assault Helicopter Company circled the crash site searching for signs of survivors. Overhead, after his first several passes turned up empty, the 176th's commanding officer, Major Ronald C. Metcalf, concluded that no one had survived the crash. However, with enemy fire increasing as the helicopters searched lower and lower, another of the pilots sighted a strobe light blinking from the middle of a nearby rice field.

Lying on his back, Lunt had crawled into the paddy and, using Bristow's strobe light, signaled to the helicopters overhead. Immediately the three ships pulled into formation, and with two acting as cover the third dropped down to the stranded crew. Despite heavy ground fire, Lieutenant Bristow and his men reached the helicopter safely, and the aircraft quickly lifted off, successfully completing the rescue. Twenty aviators received medals for their heroic efforts in the battle.

A new breed

Although the helicopter proved an invaluable asset to the Army in Vietnam, flying proved a dangerous occupation. By the end of 1971, nearly 4,700 helicopters had been lost in Vietnam. Enemy soldiers had gunned down nearly half of these, mostly by rifle fire or hand grenades, while accidents or mechanical failure had claimed the other half. The losses, which cost nearly $1.75 billion, also included the lives of 5,289 American soldiers. Military officials repeated that the number of deaths was extremely low in comparison to the number of sorties flown. For example, in the month of April 1969, forty-six helicopters were lost in combat out of a total of 588,700 sorties. But pilots still strapped themselves into their cockpits each day certain that they were performing one of the most dangerous jobs in the war.

Despite the risks, helicopter pilots welcomed the opportunity to fly. "Army aviators are different from other people," explained Major Charles J. Mix, commander of the 117th Aviation Company. "It's the challenge, the danger, taking chances. When you're flying and you hear one of your own men at night on the ground, whispering messages into his radio set because the enemy is nearby, that's when the adrenalin really flows."

In the flying-by-the-seat-of-your-pants atmosphere that prevailed for much of the Vietnam era, many helicopter pilots saw themselves as throwbacks to an earlier era in aviation. "We go about the same speed as the Spads [in WW I] did," said one gunship commander, "and that's the kind of flying a man can comprehend." Close contact was especially appealing to many pilots. "We're the last of the hand-to-hand warriors," boasted one pilot. "We can see the enemy and he can see us. The jet jockeys and even the infantry often don't get that chance."

For the pilots in Vietnam, many of them barely twenty years old, flying seemed the most glamorous job in the war. Very few wanted to make the Army their career. They wanted only to fly. But, as Warrant Officer Wayne Forbes pointed out, you needed a lot more than glamor to survive. "Some guys think this job is glamorous, but they find out pretty fast that it isn't. They see people getting messed up, and then they're afraid. But me, I've been afraid the whole goddamned time, and that's why I'm alive."

In 1969 the U.S. announced its plans to begin withdrawing its troops from Vietnam and to allow the South Vietnamese to assume responsibility for the war under the new Vietnamization program. While ground troops began leaving almost immediately, the 1st Aviation Brigade still faced four more years of war. Once the U.S. troops left, the brigade assumed the responsibility for providing air support for the ARVN troops and also for training the South Vietnamese pilots who would eventually replace them.

The brigade first began training South Vietnamese pilots in August 1966. Over the next three years they trained an average of sixty pilots per year in four three-month courses. In 1969, as the Army initiated its Vietnamization program, the brigade quickly expanded its training program. By October, more than 130 South Vietnamese were receiving training from brigade units. The Army also began sending Vietnamese pilots to the U.S. for training at Fort Rucker, Alabama, and Fort Wolters, Texas.

In September 1969, the Army completed the first phase of the South Vietnamese Air Force (VNAF) Improvement and Modernization Program, which consisted of the conversion of four VNAF squadrons from the older model CH-34 to the Huey. Phase II of this program, completed in July 1971, added eight more Huey squadrons to the VNAF and one CH-47 squadron. Phase III, begun in November 1971, allowed for the conversion of one CH-34 squadron to the latest model Huey, the UH-1H, and the activation of three more UH-1H squadrons and a single CH-47 squadron. In all cases, the 1st Aviation Brigade provided both the aircraft and trained the Vietnamese crews in their use, flying approximately 180 hours with the Vietnamese to familiarize them with the new machines. By the end of 1972, the VNAF helicopter fleet boasted more than 500 new helicopters—a major improvement over the 75 outmoded CH-34s that constituted the VNAF helicopter force in early 1968. More than 1,600 VNAF pilots had completed training at Forts Rucker and Wolters.

Despite the program's impressive appearance, many within the 1st Aviation Brigade felt those figures belied the truth of the situation. At the end of 1969, as the VNAF Improvement and Modernization Plan moved into full swing, the brigade's commanding officer, Major General Allen M. Burdett, Jr., declared it "replete with problem areas which will grow in complexity." By 1971, those problems had surfaced on the battlefield.

In February of 1971, a helicopter flying out of Bien Hoa air base carrying South Vietnamese General Do Cao Tri, eight other Vietnamese, and *Newsweek* correspondent Francois Sully crashed shortly after takeoff, killing everyone aboard. An investigation revealed that the crash was the result of shoddy maintenance by South Vietnamese mechanics. Only two days before the crash a maintenance expert from the 1st Aviation Brigade, Sergeant First Class John Keith, had inspected several other helicopters from the same squadron and found their condition "worse than the worst U.S. helicopters" he had ever seen.

Less than a month later, photographers Larry Burrows of *Life*, Henri Huet of the Associated Press, Kent Potter of the United Press International, and Keisaburo Shimamoto, on

assignment for *Newsweek*, all died when their helicopter, flown by a Vietnamese pilot, was shot down over Laos. Observers attributed the crash to pilot error, charging that he lost his way and strayed over an enemy stronghold.

Both of these incidents pointed out the problems in the Army's attempt to Vietnamize the helicopter war. On the most basic level, the problem of language hindered efforts to train South Vietnamese pilots. Cadets chosen to learn to fly helicopters first had to undergo English language training at Tan Son Nhut Air Base in Saigon, followed by another six weeks of intensive study in English at Lackland Air Force Base in Texas. Even then, most only attained a limited proficiency in English. One U.S. instructor put the whole process in perspective: "I couldn't imagine myself going over there to learn Vietnamese and fly."

Soldiers from the 1st Infantry Division launch an air assault into War Zone D in June 1967.

In addition to the language barrier, most South Vietnamese lacked the technical training and background necessary to become a good pilot or mechanic. Lieutenant General James Gavin viewed the whole idea of equipping the Vietnamese with the sophisticated Army helicopters as ludicrous. "I don't see leaving sophisticated helicopters and continuing to replace them. That would be like dropping them in the Pacific Ocean." Supporters of the plan contended that the Vietnamese only needed more time. But time was one thing they did not have. After watching South Vietnamese pilots commit a number of accidents during Operation Lam Son 719, the ARVN invasion of NVA strongholds in Laos, one frustrated U.S. pilot observed, "I wish the clowns would catch on—then I could leave."

As the war progressed into 1972, the pilot received at least half of his wish. From July 1971 to July 1972, more than 19,000 of the brigade's 24,000 personnel redeployed out of Vietnam. At the same time, it reduced its number of aircraft through redeployment and transfer to the VNAF from 3,200 to 984. On March 29, 1973, the last members of the brigade departed, carrying the unit's colors to its new home at Fort Rucker.

The 1st Aviation Brigade was the last major U.S. combat unit to leave Vietnam. Although formed officially in 1966, its units had participated in U.S. operations in Vietnam from 1961 onward. In that time, the brigade and its many units not only flew more than 30 million sorties ranging from medevac missions to air assaults to close air support but also helped to develop the concept of airmobility that drastically altered modern warfare.

The Sky Cavalry

"Harry, your job with your division is to prevent the enemy from cutting the country in two." Such, recalled Major General Harry W. O. Kinnard, were the terse, straightforward orders he received in the late spring of 1965 upon learning that he would lead the U.S. Army's newly formed 1st Cavalry Division (Airmobile) to Vietnam. The assignment was not unexpected. As the commander of the Army's 11th Air Assault Division, an experimental unit based at Fort Benning, Georgia, Kinnard had spent the previous two years developing the tactics and techniques of "airmobile" warfare under the watchful eye of the Pentagon. Using fleets of helicopters and other light aircraft, the general and his staff had conducted a series of extensive field exercises designed to increase battlefield mobility. On the whole the tests had gone well, and even though they had not been conceived with Vietnam specifically in mind, by early 1965 rumors abounded that the division would soon be deployed to the war zone.

Nevertheless, when the activation of the test formation, redesignated the 1st Cavalry Division (Airmobile), became official on July 1, 1965, Kinnard knew that he faced a formidable challenge. Given only four weeks to achieve RECON-1—readiness condition of the highest combat priority—the general quickly had to find a way to bring his brigade-sized unit to full division strength and prepare it for combat 12,000 miles away. The manpower shortage was solved in part by the decision to exchange the colors of the 1st Cavalry Division, then stationed at Tonggu, South Korea, with those of the 2d Infantry Division at Fort Benning. But even the absorption of the Fort Benning soldiers did not fully meet the division's needs. Additional soldiers had to be pulled from the fort's parachute school as well as from the 197th Infantry Brigade, while some 300 critically needed aviators were whisked in from Army outposts around the globe.

After tacking on the oversized, bright yellow insignia of their new unit, the fresh troops were hurriedly organized into companies, issued equipment, and processed for overseas duty. Only those assigned to the airborne-qualified 1st Brigade, however, received much in the way of formal training. Many did not even have a chance to test-fire their new M16E1 rifles or practice squad tactics before they were aboard ships headed for Vietnam.

In the meantime, a 1,000-man advance party led by Brigadier General John M. Wright, Jr., the assistant division commander, was sent ahead to establish a base camp that could accommodate more than 450 aircraft, as well as the division's 15,000 troops. Told that the division's mission was to thwart a major Communist thrust across the rugged central highlands, Wright fixed upon an old French airstrip near the village of An Khe, midway between the port city of Qui Nhon and Pleiku along Highway 19 and not far from the site where twelve years before Vietminh forces had ambushed and annihilated the French Groupe Mobile 100. There, on August 27, officers and enlisted men alike began the arduous process of carving out the world's largest helipad, a two-kilometer by three-kilometer rectangle soon to be christened "The Golf Course."

A month later, the majority of the division's combat elements arrived in country and immediately assumed responsibility for the security of the An Khe hub and most of Highway 19. During the first few weeks contact with the enemy remained relatively light as the "skytroopers," at MACV's insistence, probed their narrowly delimited TAOR in a series of brief, small-scale operations. For General Kinnard, who had different ideas about what his division could and should be doing, it was a frustrating time. "I just don't know how to fight that way," he remembered telling

General Stanley "Swede" Larsen, the Field Force I commander. "If you'll just give me a mission-type order to go into some province, develop the enemy situation and fight it as I find it, that I can do."

"Give Kinnard his head"

The opportunity Kinnard sought came soon enough. On October 19, Communist forces launched their long-anticipated central highlands offensive with a furious division-sized assault on the Plei Me Special Forces camp in western Pleiku Province. Though the attackers were ultimately driven off, General Westmoreland was determined not to let them get away. On October 27 he told General Larsen to "give Kinnard his head" and ordered the 1st Air Cav to "find, fix, and destroy" the 32d and 33d North Vietnamese Army regiments as they retreated through the trackless jungle toward the Cambodian border.

Kinnard promptly dispatched the aerial reconnaissance arm of the division—the 1st Squadron, 9th Cavalry—to scout possible enemy routes of withdrawal within his newly expanded, 2,500-square-kilometer area of operation. Under the command of Lieutenant Colonel John B. "Bullwhip" Stockton, a daring aviator renowned for his high-speed contour flying, the OH-13 light observation helicopters of the 1/9's aero-scout platoons, designated "White teams," spent the next few days combing the western highlands for signs of the elusive enemy. Though small groups of soldiers were occasionally spotted, no significant contact occurred until November 1, when the squadron stumbled upon a major regimental aid station defended by a battalion of NVA regulars. In a textbook display of "air cavalry" tactics, heliborne infantrymen of the unit's aero-rifle platoons, or "Blue teams," were quickly inserted on the ground under covering fires provided by heavily armed gunships of the aero-weapons platoons—the "Red teams." The cavalrymen soon discovered that their adversary had some tactical tricks of his own. To neutralize the firepower of the hovering gunships, the North Vietnamese moved in so close to the American perimeter that aerial rockets and machine guns could not easily be fired without endangering U.S. lives. Then, as infantry reinforcements from the division's 1st Brigade began to arrive on the scene, the bulk of the enemy force broke contact and slipped away.

Convinced that the North Vietnamese were falling back toward base camps in the Chu Pong Mountains, the division command ordered the 1/9 to leapfrog over the retreating enemy and set up an ambush site in the densely wooded Ia Drang Valley. On the night of November 3, Blue team riflemen of the squadron's C Troop successfully

---

1st Cavalry Division (Airmobile)

Arrived Vietnam: September 11, 1965

Departed Vietnam: April 29, 1971

Unit Headquarters

An Khe   *Sep. 1965–June 1967*
An Khe/Bong Son   *July 1967–Jan. 1968*
An Khe/Hue   *Feb. 1968*

An Khe/Phong Dien   *March 1968–April 1968*
An Khe/Quang Tri   *May 1968*
An Khe/Phong Dien   *June 1968–Oct. 1968*

An Khe/Phuoc Vinh   *Nov. 1968–April 1969*
Bien Hoa/Phuoc Vinh   *May 1969–April 1971*

Commanding Officers

Maj. Gen. Harry W. B. Kinnard   *July 1965*
Maj. Gen. John Norton   *May 1966*
Maj. Gen. John J. Tolson III   *April 1967*

Maj. Gen. George I. Forsythe   *July 1968*
Maj. Gen. Elvy B. Roberts   *May 1969*

Maj. Gen. George W. Casey   *May 1970*
Maj. Gen. George W. Putnam, Jr.   *July 1970*

Major Subordinate Units

1st Battalion, 5th Cavalry
2d Battalion, 5th Cavalry
1st Battalion, 7th Cavalry
2d Battalion, 7th Cavalry
5th Battalion, 7th Cavalry
1st Battalion, 8th Cavalry
2d Battalion, 8th Cavalry
1st Battalion, 12th Cavalry
2d Battalion, 12th Cavalry
1st Squadron, 9th Cavalry
11th Pathfinder Company
Company E, 52d Infantry
Company H, 75th Infantry

11th Aviation Group
227th Aviation Battalion
228th Aviation Battalion
229th Aviation Battalion
11th Aviation Company
17th Aviation Company
478th Aviation Company
2d Battalion, 17th Artillery
2d Battalion, 19th Artillery
2d Battalion, 20th Artillery
1st Battalion, 21st Artillery
1st Battalion, 30th Artillery

1st Battalion, 77th Artillery
Battery E, 82d Artillery
1st Personnel Service Battalion
8th Engineer Battalion
13th Signal Battalion
15th Medical Battalion
15th Supply & Service Battalion
15th Transportation Battalion
27th Maintenance Battalion
15th Administrative Company
371st Army Security Agency Company
545th Military Police Company

5,444 KIA
(Casualty figures are "Vietnam Era.")

26,592 WIA

25 Medals of Honor

The Real
Air Cav

Perhaps no image came to symbolize the American military presence in Vietnam more than the hovering silhouette of the Army helicopter. Modern warfare's flying horses granted unprecedented speed and battlefield mobility to U.S. ground forces throughout the war. Initially conceived by military aviators in the years after World War II, the notion of air cavalry was slow to gain acceptance. Despite the obstacles, a few outspoken supporters continued to push the idea. Pointing out that armored cavalry had lost some of the tactical advantages of traditional horse cavalry, enthusiasts such as General James Gavin became determined to see the cavalry of old reborn in the skies.

By tradition, cavalry screened ahead for the infantry or served as a shock force, using speed and mobility to achieve surprise. It also had screened for slower infantry by delaying enemy advances and had conducted scouting and reconnaissance missions. When used with larger infantry units, cavalry could successfully protect the flanks while scouting for weaknesses in enemy defenses. From his Korean War experiences, Gavin found armor to be an inadequate replacement for horses. First, tanks were limited in the terrain they could traverse, making them useless in some situations. Second, to be effective, cavalry had to be faster and more mobile than infantry troops, yet motorized infantry was as fast and mobile—if not more so—than armored cavalry. For these reasons he saw in the modern Army a need for a new airmobile cavalry.

Through the rest of the decade, Army aviators conducted small tests trying to adapt cavalry doctrine to the slowly evolving helicopter technology. While reaching for the future, the aviators stole from the past, often relying heavily on old horse cavalry field manuals to develop their airmobile tactics.

In 1962, Secretary of Defense Robert S. McNamara ordered the Army to set up a board, headed by Lieutenant General Hamilton H. Howze, to investigate the applications of airmobility in the modern Army. After months of intensive field tests, the Howze Board came forth with its proposals, including the formation of an air assault division, an air cavalry combat brigade (ACCB), and several smaller air transport brigades. The ACCB was, in Howze's opinion, at the core of air cavalry doctrine. He envisioned a homogeneous brigade of three squadrons, where "within the squadrons, each troop looked alike, and within the troop, each platoon." Each platoon in turn was to be composed of scout helicopters, gunships, and helicopters carrying riflemen.

Only the air assault division, however, continued its testing. During the following two years, Brigadier General Harry W. O. Kinnard oversaw field applications of the experimental 11th Air Assault Division. In June 1965 the test division was rechristened the 1st Cavalry Division (Airmobile) and quickly began preparations for deployment to Vietnam. Although the entire division was designed to be airborne-qualified, the hurried pace of training and an acute shortage of parachutists permitted the formation of only one airborne brigade. Helicopters were used for transport—essentially as flying trucks—and the majority of the division never received training in the cavalry tactics explored by the Howze Board. The exception was the division's reconnaissance arm, the 1st Squadron, 9th Cavalry.

Dubbed the "Cav of the Cav," or as some would have it, the "Real Air Cav," the 1st of the 9th was the only unit in the division that conformed to General Howze's original conception of air cavalry. With its Red, White, and Blue teams coordinating firepower, reconnaissance, and shock troops, the squadron proved enormously effective, time and again initiating major division battles. Despite its success, the Army did not expand the 1st of the 9th, which was a fraction of the size of the ACCB recommended by the Howze Board, until 1970.

Under General Putnam, the squadron was finally augmented to become the 9th Air Cavalry Brigade. Putnam hoped to continue combat-testing ACCB tactics as explored by the Howze Board years earlier. He placed gunships formerly used with infantry battalions into the new cavalry units to give them more power and attempted to create a special corps cavalry reserve. By late 1970, however, the dwindling American commitment in Vietnam prevented Putnam from maintaining a cav reserve or even enough qualified maintenance crews. Some innovations were introduced as helicopter technology continued to improve. The new, deadly AH-1G Cobra of the Red teams began flying with visual reconnaissance helicopters of the White teams to form devastating Pink teams. Over the battlefield, however, the brigade never reached its potential, flying an increasing number of support missions not with the Blue teams of the Air Cav but with inexperienced ARVN infantry troops.

When the majority of the 1st Cavalry Division (Airmobile) returned to the United States in April 1971, the future of air cavalry remained unclear. Lieutenant General Harry Kinnard, then head of the Army Combat Developments Command, wanted to continue intensive ACCB tests at Fort Hood, Texas. But Chief of Staff General William Westmoreland had other plans. Curious about the possibilities of a "triple capability" (TRICAP) division incorporating armor, airmobile, and cavalry brigades, Westmoreland converted much of the 1st Cavalry Division into ground-based armor units. With its wings clipped, the division's air cavalry tests virtually ceased. Within a few years, the forgotten hopes of the Howze Board became buried under a sea of paperwork.

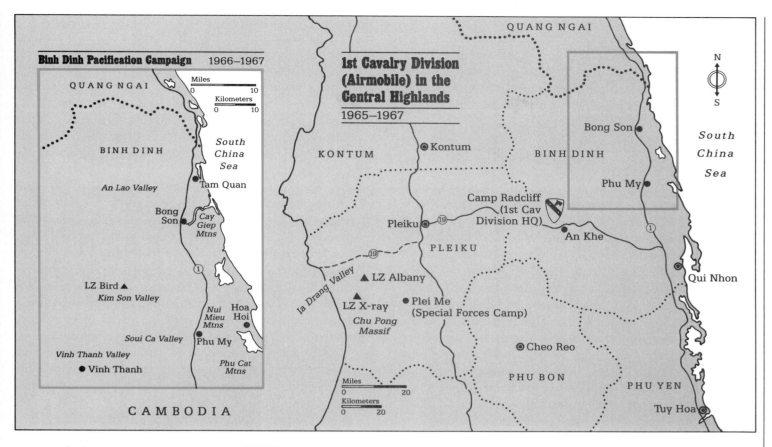

Binh Dinh Pacification Campaign 1966–1967

QUANG NGAI

BINH DINH

An Lao Valley

Tam Quan

Bong Son

Cay Giep Mtns

South China Sea

LZ Bird ▲

Kim Son Valley

Nui Mieu Mtns

Hoa Hoi

Soui Ca Valley

Phu My

Vinh Thanh Valley

● Vinh Thanh

Phu Cat Mtns

CAMBODIA

1st Cavalry Division (Airmobile) in the Central Highlands 1965–1967

QUANG NGAI

KONTUM

◉ Kontum

Bong Son

BINH DINH

Phu My

Camp Radcliff (1st Cav Division HQ)

Pleiku ●

PLEIKU

An Khe ●

South China Sea

Ia Drang Valley

▲ LZ Albany

▲ LZ X-ray

● Plei Me (Special Forces Camp)

Chu Pong Massif

◉ Cheo Reo

PHU BON

Qui Nhon ◉

PHU YEN

Tuy Hoa ◉

---

sprang their trap on an unsuspecting NVA heavy weapons company, only to fall prey to a ferocious battalion-sized counterattack less than an hour later. Though the Americans managed to fight off the enemy's initial assaults, that night they were in danger of being overrun when Company A, 1st Battalion, 8th Cavalry, staged an assault and reinforced their position. By morning the attack had been broken and the perimeter secured by the arrival of the rest of the "Jumping Mustangs" of the 1/8 Cav, backed by the 105MM howitzers of Battery B, 2d Battalion, 19th Artillery. The battle of the Ia Drang Valley, the first major confrontation between regular soldiers of the American and North Vietnamese armies, was now joined.

During the next three weeks the soldiers of the 1st Air Cav took on the NVA in a series of bloody clashes that were, in the words of General Westmoreland, "as fierce as any ever experienced by American troops." In the biggest battle of the campaign, the fight for LZ X-ray at the base of the Chu Pong Massif, elements of three battalions from the division's 3d Brigade held their ground for three days in the face of savage attacks from two North Vietnamese regiments. The battle nonetheless ended on a somber note when men of the 2d Battalion, 7th Cavalry, stumbled into an ambush near LZ Albany on November 17 and were nearly annihilated; only 84 of the original 500 men were able to return to immediate duty. By the time Operation Silver Bayonet (its official code name) came to an end ten days later, 240 air cavalrymen had been killed in action. Enemy losses, however, had been far more severe. In

addition to the nearly 1,500 KIAs established by body count, as many as 2,000 more NVA soldiers were estimated to have died on the battlefield.

While MACV was quick to publicize the 1st Cavalry Division's victory in the Ia Drang, General Kinnard was even more pleased by the extent to which the campaign "established the validity of a new concept of land warfare." During the course of the thirty-five-day operation, entire infantry battalions and artillery batteries had been moved by helicopter and inserted into otherwise inaccessible terrain. Division aircraft had also delivered over 5,000 tons of supplies to troops in the field and extracted approximately 2,700 refugees to safety. Perhaps most impressive of all, some 50,000 helicopter sorties had resulted in only fifty-nine ships hit by enemy fire, four shot down, and one unrecovered. Helicopters, it seemed, were not quite so vulnerable to ground fire as many skeptics within the military establishment had long presumed.

Yet if the bloody Ia Drang campaign clearly demonstrated that airmobility had come of age, it also taught the soldiers of the 1st Air Cavalry some hard but invaluable lessons about the nature of the Vietnam War. Time and again the enemy's "hugging" tactics frustrated American efforts to bring the full weight of their vastly superior firepower to bear on the battlefield. As a result, much of the fighting in the Ia Drang Valley took the form of pointblank shoot-outs and vicious hand-to-hand combat in which the North Vietnamese showed themselves to be well trained, highly disciplined, and ready to fight to the death. At the same time, the Communists seemed willing only to engage the Americans when they had a decisive numerical advantage and all too willing to flee when they did not. Only by maintaining the initiative could the U.S. air cavalrymen hope to subdue their determined foe, and even then, they knew, ultimate victory would not come easily.

The Year of the Horse

In the wake of the Ia Drang campaign, the division command shifted its attention away from the remote western highlands and began laying plans for a large-scale sweep of northeastern Binh Dinh Province, a populous, rice-rich coastal area that had been dominated by the Vietminh and Vietcong since World War II. Despite the presence of the 22d ARVN Division and the Republic of Korea Capital Division along Highway 1, intelligence reports confirmed that three regiments attached to the 3d NVA, or "Yellow Star," Division—the 2d VC and the 18th and 22d NVA Regiments—were operating freely throughout the region from mobile mountain base camps. General Kinnard therefore decided to launch a series of airmobile "hammer-and-anvil" operations designed to flush the enemy forces into the open and trap them against pre-established blocking positions. Code-named Masher in its initial phase, and later White Wing, the campaign was scheduled to begin on January 25 following a three-day Tet holiday truce to mark the advent of the lunar new year. To the men of the 1st Cavalry Division, whose insignia features the silhouette of a horse's head, the fact that 1966 was to be the Buddhist Year of the Horse seemed an especially auspicious sign.

Led by Colonel Harold G. "Hal" Moore, a recent recipient of the Distinguished Service Cross for his actions as commander of the 1/7 Cav at LZ X-ray, the 3d Brigade spearheaded the campaign with support from the ARVN Airborne Brigade, the 22d ARVN Division, and the ROK Capital Division. After establishing a central base of operations near the village of Bong Son, the cavalrymen first moved northeast into the flat Bong Son Plain, then west and southwest through the mountains and valleys bordering the coast of the South China Sea. Operating in weather that alternated between steady drizzle and thick fog, the skytroopers repeatedly clashed with all three regiments of the Yellow Star Division, ultimately rendering five of its nine battalions combat ineffective.

They did not remain ineffective for very long, however. Within two months the 3d NVA Division had recouped its losses and infiltrated back into the Bong Son Plain, prompting the 1st Air Cavalry to return to the area in early May in Operation Davy Crockett. Shortly after the new campaign got under way, Major General Kinnard, having nurtured his experimental airmobile formation to full maturity, relinquished command of the division to Major General John B. Norton. A former World War II paratrooper who had most recently served as commander of the Army Support Command, USARV, Norton barely had time to unpack his bags when he was confronted by reports of an impending attack on the Vinh Thanh Special Forces Camp in western Binh Dinh Province. In response, on May 16 Davy Crockett ground to a halt and a new operation, eventually dubbed Crazy Horse, was launched.

It began with an air assault by Company B, 2d Battalion, 8th Cavalry, into LZ Hereford, a small patch of elephant grass midway up the highest mountain east of the Special Forces camp. After a hard climb to the ridge line along a narrow jungle trail, the lead platoon spotted and fired upon six enemy soldiers moving ahead of them along the same path. For a moment there was silence. Then, suddenly, a fusillade of automatic weapons fire tore into the column from the east, killing three men and pinning down the rest of the platoon. Forced to pull back after one squad was decimated in an abortive flanking action, the platoon eventually linked up with the rest of the company. Any hope of regaining the offensive was abandoned. As the battalion-sized enemy force pressed its attack and American casualties multiplied, Captain John D. Coleman hastily organized his troops into a roughly defined perimeter and awaited reinforcements.

In the meantime, two gunships of the 2d Battalion, 20th Artillery, eased their way up the mountain through a torrential downpour, trying to locate the company's position beneath the 200-foot-high jungle canopy. Guided by radio, they eventually found their target and began firing salvo after salvo of 2.75-inch rockets beyond the edge of Company B's collapsed perimeter. The aerial artillery bombardment temporarily broke the attack, allowing Company A of the 1st Battalion, 12th Cavalry, to reach the mountaintop shortly after nightfall. Early next morning the enemy resumed their ground assaults behind an intense barrage of grenade, rocket, and recoilless rifle fire. During the next two hours the survival of the two American companies was much in doubt, until the approach of an additional relief column from Company C of the 1/12 Cav caused the enemy to break contact and fade back into the jungle.

The vicious firefight above LZ Hereford was costly to the 1st Cav. Twenty-eight soldiers were killed and nearly 100 had been wounded. But it had also tipped off the division to the presence of a sizable enemy contingent in the area, which subsequent intelligence revealed to be the 2d VC Regiment—one of the same units the Cav had tangled with in Masher/White Wing. During the next three weeks the cavalrymen plunged into some of the most forbidding terrain in the central highlands, an area of steep, thickly forested mountains rising up to 3,000 feet above sea level.

A wounded grenadier of the 1st Cav is treated by medics after his company stumbled into a firefight with Vietcong troops during Operation Paul Revere in August 1966.

A cavalryman of Company C, 2d Battalion, 8th Cavalry, leads a Vietcong suspect captured near Bong Son toward the company command post during Operation Thayer in late September 1966.

To insert troops on the ground, air commanders often had to rely on single helicopter landings through narrow shafts in the triple canopy jungle or use "Jacob's ladders" strung from hovering CH-47 Chinooks. Though sporadic contact was made, ground operations were eventually brought to a halt after efforts to bottle up the VC proved fruitless. Division artillery then began pounding suspected enemy positions with 12,000 to 13,000 rounds per day, while the Air Force assisted with tactical air strikes, including B-52 raids. Just how many enemy soldiers were killed in the firestorm could never be known, but the powerful 2d VC Regiment did not reappear on the battlefield for months.

After Crazy Horse there was a temporary pause in the ongoing battle of Binh Dinh, as the 1st Cav split up to conduct a series of far-flung operations, Paul Revere in Pleiku Province, Hawthorne in Kontum Province, and Nathan Hale in Phu Yen Province. Already suffering from a shortage of pilots, trained mechanics, and standard re-

placement parts for its helicopters, the division soon found its logistical system strained to the limit. Nor were these the only problems facing General Norton and his staff. The division's infantry units were also severely under strength, in part because of casualties and in part because of the rotation of some 9,000 officers and enlisted men back to the U.S. By midsummer 1966, the 1st Cav's 920-man battalions were commonly fielding fewer than 550 troops, while rifle companies often went into combat at two-thirds of their authorized strength.

In early September 1966, the division returned to its base at An Khe to resume what had come to be called the Binh Dinh Pacification Campaign. In Operation Thayer I (September 13 to October 1), a sweep of NVA/VC staging areas in the Kim Son and Soui Ca Valleys, the 1st and 2d brigades uncovered numerous arms caches as well as a regimental hospital and a munitions factory. Though contact was minimal, the action forced the enemy to flee eastward toward the coastal plain, where two battalions of the 18th NVA Regiment were later trapped in the hamlet of Hoa Hoi and severely battered during a follow-up operation code-named Irving (October 2 to 24). Irving in turn dovetailed into Operation Thayer II, in which all three brigades of the 1st Cavalry were committed to Binh Dinh in an effort to keep pressure on the resilient 3d NVA Division.

For all the inroads the division made during its various Binh Dinh operations, however, pacification of the longtime Communist stronghold remained a distant goal. As if to remind the cavalrymen of that sobering fact, the 22d NVA Regiment launched a surprise attack on the 1st Cav's artillery base at LZ Bird on December 27, only hours after the end of a tense Christmas truce. After silently defusing the trip flares and claymore mines protecting the LZ's perimeter, the NVA rushed forward with bayonets fixed and overpowered several gun crews. Only the firing of two devastatingly lethal beehive rounds at pointblank range prevented the enemy from overrunning the base entirely. Fifty-eight U.S. soldiers were killed in the attack and another 77 wounded, while enemy losses were reported as 266 KIA. As the Year of the Horse drew to a close, the battle of Binh Dinh had just begun.

Operation Pershing

In order to break the Communists' grip on the 800,000 inhabitants of Binh Dinh, in early 1967 the division command began outlining plans for an all-out campaign aimed at destroying the local VC infrastructure as well as the enemy's Main Force units. Code-named Pershing, the operation kicked off on February 12 amid great fanfare, as hordes of journalists and photographers accompanied the troops into the field. Working in conjunction with the South Vietnamese 18th National Police Field Force, the 1st Cav spent the next eleven months combing the province's villages for members of the Vietcong political and administrative apparatus while maintaining a steady pace of combat operations against its principal nemeses, the 2d VC Regiment and the 18th and 22d NVA Regiments.

The largest engagement of the campaign occurred toward the end of the year when three infantry battalions of the 1st Cav, backed by the recently arrived 1st Battalion, 50th Infantry (Mechanized), and the 40th ARVN Regiment, fought a two-week running battle with the 7th and 8th Battalions of the 22d NVA Regiment along the coastal plain north of Bong Son. The action began on December 6, after scout ships of the 1st Squadron, 9th Cavalry, spotted a radio antenna near the village of Tam Quan, a cluster of paddy island hamlets surrounded by an expanse of rice fields. Met by machine-gun fire as they swooped down to investigate, the White team observation helicopters pulled away and called for the insertion of a Blue team rifle platoon. The riflemen of A Troop only got as far as the edge of the village before they were pinned down by intense fire from a sizable and well-entrenched NVA force. A second aerial rifle platoon then air-assaulted into an adjacent rice field, but it too became stranded as it attempted to link up with the men of A Troop.

With darkness rapidly approaching, 1st Brigade Commander Colonel Donald V. Rattan ordered his ready reac-tion force—Company B of the 1st Battalion, 8th Infantry—to reinforce and rescue the isolated reconnaissance troops of the 1/9. Again the North Vietnamese waited until the cavalrymen had closed in on the thick hedgerows and shrubbery that concealed their entrenchments, then opened up with a deafening volume of automatic weapons and grenade fire. Savage, close-range combat raged. The NVA surged out of their trenches and spider holes to finish off and loot the American wounded. In the meantime, four armored personnel carriers from Company A of the mech-anized 1st Battalion, 50th Infantry, rushed toward the scene of action, only to be halted by a dike at the edge of the village. After one of the APCs took a direct hit from a B-40 rocket, the other three pulled back and joined the men of Bravo Company to form a makeshift defensive perimeter.

Throughout the night, aircraft searchlights and illumi-nation flares lit up the sky over Tam Quan, as helicopter gunships and artillery continually pounded the NVA forti-fications. Taking advantage of the covering fires, one of

Soldiers of the 1st Cav, in search of Vietcong, flush civilians out of their air–raid shelters shortly after aircraft and artillery struck the village, as part of the Binh Dinh pacification cam-paign, 1966.

the relief force's APCs churned through the rice fields and extracted the beleaguered aerial riflemen of the 1/9. By early morning, troops of the 40th ARVN Regiment had taken up blocking positions around the general area, while the rest of the 1st Battalion, 8th Infantry, moved in to reinforce Company B.

At 9:00 A.M. on December 7 the soldiers of the 1/8, backed by four self-propelled 40MM Duster guns and additional armored personnel carriers, renewed their attack on Tam Quan. Charging across a causeway created by bulldozer crews of the 8th Engineer Battalion, the infantrymen once again ran into a wall of machine-gun, rifle, and grenade fire from the enemy's interlocking defensive positions. Casualties mounted as NVA snipers zeroed in on the armored tracks, disabling several vehicles and killing their commanders and drivers. Forced to fall back, the cavalrymen called for more artillery and air strikes, then regrouped for a follow-up assault. This second advance proved even more costly than the first, as twenty men from Company B were cut down trying to cross a low hedgerow less than 100 meters from the point where they started.

By early afternoon, so many Americans had fallen on the battlefield of Tam Quan that twelve helicopter sorties were required to evacuate the wounded. Despite the heavy toll, the battalion mounted a third attack, this time moving in line behind a shield of armored personnel carriers and a mechanized flame thrower. Hit by steadily intensifying recoilless rifle fire and rocket-propelled grenades as they rumbled forward, one of the APCs exploded and another became immobilized. The flame thrower retaliated by immolating an NVA antitank weapon site. Moments later, the remaining three armored personnel carriers suddenly and unexpectedly accelerated to maximum speed and smashed into the enemy's forward trench line. Caught by surprise, many of the North Vietnamese troops began to flee. Others attempted futilely to climb atop the onrushing vehicles, only to be crushed beneath their steel tracks or shot down by their crews. The infantrymen quickly closed in behind the armored carriers, and by nightfall the NVA's main line of defense was in American hands.

The following morning the air cavalrymen resumed the offensive, though it soon became apparent that the enemy's resistance had weakened considerably. Heavy fighting nevertheless continued for ten more days as infantry, armor, and engineering forces combined to drive the 22d NVA Regiment from the surrounding area. By the time the battle of Tam Quan came to an end on December 20, both sides had paid heavy prices. Fifty-eight soldiers of the 1st Cavalry Division had been killed and another 250 wounded, while enemy losses, established by body count, exceeded 600.

Cav troopers of Company D, 2d Battalion, 8th Cavalry, charge through enemy fire to overrun an enemy position on the Bong Son Plain during Operation Pershing, May 1967.

Total division casualties for Operation Pershing—852 troops killed in action, 286 killed in noncombat circumstances, 4,119 wounded, and 22 missing in action—surpassed all operational losses suffered in 1966 and amounted to 27 percent of available manpower. By contrast, the Americans claimed to have killed more than 5,300 NVA and VC troops and captured 2,323, while rendering 50 percent of the Vietcong political and administrative cadres in Binh Dinh Province "ineffective." As a result, when the Tet offensive erupted across the length and breadth of South Vietnam in late January 1968, Binh Dinh was one of the least affected provinces.

Although Pershing occupied most of the division's attention and assets during the year, it was not the only operation in which the 1st Cavalry participated. In early April, shortly after Major General John J. Tolson III succeeded Gen. Norton as the division commander, the 1st Cav made its first foray outside of II Corps when it was called upon to relieve a Marine unit in southern Quang Ngai Province. Seizing the opportunity to enter an area that had long served as a sanctuary for NVA/VC forces operating in Binh Dinh Province, Tolson dispatched the 2d Brigade into I Corps with orders to seek out the headquarters of the 3d NVA Division. Two weeks of sweeps yielded little contact, however, and on April 19 the cavalrymen returned to Binh Dinh after relinquishing control of the area to the 3d Brigade of the 25th Infantry Division.

Two months later, in early August 1967, the 1st Cav returned to Quang Ngai to conduct a "reconnaissance in force" of the Song Re Valley. Begun with high hopes of penetrating another previously unexplored VC stronghold, the operation nearly ended in disaster when the 2d Battalion, 8th Cavalry, air-assaulted into a hornet's nest called LZ Pat on the morning of August 9. As soon as the lead company hit the ground, it was greeted by a torrent of heavy automatic weapons, mortars, and recoilless rifle fire from an estimated eighty NVA soldiers, reinforced by a Vietcong montagnard rifle company. Firing from well-concealed bunkers surrounding the small clearing, the enemy shot down two command helicopters and pinned down the company for four hours until aerial rocket artillery and a series of tactical air strikes finally broke the attack. In the days that followed the cavalrymen pursued their attackers but were unable to reestablish contact, and on August 20 the operation ended.

During the fall of 1967, amid criticism from some quarters that the 1st Cav was stagnating in Binh Dinh Province, the division's forces were channeled in a variety of directions. At the beginning of October, growing concern over the enemy buildup in I Corps led to the deployment of the 3d Brigade to Chu Lai, where it joined Operation Wheeler/Wallowa under the operational control of the newly formed American Division. In November, the 1st Brigade rushed west to Kontum Province to bolster the 4th Infantry Division and the 173d Airborne Brigade at Dak To, only to be called

back to the Bong Son plains a month later during the nine-day battle of Tam Quan. In the meantime, MACV ordered the 1st Cavalry Division to I Corps to reinforce the Marines, hoping that the Marines would improve their airmobile tactics by observing the 1st Air Cav. On January 17, 1968, the 1st Brigade moved up to Hue-Phu Bai and from there to the outskirts of Quang Tri City. Then came Tet.

Tet 1968

It was 4:20 A.M. on January 31, 1968, when the 812th NVA Regiment, backed by the 808th and 814th VC Main Force Battalions, launched its attack on the city of Quang Tri. Striking from the north, east, and southeast, the NVA quickly penetrated the city at several points. Though the local defense forces, including the 1st ARVN Regiment and the 9th ARVN Airborne Brigade, put up a good fight, by noon the enemy seemed poised to capture its prize.

Recognizing the need for immediate action, Colonel Donald V. Rattan, the commander of the 1st Cavalry Division's 1st Brigade, called division headquarters and received authority to counterattack. Several hours later, around 3:00 P.M., the 1st Battalion, 12th Cavalry, and the 1st Battalion, 5th Cavalry, staged a series of combat assaults east and southeast of Quang Tri. After sealing off the enemy's main infiltration routes and neutralizing two fire support bases, the cavalrymen pushed west toward the city shortly after nightfall. Wedged between the Americans at their rear and the city's ARVN defenders, and steadily pounded by aerial rocket fire from the Cav's new Cobra gunships, the young, inexperienced soldiers of the 812th NVA Regiment were forced to scatter and flee. By morning only a few small pockets of resistance remained, and by midday the capital of Quang Tri Province was once again secure.

The next day, February 2, the 1st Cavalry's 3d Brigade rushed into action outside the city of Hue, where one of the most decisive battles of the countrywide Tet offensive now raged. Ordered to block the enemy's principal reinforcement and supply routes, the 2d Battalion, 12th Cavalry, and the 5th Battalion, 7th Cavalry, air-assaulted into positions west of the city and soon became embroiled, in the words of Gen. Tolson, "in some of the most furious combat" of the Vietnam War. Reinforced by the arrival of the 2d Battalion, 501st Airborne, on February 15 and the 1st Battalion, 7th Cavalry, four days later, the 3d Brigade advanced steadily along a four-battalion front behind a shield of heavy artillery fire, tactical air strikes, and off-shore naval gunfire. On February 24 the cavalrymen finally reached the walls of the enemy-occupied Citadel, as the three-week battle of Hue came to an end.

Back at division headquarters, Gen. Tolson and his staff were already making preparations for the 1st Cav's next major assignment, the relief of the besieged Marine garrison at Khe Sanh combat base in western Quang Tri

Province. Code-named Pegasus/Lam Son 207, the operation began on the morning of April 1 with a drive westward along Highway 9 by two battalions from the 1st and 3d Marines. Then the 1st Cav took over. As the Marines trudged along, clearing and repairing the road, waves of helicopters carrying seven infantry battalions from all three of the division's brigades leapfrogged ahead in a spectacular display of airmobility. Although delayed by poor weather and sporadic enemy resistance, the skytroopers reached Khe Sanh within a week, marking the end of the seventy-seven-day siege on April 8.

The cavalrymen barely had time to catch their breath before they were on the move again, this time into the A Shau Valley, a major North Vietnamese base area in Thua Thien Province that Gen. Tolson later described as "the enemy's Cam Ranh Bay." Following six days of intensive B-52 raids and tactical air strikes, the 3d Brigade initiated Operation Delaware/Lam Son 216 with an air assault into the northern end of the valley on the morning of April 19. Though the first troopships landed without incident, subsequent lifts were met by withering fire from interlocked antiaircraft batteries that blasted ten helicopters out of the sky and damaged thirteen others. "There were white puffs of smoke everywhere," one aviator remembered. "I mean,

when I came in the ground *erupted* right at me." Thick fog and intermittent thunderstorms brought on by a late-season monsoon only made matters worse, forcing pilots of the 11th Aviation Group to search for holes in the low cloud ceiling before making their descent.

On April 23 the weather finally improved, allowing the division's huge CH-54 Flying Sky Cranes to haul in 105MM and 155MM artillery guns in support of the ground troops. Riflemen of the 1st Battalion, 7th Cavalry, meanwhile, moved out across the valley floor, where they discovered an NVA maintenance area containing Soviet-made bulldozers, trucks, and other engineering equipment. After the 1/7 secured an abandoned airfield near A Luoi, three battalions of the 1st Brigade swept into the valley and joined the operation on April 25. In the days that followed, the cavalrymen continued to find enormous caches of war materiel, including thousands of small arms, hundreds of thousands of ammunition rounds, and tons of supplies, as well as thirteen 23MM and 37MM antiaircraft guns and one Soviet-made PT76 tank. What they rarely encountered,

In February 1968, two 1st Cav troopers drag a wounded buddy across Highway 1 by an M42 self–propelled artillery piece after being ambushed on their way to Hue.

Off Duty

The cavalrymen did not spend all their time in combat. The stress and terror of war were relieved by precious moments of recreation, quiet reflection, and the mundane chores of everyday life. For some the day's end found them at a base camp, away from the immediate danger of patrols. For others, a short relief from perimeter guard duty was the only chance to prepare for the uncertainties of the next day.

Above. Members of Troop C, 1st Squadron, 9th Cavalry, enjoy a basketball game at base camp after returning from missions in Binh Dinh Province, July 1967. Right. M16 gripped in hand, a cavalryman pauses to read his Bible while on patrol in the An Lao Valley in 1967. Opposite above. A soldier near An Khe uses time away from patrol to wash his laundry. Opposite below. Men of the 1st Cav attend Mass near LZ X–ray.

however, were enemy soldiers. Once again the NVA chose not to fight, instead retreating to the hills to harass the Americans with 122MM rockets and heavy artillery fire. During the second week of May, as the monsoon rains returned, the 1st Cavalry Division began pulling out of the A Shau, completing their withdrawal on May 13.

The Cav moves south

As the American command shifted its priorities toward Vietnamization and the security of the population centers in the wake of the 1968 Tet offensive, the mission assigned to the 1st Cavalry Division changed as well. In late October 1968, two months after Major General George I. Forsythe took over the division, new COMUSMACV General Creighton Abrams ordered the redeployment of the 1st Cav from I Corps to III Corps. Concerned about the steady buildup of North Vietnamese forces along the Cambodian border, Abrams wanted to establish a screen that would protect the Saigon-Bien Hoa area and at the same time allow the 1st and 25th Infantry Divisions to focus on pacification. The Cav, with its unparalleled mobility and flexibility of organization, seemed ideally suited to the job.

The division's new area of responsibility encompassed a vast expanse of largely uninhabited territory bordering Cambodia from a point just west of Tay Ninh City to the boundary between III Corps and II Corps. Over the years, the enemy had developed an elaborate network of supply caches and campsites in the region, linked together by a maze of trails leading toward Saigon. Placed roughly a night's march apart, the depots allowed enemy troops to pick up their equipment and rations as they moved along, thus enabling them to travel very lightly and very fast. It was by this means that the enemy had infiltrated troops into position for the Tet 68 attacks on Saigon. Now, as the end of the year approached, intelligence indicated that the NVA was using the same system to prepare for another major assault on the capital in 1969.

To curb the flow of infiltrators along the extensive frontier, the division command organized its forces around a network of interlocking fire support bases. Screening patrols were then sent out to comb the countryside for cache sites and set up ambushes along the trails. In December the 1st Brigade took up position east of Angel's Wing in Tay Ninh Province, where they uncovered more than 150,000 small arms during a series of sweeps code-named Navajo Warhorse. In the meantime, the 2d Brigade conducted similar interdictory operations south of the Fishhook region, while the 3d Brigade plunged into War Zone D. The combined impact of these maneuvers severely disrupted the enemy's logistical system and forced the NVA and VC units to break up into small cells in order to elude the 1st Cav's screen.

The Communists nevertheless pressed forward with preparations for their 1969 spring offensive. The general outline of the plan, gleaned from captured documents and prisoners, called for coordinated attacks by four Main Force divisions. Striking out of War Zone D, the 5th VC Division was to initiate the campaign with attacks on key U.S. installations outside Saigon. The 1st NVA Division would meanwhile move out of War Zone C and take up position near Highway 1, a diversionary effort designed to lure the U.S. and South Vietnamese mobile reserves out of position and open the way for the 7th NVA Division and the 9th VC Division to attack the capital.

The offensive, which began on February 23 following a five-day Tet cease-fire, never achieved its ultimate objectives. The attacks launched by the 5th VC Division, including regimental-sized ground assaults on the 1st Infantry Division base at Dau Tieng and the Long Binh complex, were quickly repulsed, while the 1st NVA Division remained bottled up in War Zone C. Operating out of Fire Support Base Grant, the 2d Battalion, 12th Cavalry, cut the 1st NVA Division's lines of communication and supply, making it impossible for them to fulfill their diversionary mission. In an effort to break out, the enemy division's 95C Regiment attacked Grant on the night of March 8 and nearly overpowered its defenders before a combination of aerial rocket fire, tactical air strikes, and tube artillery from other FSBs finally forced the enemy to withdraw. A followup attack three nights later met with the same result.

Once it became clear that the enemy's offensive had stalled, the U.S. command decided to initiate a counteroffensive of its own. Beginning on March 17, the 1st Cavalry Division teamed up with elements of the 11th Armored Cavalry to drive the 7th NVA Division from the Michelin rubber plantation in Operation Atlas Wedge. In April, the 11th Armored Cavalry again joined the air cavalrymen for Operations Montana Scout and Montana Raider. Designed to keep pressure on the 1st and 7th NVA Divisions, the Montana series involved coordinated air and ground assaults into War Zones C and D in the wake of massed B-52 Arc Light strikes.

Whatever damage these blows may have inflicted on the North Vietnamese, they did not deter the enemy from continuing offensives. By early May, plans for a large-scale attack on Tay Ninh City, scheduled for Ho Chi Minh's birthday on May 19, were already well under way. To facilitate the movement of men and supplies prior to the main attack, the NVA launched a series of ferocious ground assaults on 1st Cavalry Division firebases in War Zone C.

The largest attack took place on the night of May 6, the day after Major General Elvy B. Roberts took command of the division, when the 95C NVA Regiment slammed into FSB Carolyn behind an intense barrage of rocket, mortar, and recoilless rifle fire. "Everybody knew we were going to be hit," recalled Private First Class Wayne Decker, a gunner with Battery A of the 2d Battalion, 19th Artillery, "because our patrols had been making steady contact with enemy forces in the area for several weeks." After piercing the northern perimeter, the enemy overran six bunkers and blew up an ammunition dump. The defenders of the base—two companies of the 2d Battalion, 8th Cavalry, as well as Battery A, 2d Battalion, 19th Artillery, and Battery B, 1st Battalion, 30th Artillery—retaliated by calling in high-explosive artillery fire from nearby firebases Ike and Barbara as well as the AH1-G Blue Max gunships of the 1/9 Cav. Once the helicopters arrived and began showering the NVA with rockets and minigun fire, the attack ebbed, and by dawn the battle was over. When attempts to overrun Firebases Grant, Jamie, and Phyllis a week later also ended in failure, the enemy suspended its plan to attack Tay Ninh City and instead focused on rehabilitating its battered units.

Into Cambodia

Throughout the summer and fall of 1969, the 1st Cav continued to conduct screening operations along the Cambodian frontier, rooting out enemy cache sites and bunker complexes and engaging North Vietnamese units wherever they could be found. Skirmishes with the NVA became increasingly rare toward the end of the year, however, as the division assumed responsibility for training ARVN's elite airborne units in the sophisticated tactics of airmobile warfare. In early 1970, the Cav's sponsorship role grew even greater, as MACV pressed ahead with plans for a joint U.S.-ARVN "spoiling attack" against NVA base camps and supply depots across the Cambodian border.

Regarded as a crucial test of Vietnamization, the cross-border incursion, code-named Toan Thang ("Total Victory") 43, kicked off on April 29, 1970, with a thrust into the protrusion of Cambodian territory known as the Parrot's Beak by several battalions of the 3d ARVN Airborne Brigade. Two days later, on the morning of May 1, tanks and armored personnel carriers attached to the 1st Cavalry Division's 3d Brigade roared across the border as scout helicopters and gunships of the 1/9 Cav raced ahead seeking targets of opportunity. Behind them came waves of CH-47 Chinooks carrying South Vietnamese paratroopers and American cavalrymen into landing zones that had been carved out by massive, 15,000-pound Commando Vault bombs. Met by only light, scattered resistance as they hit the ground, the infantrymen consolidated their positions and fanned out in search of the enemy, only to discover that the North Vietnamese had once again decided not to stand and fight.

Aerial view shows Fire Support Base Wade, near the Cambodian border in June 1970. The base is manned by men of the 2d Battalion, 5th Cavalry.

Although aerial observer and gunship teams of the 1/9 continued to spot and fire upon groups of fleeing enemy soldiers, any hopes of luring the NVA into open battle were soon discarded. Instead the men had to content themselves with seizing and destroying the enormous caches of equipment and supplies that the enemy left behind. The largest of these logistical complexes, discovered on May 5 by Company C of the 1st Battalion, 5th Cavalry, and immediately dubbed "The City," contained 182 storage bunkers brimming with weapons, munitions, foodstuffs, and medical supplies, as well as eighteen mess halls, a training area, and a variety of livestock. Even after all thirteen of the 1st Cav's battalions were committed to the campaign, supplies were still being discovered faster than the cavalrymen could destroy them.

Despite the enemy's evasive tactics, the American command was satisfied with the overall results of Operation Toan Thang 43. Not only had the destruction of the enemy's Cambodian sanctuaries significantly reduced the vulnerability of Saigon, but, perhaps more important, it had bought valuable time to strengthen ARVN further in anticipation of a total U.S. pullout. The campaign nevertheless ended on a tragic note for the 1st Air Cav when on July 7—eight days after the last American troops left Cambodia—division commander Major General George W. Casey was killed in a helicopter crash while en route to visit wounded soldiers. Major General George Putnam, the former commander of the 1st Aviation Brigade, was immediately named as Casey's successor.

Standing down

Faced with expanded operational responsibilities as other American units returned to the U.S., Putnam initiated a major reorganization of the 1st Cavalry Division shortly after he assumed command. In order to stretch the division's assets to the limit, he enlarged the highly successful 1st Squadron, 9th Cavalry, by converting two assault weapons companies of the 227th and 229th Assault Helicopter Battalions into aerial reconnaissance troops. Three more troops—each containing the customary White, Red, and Blue teams—were added a short time later, when the division was given control of a separate air cavalry squadron, the 3d Battalion, 17th Cavalry. As the multibattalion operations of the past gave way to smaller platoon- and squad-size actions, Putnam's reforms greatly enhanced the 1st Cavalry Division's ability to cover its far-flung responsibilities rapidly and effectively.

Although the skytroopers of the 1st were not immune to the morale problems that afflicted other withdrawing American combat units, their performance in the field during their final days in Vietnam tended to reflect the better side of soldiering. In some instances, the aggressiveness displayed by cavalrymen of the 1st and 2d Brigades prior to withdrawal was nothing less than extraordinary. Men of the 1st Battalion, 5th Cavalry, for example, fought fifteen skirmishes with the NVA during the nine days before they were yanked out of the jungle in March 1971 to stand down and await redeployment.

After the bulk of the division left for Fort Hood, Texas, in April, an oversized, 7,000-man 3d Brigade stayed behind as a security force. Placed under the direct operational control of USARV, the brigade took up defensive positions northeast of Saigon in the area surrounding the town of Xuan Loc. A year later the 3d Brigade also went home, its last remaining battalion, the 1/7 Cav, departing on August 22, 1972. For the unit that had come to be known as "The First Team," the first full Army division deployed to Vietnam, the war was over.

Left. *Cavalrymen sit near captured Communist weapons and ammunition at FSB Gonder in Cambodia in June 1970.*
Right. *A mine-detecting dog and his trainer lead an M551 Sheridan and men from Troop C, 3d Squadron, 5th Cavalry, on patrol in late August 1970.*

Combat Assault

To the soldiers of the 1st Cavalry Division (Airmobile) it was known as a "Charley Alpha," derived from the military's phonetic abbreviation for *combat assault.* Their commanders preferred the term *air assault.* Yet no matter what label was applied, the use of helicopters to carry troops into battle was perhaps the single most important tactical innovation of the Vietnam War.

A modern variation on the light horse cavalry tactics of old, the combat assault was designed to maximize the shock effect of a sudden massing of troops, catching enemy forces by surprise before they could flee or mount an effective defense. Unlike traditional cavalrymen, however, the heliborne troops of the 1st Air Cav could leapfrog over enemy positions, penetrate otherwise inaccessible terrain, and strike from any direction.

Throughout the war, the rifle platoons of the 1st Squadron, 9th Cavalry—the division's crack reconnaissance formation—were often in the forefront of the action. Once an NVA or a VC force had been spotted by White team scoutships and fired upon by Red team gunships, Blue team riflemen were placed on the ground to confront the enemy. If the opposing force proved larger than anticipated, infantrymen from the division's maneuver battalions would be dispatched in waves to "pile on" until the American forces had established a tactical advantage.

In other instances, combat assaults were planned long in advance. In response to intelligence indicating the presence of enemy troops in an area, commanders would select at least one and

Red team gunships of Troop B, 1st Squadron, 9th Cavalry, pour rocket and machine-gun fire into a preselected landing zone as Blue-team riflemen prepare to assault into the An Lao Valley during Operation Pershing in Binn Dinh Province in 1967.

usually several alternative landing zones large enough to accommodate troop-carrying helicopters. Artillery and perhaps even air strikes were then directed on the sites to eliminate or weaken enemy resistance. In the meantime, troop-laden UH-1 Hueys or larger CH-47 Chinooks raced at treetop level toward the scene of action, accompanied by helicopter gun-

Left. *Soldiers of the 1st Squadron, 9th Cavalry, leap from the skids of a hovering UH-1 Huey helicopter during a reconnaissance mission near Chu Lai in 1967.*

Above. *1st Cavalry Division (Airmobile) troops unload a 105MM howitzer from a CH-47 Chinook helicopter during an air assault into the Suoi Ca Valley, a long-time Vietcong stronghold in Binh Dinh Province, in October 1965.*

Right. *Artillerymen of the 1st Air Cav fire a 105MM howitzer in support of ground forces during the bloody battle of the Ia Drang Valley, November 1965.*

ships. As the lead helicopters entered the "assault corridor," door gunners began a steady stream of tracer-laced machine-gun fire while pilots searched for the white plume of smoke signaling the end of the preparatory fires.

Since the assaulting infantrymen never knew for sure whether a landing zone would be "hot" or "cold," tension mounted quickly as the helicopters banked into their final approaches and started to descend. Measuring their vulnerability in fractions of seconds, some soldiers lowered themselves onto the outboard skids of the Hueys while airborne, ready to leap out as soon as the ground came within range. Once the first wave of troops had fanned out and formed a defensive perimeter, reinforcements arrived in rapid succession until the landing zone was deemed secure. Artillery guns were then flown in to provide support for the infantrymen as they set off in search of the NVA and the VC.

If the patrolling ground troops succeeded in engaging the enemy, additional forces could be quickly inserted to block an anticipated withdrawal. If they failed to make contact, the cavalrymen could be pulled out and redeployed to another area. The tactics of airmobility, in short, afforded American commanders unprecedented flexibility and made Charley Alphas a way of life for the men of the 1st Air Cav.

Refuel bladders litter the helipad at the division's An Khe base, better known as the "Golf Course" because of its immense size, as helicopters return from a mission in the central highlands.

143

The Nomads of Vietnam

"Take a break! We're here," the soldier shouted from the deck of the ship to the troops standing guard on the dock below. The soldier, a paratrooper from the 1st Brigade, 101st Airborne Division, had just arrived at Cam Ranh Bay on July 29, 1965, after a three-week ocean voyage. His ship, the USNS *General Leroy Eltinge*, a WW II liberty ship, had been reactivated recently to ferry U.S. troops to Vietnam. With a listed capacity of only 2,800, the ship could barely accommodate the nearly 4,000 soldiers of the 1st Brigade. Many of the troops itched to leave their cramped quarters behind and take to dry land.

At a welcoming ceremony, two former commanders of the 101st, Maxwell Taylor, then ambassador to Vietnam, and General William Westmoreland, commander of U.S. forces in Vietnam, greeted the men of the Screaming Eagles Division, led by their commander, Colonel James S. Timothy. Ambassador Taylor, whose son Thomas was a captain in the 1st Brigade, warned the troops that they would find the Vietcong a formidable foe. At the same time, he

admonished them to remember the division's proud past "when the Vietcong are pressing you from all sides."

As Taylor noted, the 101st arrived in Vietnam with a storied tradition. Formed at the end of WW I as an infantry division, it had been redesignated as the Army's second airborne division during WW II and gained distinction for its role in the invasion of Normandy and the famous siege at Bastogne.

The arrival of the 1st Brigade of the 101st in Vietnam—it would be over two years before its other two brigades arrived—brought the total of U.S. soldiers serving in Vietnam to 79,000. Additional troop deployments soon brought that figure to 125,000, as the U.S. rapidly escalated its forces. With most arriving units still occupied with the construction of their base camps and the securing of their own areas, MACV decided to employ the 1st Brigade as a mobile reaction force, shuttling the brigade around the country as the tactical situation demanded. Over the next two and a half years, until the arrival of the remainder of the division, the 1st Brigade executed thirty-one tactical deployments spanning more than 2,500 miles and twenty-five major operations. Constantly on the move, the soldiers joked about changing their nickname from the Screaming Eagles to the Nomads of Vietnam.

The battle begins

At the outset the 1st Brigade conducted a series of clearing operations around Cam Ranh Bay. Next, the Screaming Eagles moved north to An Khe to secure a base for the 1st Cavalry Division, scheduled to arrive in Vietnam in September. On September 18, as part of Operation Gibraltar, a combined ARVN-U.S. search-and-destroy mission, the 2d Battalion, 502d Infantry, from the 1st Brigade air-assaulted into a landing zone thirty kilometers northeast of An Khe in a suspected VC location in the Song Con Valley.

The troops went in light. Because of the difficult terrain, the battalion left behind its mortars and other heavy weapons. It was also operating without the support of an artillery task force, which failed to negotiate the muddy roads leading to its assigned position. Just after 7:00 A.M., following air strikes around the landing zone by Air Force Skyraiders, the first helicopters touched ground. The first landing encountered scattered sniper fire. But on the second landing, the LZ erupted.

Automatic weapons fire raked the landing zone. Within seconds, radio operator Kenneth L. Moore saw his company commander fall dead beside him, killed by a bullet that passed only inches from the young soldier's face. "I was spoiling for a fight with the Vietcong," the twenty-one-year-old Moore said later. "But when those machine gun

bullets started flaking pieces off my radio on my back, I wanted to be 200 miles away." As he watched his headquarters group fall around him, Moore crawled out of the line of fire, advancing 200 meters along the paddies until he reached another platoon. When he tried to use his radio he found it clogged with his commanding officer's blood.

As soldiers ran for cover, door gunners from the helicopters fired hundreds of rounds into the tree line with no apparent effect. Unable to hold their position, the vulnerable aircraft hovered long enough for the paratroopers to jump to the marshy ground before pulling out. As they lifted out, they waved off a third group waiting to land.

On the ground, Lieutenant Colonel Wilfrid K.G. Smith assessed his situation. Four helicopters had been lost in the landing and a number of soldiers killed or wounded, including all three rifle company commanders. Company B had lost its commander even before it landed, and a young first lieutenant now led that unit. In all, Smith had 224 men on the ground, including the wounded.

The commander needed to call in air strikes but the enemy was too close. Unable to retreat, Smith ordered his men to attack to put some room between them and the VC. "This was the dirtiest kind of fighting," he recounted. "Platoons, squads would charge the jungle trenches, gain entry at one point and fight their way along with rifles and grenades."

After more than an hour of vicious fighting, the paratroopers succeeded in pushing the VC back. At 9:00 A.M., the first Air Force fighter-bombers arrived, swooping down low to unload incendiary bombs on the nearby VC positions. "The air strikes were coming in so close that our own men were getting hit with shrapnel," recalled radio operator Moore. "That's how I got wounded. But we were not complaining. We were on a bald little hill with no cover. We needed that air."

Soon, helicopter gunships joined the fighter-bombers, strafing the enemy positions with heavy machine-gun and rocket fire. Smith also was able to direct artillery fire from a battery lifted into position by the 1st Air Cavalry. Despite the heavy fire support, the soldiers could neither advance upon nor drive off the attacking forces. From their superior, well-fortified positions atop a nearby hill and along the banks of a river, the VC pounded the exposed troopers without respite, eventually forcing Smith to pull his men into a smaller perimeter.

On several occasions, only continuous air support kept them from being overrun. The Air Force and Navy jets halted one attack with what Smith called a "long belt of fire." Army and Marine helicopters also aided the embattled troops, flying supply and medevac missions despite the heavy fire.

That afternoon, the 101st attempted to land the rest of the battalion at an LZ to the south. This time they landed only thirty-six men before enemy fire drove them off. Every one of the twenty-six helicopters used in the assault had to

Preceding page. *Soldiers of the 101st Airborne Division rush toward UH–1D helicopters arriving to carry them out of Fire Base Saber on October 12, 1969.*

146

101st Airborne Division (Airmobile)*

Arrived Vietnam: November 19, 1967
(1st Brigade: July 29, 1965)

Departed Vietnam: March 10, 1972

Unit Headquarters

Bien Hoa   *Nov. 1967–Feb. 1968*
Bien Hoa/Phu Bai   *March 1968–April 1969*

Bien Hoa/Gia Le   *May 1969–Sep. 1969*
Bien Hoa/Hue/Phu Bai   *Oct. 1969–Nov. 1969*

Hue/Phu Bai   *Dec. 1969–March 1972*

Commanding Officers

Maj. Gen. Olinto M. Barsanti   *Dec. 1967*
Maj. Gen. Melvin Zais   *July 1968*

Maj. Gen. John M. Wright, Jr.   *May 1969*
Maj. Gen. John J. Hennessey   *May 1970*

Maj. Gen. Thomas M. Tarpley   *Feb. 1971*

Major Subordinate Units

1st Brigade (1/327; 2/327; 2/502; 3/506)	2d Battalion, 11th Artillery	801st Maintenance Battalion
2d Brigade (1/501; 2/501; 1/502)	1st Battalion, 39th Artillery	101st Administration Company
3d Brigade (3/187; 1/506; 2/506)	4th Battalion, 77th Artillery	265th Army Security Agency Company
2d Squadron, 17th Cavalry	2d Battalion, 319th Artillery	10th Chemical Platoon
Company F, 58th Infantry	2d Battalion, 320th Artillery	20th Chemical Detachment
Company L, 75th Infantry	1st Battalion, 321st Artillery	36th Chemical Detachment
101st Aviation Group	Battery A, 377th Artillery	22d Military History Detachment
101st Aviation Battalion	5th Transportation Battalion	101st Military Intelligence Company
158th Aviation Battalion	326th Medical Battalion	25th Public Information Detachment
159th Aviation Battalion	326th Engineer Battalion	34th Public Information Detachment
163d Aviation Company	426th Supply & Service Battalion	45th Public Information Detachment
478th Aviation Company	501st Signal Battalion	

4,011 KIA
(Casualty figures are "Vietnam Era.")

18,259 WIA

7 Medals of Honor

*Officially redesignated 101st Airborne Division (Airmobile) on December 15, 1968.

be scrapped or grounded. The force left stranded on the ground had to stave off three attacks before they were rescued the following day. The U.S. finally landed the 1st Brigade's 2d Battalion, 327th Infantry, and two companies of the 23d ARVN Ranger Battalion 3,000 meters to the east that afternoon. However, the rough terrain prevented them from linking up with the 2/502 before nightfall.

When day dawned, the relief force finally reached the 2/502. The enemy, however, had fled under the cover of darkness. As the soldiers searched the area, they discovered the bodies of 257 enemy soldiers and an extensive bunker system that they identified as a major base camp. U.S. commanders estimated that the paratroopers had faced a force of more than 600, nearly three times as large as the American unit on the ground. However, the heavy and accurate air support, which included more than 100 air strikes and 11,000 rounds of artillery, effectively evened those odds. U.S. losses in the battle amounted to thirteen killed and twenty-eight wounded. For its actions in the battle, the 2/502 received the Presidential Unit Citation.

Although Operation Gibraltar provided the 1st Brigade its first major contact of the war, it also marked the only large-scale encounter for the year. As the year-end neared, the Screaming Eagles developed new tactics to locate the increasingly elusive enemy. In October 1965 they moved to Phan Rang, where they established a base camp. There, under the command of Lieutenant Colonel Henry "The Gunfighter" Emerson, the men of the 2/502 employed a saturation patrolling technique dubbed "checkerboard

patrols." In a checkerboard operation, Emerson deployed his men in multiple small patrols across a small square of terrain that they searched thoroughly before moving on to another square. Each man carried with him three to five days' rations and as much armament as he could manage. By equipping his men in this manner, he hoped to make them self-sufficient, able to sustain themselves for several days in the field without need of resupply, in much the same way as the guerrillas did. Thus, Emerson became one of many American commanders to declare that he would "beat the damned guerrilla at his own game."

Emerson's emphasis upon guerrilla tactics received active support from the brigade's new commander, Brigadier General Willard Pearson. Pearson assumed command of the brigade on January 28 from Col. Timothy. A veteran of WWII and Korea, Pearson increased the brigade's night operations, both ambushes and airmobile assaults, and its reconnaissance operations. Under his supervision, each battalion developed its own reconnaissance unit in addition to the brigade's long-range reconnaissance patrol (LRRP). Every member of these units volunteered to serve in them, and as Pearson noted they were all "men who enjoy a good firefight."

Expanding upon one of Emerson's innovations, Pearson occasionally allowed his men to carry rice and powdered soup in place of the heavier C rations. As one platoon leader explained, "There is nothing worse for a trooper's morale than to be handed a week's supply of C-rations weighing upwards of 30 pounds." The new brigade com-

mander also believed in "clandestine entry to the battle-field." He preferred to insert troops by foot, making it difficult for the enemy to locate the U.S. forces.

Operation Hawthorne

Throughout the early part of 1966, the brigade made extensive use of Pearson's guerrilla tactics. It carried out a variety of operations beginning with a series of rice protection maneuvers in Phu Yen Province near Tuy Hoa and continuing along the Cambodian border in Quang Duc Province during Operation Austin VI. There the U.S. forces attempted to block suspected NVA infiltration routes. However, as the monsoon season approached and the enemy prepared for a new, large-scale offensive, the 101st temporarily abandoned its guerrilla tactics and substantially increased the size of its operations to meet the new threat.

In June, the brigade moved into the central highlands in response to increased enemy presence. One year earlier, during the 1965 monsoon offensive, the VC had attacked and overrun the Regional Force outpost at Tou Morong located twelve kilometers northeast of Dak To in Kontum Province. As the rains and the enemy returned, MACV planners anticipated a similar attack. According to 1st Brigade commander Pearson, "Unless Tou Morong could be relieved or reinforced, it was certain to fall." To thwart the enemy's plans, the U.S. and ARVN forces launched a major spoiling attack—Operation Hawthorne.

As their troopships depart, soldiers from the 2d Battalion, 502d Infantry, move to secure a pass along Route 19 east of Pleiku during Operation Highland on August 26, 1965.

On June 3, the 1st Battalion, 327th Infantry, joined by the 21st ARVN Ranger Battalion and a second South Vietnamese unit, the 1st Battalion, 42d Infantry Regiment, boarded helicopters in Dak To on their way to secure Tou Morong. By June 6, the three battalions had closed on the outpost encountering only light resistance. Both ARVN battalions departed that evening, leaving the 1/327 to man the outpost. The battalion was supported by an artillery position at Dak Pha, to the west of Tou Morong, manned by Battery B, 2d Battalion, 320th Artillery; Company A, 2d Battalion, 502d Infantry; and the 326th Engineer Battalion.

At 2:00 A.M. on June 7, NVA forces unleashed a fierce attack upon the artillery battery. Raking the U.S. position with automatic weapons fire, mortars, and grenades, the enemy followed with an all-out assault. The guerrillas quickly smashed through the perimeter. A bloody contest developed for control of a howitzer. Twice the enemy overran the gun site, and twice the artillery crew, bayonets drawn, drove them out. For nearly seven hours, the battle raged back and forth until the NVA finally broke off the attack and withdrew. They left behind eighty-five dead, thirteen inside the wire.

That morning the 1/327, patrolling to the north of the artillery position, encountered heavy resistance from the

24th NVA Regiment. Brigade headquarters now released its reserve battalion, the 2d Battalion, 502d Infantry. The men air-assaulted into a position to the north to form the northern arm of a double envelopment with the 1/327 in hopes of catching the NVA.

With no results to show for operations on the seventh, the 2/502 resumed its sweep the following day after breaking into companies. Charley Company proceeded to the base of Hill 1,073. Its commander, Captain William S. Carpenter, Jr., hoped that this hunt would be more than another futile day of bushwhacking. Carpenter was not a man accustomed to poor results. Several years earlier he had gained renown as the All-American "Lonesome End" on West Point's football team. He had seen his first action in Vietnam in 1963 as an adviser to the South Vietnamese army, and by 1966 he could pass as an old hand in Vietnam. However, he had only recently joined Charley Company, and this was his first opportunity to lead the men into battle.

Following orders, Carpenter started the company toward Hill 1,073 early that morning. Although the hill lay little more than 500 meters to the south, even this short march proved difficult in the steamy jungle. Moving slowly, the company reached the base of the hill in mid-morning. The point squad surprised a solitary VC emerging from a bamboo thicket. Several soldiers fired simultaneously, killing the enemy soldier. They found the body laden with medical supplies.

The squad radioed for permission to advance up the hill, but before Carpenter could order them on, Col. Emerson ordered him to turn north to avoid a tactical air strike being called upon Hill 1,073 by the commander of the 1/327, Major David Hackworth, whose troops had engaged the enemy on the far side of the hill. Carpenter reluctantly led his men away from the battle to another hill 1,000 meters to the north. Conducted in the middle of the day under a blazing sun, the march exhausted Charley Company. At the top of the first ridge, Carpenter called for a halt. When the company resumed its march after a short rest, Carpenter turned to the east to avoid climbing straight up the hill, a task that would have spent his already tired troops.

The company crossed over the first ridge and had just crested the second when Sergeant Thomas Delemeter, walking point for the lead 1st Platoon, reported that he heard voices speaking Vietnamese only 200 meters away. Lieutenant William Jordan relayed Delemeter's observation to Carpenter by radio: "I've got Charley 200 meters to my front. Shall I continue on the present azimuth or go for Charley?" After a day and a half of first not being able to find the enemy and then being denied the opportunity to chase him, Carpenter replied without hesitation: "We'll go for Charley." Carpenter then radioed Lt. James Baker, leader of the 3d Platoon, and said, "Get ready for a fight."

Advancing up the ridge, Jordan's platoon stumbled upon four more NVA. Obviously unaware of the U.S. soldiers, three of the guerrillas carried with them cooking utensils to clean in the nearby stream. The fourth held a roll of toilet paper and had already squatted in a spot beside the stream when the U.S. soldiers opened fire. He died in the first volley, but the other three escaped into a nearby bamboo thicket unscathed.

Having caught the enemy by surprise, Charley Company rushed to press its advantage only to have the NVA suddenly turn the tables on them. Beginning with a few sporadic bursts of automatic weapons fire, the enemy fire swelled in volume until within five minutes every man from the 1st Platoon lay belly to the ground. They could see nothing but bamboo shattering about them under the intense fire. "They plastered us so we couldn't move," recalled 1st Lieutenant Bryan Robbins. "We just lay there and hugged old Mother Earth and kissed it and prayed."

Carpenter radioed Emerson that his 1st Platoon was heavily engaged and that he was committing his 3d Platoon in support. Unaware of the seriousness of the situation, Emerson, from his isolated post 1,400 meters away, replied, "Go right ahead; be sure to police the field of all weapons when the fight is over." "Believe me," Carpenter answered, "it's not a question of doing anything like that. We're under heavy fire, repeat, heavy fire."

Ten minutes later, the 3d Platoon, under Lt. Baker, arrived. At the same moment, the enemy redoubled its attack. In the next few moments every soldier at the company command post, except for Carpenter and two others, was wounded. Carpenter ordered the 4th Platoon under Lt. Robbins to clean out an enemy gun position on a nearby ridge. Two NVA machine guns stopped their charge after only fifteen meters.

Pinned down, unable to advance or retreat, the company was taking casualties at a furious rate. Third Platoon commander Lt. Baker was killed by a machine-gun burst. Sergeant Robert Hanna informed Carpenter by radio of Baker's death. He also reported that the enemy was closing to within grenade range. "I think most of our platoon is done," he told the company commander. At that moment two grenades rolled next to him. As Hanna rolled away, both grenades exploded, ripping off his legs and shattering his skull. Sergeant James Harding, already wounded himself, crawled to the radio and screamed into the receiver, "Hanna's dead. The lieutenant's dead. I'm the only live person left here. I can't see anybody. Grenades are coming in on me!"

Harding broke off transmission before Carpenter could identify him or verify his information. However, the commander needed only to look around to recognize the seriousness of the situation. Nearly every man around him lay either dead or wounded, and not one of those alive was returning the enemy's fire. He made a desperate decision. "They're right in among us," he radioed Emerson. "We're being overrun. I've got to have napalm dropped right on my position." According to many reports, he added, "We'll

take some of them with us." (Carpenter later said that he had no recollection of saying this.)

At the battalion command post, Emerson stood momentarily stunned by Carpenter's request. He had not realized how desperate Charley Company's position was. However, he quickly recovered and relayed Carpenter's request and told Carpenter, "I want you to know that I am putting you in for the Medal of Honor. You can be sure of that." He did not expect to see Carpenter alive again.

Not realizing that the planes were already circling overhead, Carpenter had expected that he would have some time to warn his men of the incoming air strike. However, less than thirty seconds after his request, the planes arrived, dropping their loads of napalm. The burning liquid struck the tops of the thick bamboo forest, splitting into exploding sheets of flame. Fortunately, most of the napalm spilled forward onto the enemy positions. Some, however, landed upon the prone U.S. soldiers. Twelve were burned by the napalm, two seriously.

If the men were uncertain about what had happened, they quickly recognized the result. Almost immediately, the fire from their front stopped entirely. After a minute, the company rose from the ground, gathered the wounded, and regrouped. Despite this momentary reprieve, Carpenter, viewing the men wounded by the napalm, despaired of his decision. "I've stopped them," he radioed, "but I also hurt myself terribly."

As Carpenter reorganized his men, he attempted to assess the situation. First Sergeant Walter Sabalauski, a twenty-six-year veteran, took a head count. He could not locate most of the 3d Platoon, and he estimated that "about fifty have been killed." Carpenter then relayed that information to Emerson. Believing that Carpenter had engaged an enemy regiment, Emerson ordered him to establish a tight perimeter and to hold his position while he surrounded him with air and artillery strikes and dispatched another company to rescue the men.

In the twenty-minute lull that followed the napalm strike, Carpenter established a perimeter about forty-five meters in diameter. Emerson, meanwhile, moved with his plans to rescue the embattled company. He ordered Alpha Company, under Captain Walter R. Brown, to advance toward Carpenter's position. He also reoriented Major Hackworth's battalion to ease the pressure upon Carpenter. However, Hackworth was also heavily engaged and unable to offer assistance.

Finally, Emerson readied another relief column, led by Captain Walter B. Wesley, and consisting mostly of soldiers preparing to return to the U.S. and an assortment of clerks, cooks, and other support personnel. Emerson ordered them to advance along the first ridge crossed by

Operation Hawthorne. Men of Capt. William Carpenter's Company C, 2d Battalion, 502d Infantry, load their dead onto a CH–46 Sea Knight near the Dak Ta Kan Valley.

The grimness of war etched deeply into his face, Capt. Carpenter enjoys a cigarette and a brief respite from battle after Operation Hawthorne.

Carpenter. However, the force stalled and established a position several hundred meters short of Carpenter.

The fall of darkness brought torrential rains. Great sheets of water, illuminated by occasional bolts of lightning, washed across the bamboo forest. Soon Carpenter's men found their hastily dug foxholes overflowing. Many simply squatted deeper into the holes, displacing the water with their bodies rather than trying to bail with their helmets. The rain also slowed the advance of Capt. Brown and Company A, as the red-clay earth turned into knee-deep mud. They slogged on until, just after midnight, they hooked up with Carpenter. "You're the prettiest thing I ever saw," an exhausted Carpenter told Brown.

Soon after Brown arrived, six men from the 3d Platoon, whom Carpenter had thought were lost, suddenly appeared out of the darkness inside the perimeter. Carpenter ordered a more complete assessment of the company's losses and discovered to his amazement and relief that he had lost only six dead, sixteen unaccounted for, and twenty-five wounded, not the fifty presumed dead earlier.

The following day, the rain, which earlier had diminished to a light drizzle, once again fell in torrents. The weather precluded any chance for an aerial rescue, and continued harassing fire from the enemy kept Carpenter and Brown pinned down for the entire day. Finally, after darkness fell, Carpenter decided to attempt a move. His wounded, now numbering twenty-six, had been without medical assistance for over thirty hours and several were badly in need of attention.

At 11:00 P.M. a Huey dropped twenty litters into Carpenter's perimeter. With twenty-six men requiring litters, Carpenter tried having six men carry each of the remaining severely wounded, but the rough, uphill terrain and the rain-soaked clay slowed their advance to a crawl. By first light, his men had traveled less than 200 meters from their original position. With the skies clearing, Carpenter called a halt and waited for the trails to dry. Later that morning, he finally stumbled upon Wesley's force, and by 11:00 A.M. helicopters began evacuating the wounded and dead.

Two days later on June 13, the U.S. forces pulled back as B-52s bombarded the area. A search of the battlefield uncovered 531 dead NVA and an extensive complex of bunkers and tunnels. U.S. losses for Operation Hawthorne numbered 48 dead and 239 wounded. Although he did not receive the Medal of Honor, Capt. Carpenter was awarded the Distinguished Service Cross for his efforts, and the entire 1st Brigade won the Presidential Unit Citation. First Brigade commander Pearson called it "our biggest and best fight, our greatest battle," and White House Press Secretary Bill Moyers called it "an inspiring chapter in the Vietnam story." In view of the brigade's heavy casualties, however, Capt. Brown took a more sober point of view. "All the time before this we had a hard time finding the VC. This time we had no trouble. We found them wherever we turned. We found too many of them at once."

As the war progressed into 1967, the 101st once more found itself on the move. While General Westmoreland pursued his "big battle" strategy to the south in III Corps, the enemy increased its pressure on the northern provinces. To reinforce the two Marine divisions stationed in I Corps, Westmoreland ordered three brigades to move north: the 1st Brigade, 101st Airborne; the 3d Brigade, 25th Infantry; and the 196th Infantry Brigade. These three brigades formed the new Task Force Oregon, which assumed tactical responsibility for southern I Corps. With the 101st as its core, Task Force Oregon continued to operate in I Corps until the end of the year, when the 1st Brigade was detached to rejoin its parent division scheduled to arrive in December.

Eagle Thrust

From December first to the nineteenth, the Army airlifted the nearly 10,400 men of the 101st Division's 2d and 3d Brigades over 9,000 miles from Fort Campbell, Kentucky, to Vietnam as part of Operation Eagle Thrust. The single largest airlift of the war, it cost the Army more than $17.5

million. Greeting the division and its commander, Major General Olinto M. Barsanti, Westmoreland proudly declared, "The 101st is now, and it always has been a formidable fighting force." The following day, while visiting his former command, the 3d Battalion, 187th Infantry, Westmoreland promised to drink from the battalion's "Westmoreland Bowl" after the unit's first victory.

However, despite Westmoreland's brave words, the two brigades that arrived in country that December hardly resembled the elite fighting force that had defended Bastogne during WW II. By the end of 1967, the ranks of the 101st had been badly depleted by demands for troops from units already serving in Vietnam. Upon learning that the division's scheduled deployment to Vietnam had been accelerated from June 1968 to December 1967, Gen. Barsanti had been hard pressed to find the 4,500 men needed to bring the two brigades up to three-quarter strength. Furthermore, most of these men fell far below the standards usually demanded in the 101st. Almost none were parachute-certified. Essentially, the two brigades that arrived in Vietnam were airborne in name only.

Barsanti noted, "Because of this extreme personnel turbulence meaningful unit training was virtually impossible." To offset the lack of stateside training, Barsanti insisted that the two brigades be allowed a one-month, in-country training period. For the entire month of January, the soldiers of the 101st engaged first in training sessions and then in small-scale operations around their new bases in III Corps at Phuoc Vinh, Cu Chi, and Bien Hoa. The units had only just completed their training when the enemy launched its 1968 Tet offensive.

To counter the enemy's offensive, the Screaming Eagles once again scattered across the country. In III corps, the 2d Battalion, 506th Airborne Infantry, air-assaulted from Phuoc Vinh to protect Bien Hoa Air Base. Another unit, 3d Platoon, Company C, 1st Battalion, 502d Airborne Infantry, led by Major Hillel Schwartz, air-assaulted onto the roof of the U.S. Embassy to root out the VC sapper squad that had attacked and infiltrated the compound. To the north, in I Corps, members of the 2d Brigade of the 101st fought to wrest control of Quang Tri and Hue from the enemy. By the end of the offensive, when U.S. forces had finally driven off the attackers, the 101st had gained more battle experience in a very short time than most had dreamed.

Cordon and search

Following the Tet offensive, the 101st assumed the task of clearing and securing the area surrounding the former imperial city of Hue. The division's new area of responsibility ran from the low-lying coastal plains of Thua Thien Province in the north and east to the thickly jungled, mountainous A Shau Valley to the west. The 101st was now lacking its 3d Brigade, which spent the first half of the year shuttling about the other corps zones before rejoining the

division in September. Meanwhile, the 3d Brigade of the 82d Airborne Division had arrived in Vietnam and operated with the 101st. On March 5, the newly constituted Screaming Eagles launched Operation Carentan I, and Carentan II followed on April 1.

Combining continuous, daytime reconnaissance-in-force missions with nightly ambushes, the 101st pursued the VC/NVA forces relentlessly. According to intelligence reports, the North Vietnamese and guerrilla forces planned to launch a second attack upon Hue. Remaining well hidden within the 101st's area, they tried to avoid any major contact until they could launch their second offensive. To prevent the VC/NVA from slipping away once contact had been made, the 101st developed and implemented a series of cordon operations.

Essentially, a cordon operation required that the enemy force be entirely surrounded immediately after contact was made. That perimeter then had to be maintained until the enemy either surrendered or was killed. This necessitated extensive use of illumination flares to prevent the enemy from escaping at night and close coordination with local Vietnamese forces.

Near the end of April 1968, a combined 101st and ARVN force engaged in a textbook example of a cordon operation in a village near Hue. On the morning of the twenty-eighth, intelligence indicated that the enemy could be found in an area five kilometers northwest of Hue along a river called the Song Bo near the village of Phuoc Yen. Much of the civilian population had long ago abandoned this area, but the VC still used it as a primary base area. At midday, the Black Panther Company of the 1st ARVN Division, approaching the village on a reconnaissance mission, encountered heavy fire. Calling on elements of the 101st and local Popular Forces (PF) platoons, the ARVN and U.S. commanders moved quickly to cordon off the area.

Company A of the 1st Battalion, 501st Infantry, traveled overland to establish a blocking position to the west on the far bank of the Song Bo, while Company B of the 2d Battalion, 501st, air-assaulted into the area along the river to the east. Three PF platoons completed the encirclement on the eastern side.

By evening, the U.S. and South Vietnamese forces had surrounded nearly 80 percent of Phuoc Yen. A momentary pause to debate whether to include the nearby village of Le Van Thuong in the encirclement was settled when a twilight probe into the village encountered heavy resistance. In the first hours of the night, Company A of the 1st Battalion, 502d Infantry, arrived to complete the perimeter around the two villages, positioning itself along a hedgerow that ran from the second village to the river.

With the encirclement completed, Lieutenant Colonel Jim I. Hunt, who had assumed command of the 1/501 only two days earlier, ordered his men to dig in, their foxholes spaced no more than ten meters apart. Then he called for flareships. That night, with the area lit by the constant

3d Brigade, 82d Airborne Division

On the morning of February 15, 1968, an advance party of twenty-three soldiers from the 3d Brigade, 82d Airborne Division, stepped onto the tarmac of the U.S. airfield at Chu Lai. For this much-heralded division that had served in every major U.S. conflict since World War I, this marked a late entry into the Vietnam War. During the previous three years, as the war escalated, the division had served much closer to home. It helped end the insurrection in the Dominican Republic in 1965 and quelled civil disturbances in Detroit and Washington, D.C., in 1967. In the wake of the 1968 Tet offensive, however, the Johnson administration overrode the Pentagon's wish to keep the 82d Division in the United States and ordered its 3d Brigade to temporary duty in Vietnam.

Beginning on Valentine's Day and ending twelve days later, 160 C–141s and 6 C–133s carried the three battalions of the Golden Brigade—the 1st and 2d Battalions, 505th Airborne Infantry, and the 1st Battalion, 508th Airborne Infantry—from Fort Bragg, North Carolina, to the U.S. base at Chu Lai in Quang Tin Province. After a week of training with the 23d, or Americal, Division, the 3d Brigade, led by Colonel Alexander R. Bolling, Jr., headed north to Hue, which U.S. and South Vietnamese troops had only recently secured after a fierce struggle.

The brigade encountered problems soon after its arrival but not on the battlefield. In the rush to deploy its 3d Brigade, the division had filled it with paratroopers who had only recently returned from service in other airborne units already operating in Vietnam. The resulting protests forced the Army to offer the paratroopers a choice of staying in Vietnam or returning to the U.S. Not surprisingly, 2,513 of the brigade's 3,650 soldiers opted to go home. With no other paratroopers readily available as replacements, the Army converted it into a separate light infantry brigade making it airborne in name only.

The 3d Brigade jumped into combat almost immediately. Operating under the control of the 101st Airborne Division, the brigade took part in several of the division's operations conducted in Thua Thien Province, including Operations Carentan I and II and Operation Nevada Eagle. Confined mostly to protecting the major roads and lines of communication such as Highway 1 and the Perfume River, the brigade also conducted a number of operations along enemy infiltration routes west of Hue in an attempt to preempt any NVA troop or logistical buildup.

Frequent reconnaissance-in-force and company-size cordon-and-search missions surprised enemy troops in their staging areas. In perhaps the most successful of these operations in late August, the 1st Battalion, 508th Infantry, and the 2d Battalion, 505th Infantry, using information from an NVA rallier, caught the 22d NVA Regiment in its base camp ten kilometers southwest of Phu Bai. In a three-week engagement, the two battalions captured numerous weapons and supplies and killed 225 NVA. During that period the brigade suffered 31 killed in action and 123 wounded.

While the brigade performed well in I Corps, control of the outfit by the 101st, its long-time airborne rival, created friction between many NCOs in the two units. Antagonism between the two divisions dated from World War II, when soldiers in the 82d had felt slighted by the adulation heaped on the 101st for its defense at Bastogne. In the fifties and sixties, the two proud divisions continued their competition during training exercises. General Westmoreland, then commander of the 101st, even pitted his unit against the 82d in counterinsurgency maneuvers.

Partly as a consequence of this rivalry, MACV shuttled the 3d Brigade south to Saigon in September. Coming under control of the Capital Military Assistance Command, the 3d Brigade assumed responsibility for the western approaches to Saigon and protected the major installa-tions in the Saigon/Tan Son Nhut area from ground and rocket attacks.

In contrast to the sparsely settled and heavily overgrown countryside near Hue, where the brigade encountered mostly NVA troops, it now maneuvered mostly against the Vietcong in open swamps and canals in a heavily populated area. Concerned with protecting against both infiltration and large-scale attacks, the brigade employed a pattern of day saturation patrols and night ambushes.

Under the direction of a new commander, Brigadier General George W. Dickerson, the brigade also developed a Surveillance Task Force (STF). The first unit of its kind, the STF combined sensors, radar, and various observation craft to stem the flow of infiltrators into the Saigon area. The system was not always perfect. On one occasion, the STF called in artillery and mortars to block an apparent attack against Saigon only to discover that the shelling had eliminated sixty creatures; they were ducks, not VC guerrillas. However, by carefully charting possible launching sites, the STF virtually eliminated the threat from rockets, which had terrorized the city during the Tet offensive. No rockets were fired from the brigade's area of operations into Saigon during its one year in III Corps.

Because of the dense population in the Saigon area, the 3d Brigade placed great emphasis on its pacification programs, giving special attention to Vinh Loc village, a complex of six hamlets that the VC had used previously as a staging area. By the time it went home in December 1969, the brigade had raised the village's Hamlet Evaluation System rating from an "E" (contested village) to a "B" (secure).

In December 1969, the Army ordered the brigade to return Stateside. Originally scheduled only for short, temporary service in Vietnam, it had served for twenty-two months before returning to its home at Fort Bragg. In all, the brigade suffered 184 soldiers killed in action and 1,009 wounded.

illumination of flares, Company A, 1/502, repulsed three enemy attacks along the hedgerow, inflicting heavy casualties upon the enemy.

The following morning, U.S. and ARVN forces twice attempted to enter the two villages. Each time strong resistance forced them back. Resigning themselves to a protracted fight, they called in air and artillery strikes and waited for the enemy to surrender.

The battle situation continued unchanged until the early morning of May 1. Just after 5:00 A.M. a flareship ran out of lights before its replacement arrived. Supported by a VC/NVA mortar firing from outside the cordon, the enemy seized the opportunity to attack along the darkened left flank of Company A, 1/502. For more than two hours the battle raged, with both sides exchanging fire at close range. A single enemy platoon succeeded in breaking through the cordon, but the soldiers of the 101st quickly reestablished the perimeter. When dawn finally arrived, the main body of enemy troops retreated to their positions inside the village, leaving behind twenty-three dead on the battlefield and another ten floating lifelessly in the Song Bo. Three men from Company A died in the attack.

That morning, while U.S. jets executed several tactical air strikes against the enemy positions, a psychological

Troopers of the 2d Battalion, 327th Infantry, armed with an M60 machine gun and M16 rifles, return enemy fire near Phu Bai during Operation Carentan II in spring 1968.

warfare team began broadcasting appeals to the VC/NVA to surrender. Their efforts prompted an NVA sergeant to give up the fight. He in turn attempted to persuade his fellow soldiers to surrender. By day's end, ninety-five enemy soldiers had delivered themselves to the ARVN and U.S. troops.

That afternoon, the airborne troopers further tightened the perimeter during the afternoon, securing the village of Le Van Thuong. Resistance continued strong in Phuoc Yen, however, for another two days until finally on May 3 the troops of the 101st swept through the remaining sections of the village, wiping out the last pockets of resistance.

In all, the cordon of Phuoc Yen accounted for 429 enemy killed and 107 captured, the largest number of prisoners taken from any battle to that date in the war. By contrast, the U.S. and ARVN forces had suffered six dead and forty-three wounded. Through close coordination of U.S. and Vietnamese forces, artillery and air support, and effective intelligence, the 101st had applied the cordon technique effectively against entrenched VC/NVA forces.

Operation Carentan I-II ended on May 17 with 2,825 enemy killed and 191 captured. However, the 101st continued to employ cordon tactics in subsequent operations, notably Operation Nevada Eagle. Begun the day after Operation Carentan I-II ended, Nevada Eagle was designed to protect the rice harvest of the fertile rice fields in Thua Thien Province. During this 288-day operation, the cordon technique played an even more important role in locating and isolating the VC/NVA forces. In particular, with the disbandment of the large enemy Main Force units after the 1968 Tet offensive, the cordons were now aimed almost exclusively at the local Vietcong infrastructure.

No longer facing massed, Main Force VC/NVA units, but local political and military cadres who operated covertly within the civilian population, U.S. forces could not employ their superior firepower indiscriminately. Destroying an entire village to kill a few VC officials could be costly both in civilian lives and in support from the local population. The 101st altered its earlier cordon tactics, adopting what it called a "soft" cordon approach.

According to the 101st's new commander, Major General Melvin Zais, "the soft cordon" was "characterized by the limited use of firepower resulting in minimum property damage and injury to civilians, and slow, painstaking searches." The soft cordon also necessitated close coordination with local and national South Vietnamese forces and officials to help in the identification of VC/NVA suspects. This was done by establishing an on-site Combined Operations Center staffed by representatives of all the participating forces and a Combined Interrogation Center.

Operation Vinh Loc

After executing several smaller versions during the first part of Operation Nevada Eagle, the 101st finally saw an opportunity to conduct its first major "soft" cordon opera-

At LZ Henry in War Zone C a 105MM artillery crew from Battery C, 1st Battalion, 321st Artillery, fires in support of 101st operations in June 1968.

tion in September on the island of Vinh Loc. Located twenty-eight kilometers east of Hue, Vinh Loc Island had fallen under enemy control following the 1968 Tet offensive. With all American and ARVN forces engaged in the defense of Hue and other cities, VC local forces moved in. By July, the government controlled only the southern tip of the island. In conjunction with local South Vietnamese leaders, Gen. Zais ordered plans drawn up for a joint cordon operation of the island.

The coordination of all the forces needed to surround the island, which measured forty kilometers long and five kilometers wide, required careful and extensive planning. An Area Coordination Center (ACC) was established to control the operation. Headed by the commander of the 2d Brigade, 101st Airborne Division, this center included from the American forces the U.S. deputy sector adviser and the commanding officer and intelligence sections of the 1st Battalion (Airborne), 501st Infantry. The South Vietnamese staffed the center with the deputy province chief, the district chief, and Special Branch, National Police, and provincial and district intelligence personnel. Once the combat assault was completed, the entire center was moved to the island to oversee the operation and subsequent interrogation of prisoners and detainees.

By the morning of September 11, the cordon force was ready to move. Units involved in the operation included the 54th ARVN Regiment; the 3d Troop, 7th ARVN Cavalry; the 12th and 13th Vietnamese Navy Coastal Groups; and several Regional and Popular Forces companies. American forces employed included the 1st Battalion, 501st Infantry of the 101st Airborne Division, the U.S. Naval River Security Group, two air-cushioned vehicles from the U.S. Coastal Division 17, and U.S. Navy Swift boats. A Popular Forces platoon and members of the National Police accompanied each of the U.S. companies. This facilitated identification of the VC and gave each unit someone who knew the terrain and the people.

Just after 7:30 A.M., with the combined naval forces ringing the island, the infantry and armored units assaulted the island by water and air. Conducting thorough sweeps across the island, the U.S. and South Vietnamese troops encountered only sporadic resistance. By nightfall, they had killed only 14 enemy but had detained more than 300 suspects for questioning. Naval forces, meanwhile, maintained constant patrols around the island's perimeter, stopping any craft seeking to leave the island.

This deployment of forces continued for the remaining ten days of the operation. Only twice did the U.S. forces find themselves in an engagement serious enough to warrant artillery support, and all forces made a concerted effort to limit the amount of damage inflicted upon civilians and civilian property. The operation ended on September 20 with 154 enemy killed and 370 prisoners taken. The cordon forces suffered only two ARVN soldiers killed and seven wounded, including two U.S. soldiers. By No-

vember, the Government of Vietnam had firmly reestablished control of the island, and more than 12,000 refugees from the VC takeover returned to their homes.

Airmobile

As 1968 ended, the 101st once more expanded its area of operations, pushing farther inland, away from the populated coastline to engage larger NVA Main Force units. This change in the 101st's mission reflected both the effectiveness of its operations along the coast, which had reduced the enemy presence there to a minimum, and the onset of Vietnamization. Under Vietnamization, security for the coastal population was gradually turned over to the South Vietnamese.

The shifting of the 101st's area of responsibility had been made possible by the transition of the division into a fully airmobile unit. The Army had scheduled the 101st to be transformed into an airmobile division in January 1968. However, the needed aviation equipment and personnel were not available at that time, and the actual order for conversion to an airmobile division did not come until July 1. Initially, the Army redesignated the division the 101st Air Cavalry Division. However, this name was changed on August 26 to 101st Airborne Division (Airmobile). Despite the name change, it required more than a year for the division to become fully airmobile.

According to Gen. Zais, the reconfiguration of the 101st as an airmobile division resulted in "no major changes in operating procedures, merely an expansion of our capabilities." Zais's successor, however, Major General John M. Wright, stressed that this development could not be overlooked or overemphasized. "The 101st lived by helicopters. Other divisions had to ask for helicopter support but in the 101st, the helicopters stayed in the field. We had over 400 helicopters organic to the division able to react immediately to calls from commanders. We had the lift plus the weapons helicopters for support. It just replaced the jeep. It was that common in the 101st."

The transformation to an airmobile division proved of critical importance in March of 1969 as MACV ordered the 101st into the A Shau Valley. In this largely trackless, inaccessible area, the helicopter often proved to be the only means of inserting and extracting troops. A month earlier, MACV intelligence had reported heavy enemy activity in the valley, which had long been a major infiltration route and stronghold of the NVA. The 101st had visited the valley a year earlier during Operation Somerset Plain. That seventeen-day operation was intended primarily to forestall any possible enemy offensives against the nearby coastal areas and to develop intelligence on enemy activity and installations in the area. Now, the U.S. commanders intended to stay as long as needed to root out the Communists from their long-time stronghold.

On March 1, MACV launched Operation Massachusetts Striker, the first of three operations into the A Shau that were conducted under the overall name of Kentucky Jumper. Encountering only light resistance, the Screaming Eagles conducted a nine-week search of the southern end of the valley, which ended on May 8. MACV immediately decided to launch a second, larger operation into the A Shau. On May 10, the 101st's 3d Brigade, in conjunction with the 9th Marines and 3d ARVN Regiment, initiated Operation Apache Snow. Air-assaulting into an area along the western edge of the valley near Laos, the 101st ran headlong into fierce enemy resistance near Hill 937, called by the Vietnamese, Dong Ap Bia. For ten days the 3d Battalion, 187th Infantry, joined later by the 1st Battalion, 506th Infantry, and the 2d Battalion, 501st Infantry, sought to capture this heavily fortified and staunchly defended mountain. When they finally gained the top on May 20, the enemy had withdrawn.

The battle for Dong Ap Bia, or Hamburger Hill as the men of the 101st dubbed it, quickly became one of the most controversial of the war. Although they killed 630 enemy soldiers in taking the hill, the 101st lost 56 men of their own in addition to 420 wounded, and these came in a battle for a hill whose only significance, as Gen. Zais admitted, "was the fact that there were North Vietnamese on it." Coming at a time of growing sentiment in the U.S. to withdraw from the war, the battle outraged many Americans and led some angry 101st soldiers to place a $10,000 reward in an underground division newspaper for anyone who assassinated an officer ordering a similar attack.

Winding down

Hamburger Hill revealed a number of problems that had begun to trouble U.S. military leaders in Vietnam. As the U.S. effort wound down, soldiers became more and more reluctant to place themselves in danger to fight a war from which their country had already decided to disengage. Still, commanders were forced to fight a war while at the same time limiting casualties, both with few concrete directions on how to accomplish their mission.

Gen. Wright, who succeeded Zais as commander of the 101st only five days after Dong Ap Bia, recalled, "In commanders' conferences General Abrams stressed minimizing casualties. But I didn't need to be told this. I always looked to minimize casualties. But with all that, if you're facing an armed enemy you have to take some casualties. I could have minimized casualties by not fighting but we would have failed in our job. The enemy was very willing to take casualties. It was a matter of judgement and balance, what you will gain against losses."

The winding down of the war also brought other problems. The rapid withdrawal of forces and the lack of qualified replacements plagued the 101st during its final two years in Vietnam. To alleviate this problem among the ranks, MACV transferred to the 101st more than 3,400 enlisted men from other units in Vietnam. However, the majority of them had only two or three months left on their one-year tours, and as the 101st's new commander, Major General John J. Hennessey, noted, they "were not motivated for continued service in Vietnam. They felt they had done their job and often avoided giving their full support to their unit's mission."

The shortage of qualified personnel became particularly acute among the ranks of the division NCOs. Throughout 1970 and into 1971, the division consistently operated with only 60 to 75 percent of its authorized NCO strength. This resulted in the promotion of increasingly junior enlisted men to fill their ranks. Often, officers just out of OCS found themselves assigned to units with NCOs scarcely older or more experienced than themselves.

As disaffection grew within the ranks and days of inactivity increased, drug abuse rose dramatically, as it tended to do throughout the military in Vietnam. Gen. Hennessey admitted that drug abuse was "a serious problem in the division," and he expended considerable time and energy to combat it. Every trooper coming into the 101st received a one-hour class on drug abuse, and mobile training teams conducted periodic refresher courses for the division's units. Headquarters established a drug hot line in the office of the division psychiatrist, and the division Leadership Council was redesignated the Human Relations/Drug Control Council to focus the council's discussions upon drug abuse.

While combating these problems, the division continued to wage a war. Following Operation Kentucky Jumper, which came to a close on August 5, the 101st turned its attention to pacification and Vietnamization. The division emphasized combined operations with South Vietnamese units and measured success not by body count but by advances in pacification efforts. In Operation Randolph Glen, which began in December 1969 and ended in March 1970, the entire division devoted its efforts to the pacification of Thua Thien Province. At all times during Gen. Wright's tenure as commander, which ended in May 1970, at least one of his nine battalions was fully engaged in pacification efforts. Under Wright's successor, Gen. Hennessey, the 2d Brigade maintained twenty-two mobile training teams that traveled across the province training RF and PF forces as part of Operation Texas Star.

From late 1969 until the division's departure from Vietnam, the firebase was the center of military operations for the 101st. Located primarily along VC/NVA infiltration routes away from the heavily populated coastal lowlands, these firebases provided a first line of defense against infiltrating NVA. Although isolated, the firebases were

Soldiers from the 101st watch their supply helicopter depart before continuing their patrol in the A Shau Valley during Operation Apache Snow in June 1969.

usually located within artillery distance of other firebases, making them mutually supportable. They could also be opened and closed as quickly as the military situation dictated, and the division commonly reopened bases several months after abandoning them.

Although the firebases appeared to be an effective tactical answer to the problems of a fluid war, they actually encouraged a more static, defensive mode of operation. Soldiers stationed at firebases tended to patrol less aggressively and for shorter distances. The NVA also recognized them as fixed targets, giving them the opportunity to inflict heavy casualties. This was the case during their 1970 summer offensive when they launched a series of attacks on the division's firebases. In three weeks of fighting at Firebase Ripcord alone, the NVA killed 61 soldiers from the 101st and wounded another 345.

As the U.S. troops fought the war from within their isolated firebases, the South Vietnamese assumed control of the remainder of the fighting. However, while the U.S. troops could easily turn their areas of operations over to the ARVN troops, they could not so easily transfer their expertise and support assets, particularly their aviation equipment. During Gen. Hennessey's eight months as commander of the 101st, his division aviation companies flew over 22,000 hours in support of ARVN forces in their area. The extent of ARVN's reliance on the 101st's aviation became glaringly apparent during the 1971 invasion of Laos.

Operation Lam Son 719

In early 1971, South Vietnamese and MACV planners decided to launch an invasion of the North Vietnamese base areas located just across the border in Laos—Operation Lam Son 719. Although no American troops were allowed to cross the border on the ground, U.S. pilots and helicopters, primarily from the 101st, formed the backbone of the air support for the operation, ferrying ARVN troops into Laos and providing close air support. At the same time, infantry battalions from the 101st assumed responsibility throughout the operation for the areas in South Vietnam vacated by ARVN troops.

From the start, the U.S. pilots discovered that operating in the skies over Laos was a dangerous mission. Employing more than 200 antiaircraft weapons, ranging from 23MM to 100MM, and an even larger number of 12.7MM machine guns, the enemy barraged any U.S. aircraft entering within their range. One unnerved pilot from the 101st exclaimed, "They've got stuff out there, man, we don't even know what it is. I had things flying past me as big as basketballs." Another more laconic but no less amazed pilot, Major Burt Allen of Obion, Tennessee, said, "I've been flying for six months, took my first hit yesterday and since then I've taken 13."

As a consequence of the heavy antiaircraft fire, Brigadier General Sidney B. Berry, Jr., assistant division commander of the 101st and coordinator of the U.S. and ARVN aviation operations for Lam Son 719, noted, "Every airmobile operation, even single-ship resupply and medical evacuation missions, had to be planned and conducted as combat operations complete with fire plan, escorting armed helicopters, and plans for securing and recovering downed crews and helicopters." Berry described the antiaircraft fire during Lam Son 719 as the most intense fire experienced by helicopter pilots during the entire war. The U.S. lost 108 helicopters during the operation and another 618 were damaged. The 101st alone suffered 68 killed, 261 wounded, and 17 missing in action.

General Berry insisted that these casualty figures were remarkably low in light of the more than 164,000 sorties flown during the operation and the heavy enemy fire. However, to the men flying the missions, waiting for the end of their tour of duty or the end of the U.S. effort in South Vietnam, whichever came sooner, they seemed extremely high, especially since they came in support of a South Vietnamese operation. "This is supposed to be a South Vietnamese Army show," said one pilot, "but we're still getting our tails shot off over there, and I'd like to know why." Another pilot, David Anderson, stated the situation even more explicitly: "Face it, I'd rather hang it out for my own people—all of us would."

For the South Vietnamese, forced into retreat by the North Vietnamese, Lam Son 719 was a near total disaster. It also required the U.S. to reassess its Vietnamization program, but with plans for the American withdrawal already well under way, little time remained for major changes. Soon after Lam Son 719, the 101st, under its new commander, Major General Thomas M. Tarpley, adopted an essentially defensive posture. Although the division continued to provide combat support to the South Vietnamese, the 1st ARVN Infantry Division assumed responsibility for all offensive operations. Gradually, the 101st also turned over its firebases to ARVN troops as the division began to redeploy and pull back from outlying areas.

The withdrawal began on May 17, 1971, with the redeployment of the 3d Battalion, 506th Infantry. Other withdrawals and pullbacks followed in December and January of 1972. By February, only the 2d Brigade remained in Vietnam, where it provided security for the base at Phu Bai. A month later the 2d Brigade also departed, completing the withdrawal of the 101st and its return to its stateside base at Fort Campbell, Kentucky.

After more than six and a half years at war, the 101st had finally returned home, the last Army division to leave. During that time, the division suffered almost 20,000 casualties. It also distinguished itself with a number of individual and unit awards and as the second entirely airmobile division helped to prove and improve the airmobile concept. By the mid-1980s it was the only remaining airmobile division in the Army.

The Navy's Elite

The SEALs, the Navy's elite commandos, were highly trained but relatively untested when they entered the Vietnam War. Formed in January 1962 as the successors to the famed Underwater Demolition Teams of World War II, SEALs (for SEa, Air, and Land) spent their early years developing techniques and training the frogmen of other countries, including those of South Vietnam. Their combat operations in Vietnam began humbly. In February 1966, the Navy sent a pilot group of eighteen SEALs to the river patrol base at Nha Be, southeast of Saigon, to see if it could fight the Vietcong where other units could not—in the dense mangrove swamps and tidal mudflats of the Rung Sat Special Zone (RSSZ), long a Vietcong refuge.

The SEAL detachment quickly showed its capabilities. After spending the first weeks getting a feel for Vietcong movement on nighttime listening posts, SEAL squads of seven men each, faces painted green and black for camouflage, set nightly ambushes and conducted small

unit searches. These operations surprised the Vietcong in terrain they once considered secure. In July, for example, a SEAL squad startled three Vietcong, killing two and uncovering a major base camp with supplies and documents.

In the U.S., Rand Corporation analysts noted the success of the Navy SEALs, observing that at only a small monetary expense they were able to tax Vietcong resources to a significant degree. The experts called for more, and at the end of

The SEALs in action. Preceding page. *A Navy SEAL, wearing a protective mask, prepares for a quick strike along the Ti-Ti Canal in the Mekong Delta, following the release of helicopter-dropped CS gas, November 1967.* Above. *The SEAL squad emerges from mangrove and palm thickets along the canal after failing to find the Vietcong.* Right. *The SEALs return to Can Tho base, carried in SEAL team assault boats (STABs).*

A Navy SEAL, holding an M63A1 Stoner light machine gun, waits in ambush along a stream in October 1968. During their first weeks in the Rung Sat Special Zone and Mekong Delta studying Vietcong movement, the SEALs learned when and where to set their ambushes.

1966, the Navy earmarked five platoons from Team One and three from Team Two for duty in Vietnam.

As the new commandos arrived in 1967, the SEALs expanded their activities. Team One created three detachments, Golf, Echo, and Bravo, which conducted military operations in the RSSZ and trained South Vietnamese units. Team Two established one detachment, Alpha,

which moved into the Mekong Delta at Binh Thuy, along the Bas Sac River.

Ambush was the SEALs' staple tactic, but they also proved their versatility in missions supporting other units. SEAL demolition teams cleared blocked waterways for the Navy's Riverine Assault Force, and SEAL divers retrieved sunken equipment and bodies. Because of their stealth, SEAL squads and platoons fre-

quently acted as advance scouts for larger forces such as the Army's 199th Light Brigade. One mission took Team Two's 8th Platoon all the way to the Cambodian border. In 1967, specially trained SEALs assisted indigenous troops in the Provincial Reconnaissance Unit (PRU) program, which had been designed to dismantle the Vietcong infrastructure via terror and assassination.

From 1967 through 1969, the Navy SEALs were deeply involved in the Vietnam conflict, having an effect disproportionate to their small size. In 1967, for example, Team One's detachment Golf suffered only four fatalities but killed ninety Vietcong, destroyed twenty-seven base camps, and uncovered 4,000 pounds of rice and gear. Their guerrilla tactics kept casualties low, and their expertise

Navy SEALs keep watch for Vietcong as a Navy commander brings his craft toward shore where the SEALs will disembark, October 1968. River patrol boats and Navy helicopters often acted as decoys or created other diversions so that SEAL teams could go ashore unnoticed.

led them to be dubbed by the enemy "green-faced frogmen of the Delta."

The SEALs demonstrated that they were more than just guerrillas during the Tet offensive, when they valiantly defended cities in the Delta. They were instrumental in the retaking of Chau Doc near the Cambodian border. Team Two's 8th Platoon immediately responded to the January 31, 1968, attack on the city, rescuing sixteen American and South Vietnam-

ese civilians and fighting a running battle with Vietcong troops until the city was reclaimed.

In early 1970, SEAL advisers stopped leading PRUs, and in February 1971 the first platoon from Team Two rotated home without replacement. By the end of 1972, all but a small advisory detachment had redeployed. Nevertheless, the SEALs in Vietnam had established themselves as fierce and capable fighters.

Above. *Two Navy SEALs, backed by soldiers of a Navy river patrol unit in a heavily armored "Mike" boat, enter a Vietnamese village along the Bas Sac River during Operation Crimson Tide, September 1967.* Right. *After a search of the village, the SEALs lead a Vietcong suspect away.*

Command of the Sea

Alfred Thayer Mahan, the philosopher of sea power, likened the ocean to a broad common, open to all who wish to travel upon it. The highest aim of naval warfare, he asserted, is to deny the enemy access to this common while preserving it for oneself—a condition he called command of the sea. Usually, of course, the first order of business must be the elimination of the enemy's navy.

In the Vietnam War, American forces were spared the trouble of eliminating an enemy navy; for practical purposes, there was none. The Seventh Fleet's ability to exercise command of the sea was uncontested. For years, however, political constraints prevented that command from being fully exerted. Not until May 1972, seven years after U.S. forces entered combat, were sufficient measures taken to deny North Vietnam the advantage of access to Mahan's watery common.

The restrictions under which the Seventh Fleet operated for most of the war placed it in a situation described decades earlier by Sir Julian Corbett, Bri-

tain's greatest naval historian, who wrote that "without substantial permission to command the sea," navies cease to have meaning "except as mere adjuncts to armies." It was primarily as an adjunct to the Army that the Navy took part in the Vietnam War. Yet, considering the magnitude of that part, it can hardly be characterized as *mere*. Never in its history had the U.S. Navy undertaken a more challenging variety of missions than it did in Vietnam.

The advisory years

The Navy's involvement in Vietnam originated during the French Indochina War. A program of American aid to the French was inaugurated in June 1950, and in August the newly established Military Assistance Advisory Group, Indochina, arrived in Saigon to oversee its implementation. MAAG's Navy Section processed the first delivery of naval material in October. Over the next four years it provided to the French part of $2.6 billion of aid and equipment, including two light aircraft carriers and 500 naval aircraft.

The climax of the French-Vietnamese war brought the Navy close to entering the Southeast Asian conflict a decade earlier than it actually did. In March 1954 the Vietminh laid siege to Dien Bien Phu, giving the French their long-awaited opportunity for a large set-piece battle. As it became apparent that the Vietminh were going to win the engagement, the Eisenhower administration considered staging a massive air strike, code-named Operation

Vulture, against the forces surrounding Dien Bien Phu. The attack was to be delivered by Air Force B-29 Superfortresses from the Philippines and Guam and carrier planes from the Seventh Fleet. As a preparatory measure, the carriers *Boxer* and *Essex* were moved into the South China Sea, in position to launch on order. In the end, the administration abandoned the idea. Dien Bien Phu fell on May 7, and on July 20 France signed the Geneva agreements, acknowledging defeat in Indochina.

These agreements led to the U.S. Navy's first operational commitment in Vietnam. For 300 days following the cease-fire, the populace was allowed free movement either to the North, where the Vietminh established a Communist government, or to the South, to which the French and their supporters retired. Lacking the capability to evacuate all the Vietnamese who chose to go south, the French requested American assistance. Accordingly, in August 1954 the Pacific Fleet mounted a gigantic sea lift called Operation Passage to Freedom. Before the operation ended in May 1955, a total of seventy-four naval vessels and thirty-nine Military Sea Transportation Service ships had carried 310,800 people from Haiphong to Saigon.

In the years following Geneva, U.S. policy in Vietnam remained unchanged: to oppose the expansion of communism by financial aid and advisory assistance. MAAG, Indochina, became MAAG, Vietnam and redirected the support it had been furnishing the French forces to those of the fledgling republic organized by anti-Communist forces in the South. The Navy Section of MAAG focused its

Preceding page. *Navy crewmen of an assault support patrol boat (ASPB) return enemy fire as their damaged craft takes on water in the Mekong Delta, June 1968.*

Below. *A photograph taken from aboard the USS* Maddox *shows one of the three North Vietnamese torpedo boats that attacked the destroyer on August 2, 1964.*

U.S. Navy

Arrived Vietnam: Seventh Fleet: August 1964
Naval Forces, Vietnam: April 1, 1966

Departed Vietnam: Seventh Fleet: April 1975
Naval Forces, Vietnam: March 29, 1973

Unit Headquarters

Seventh Fleet: Honolulu

Naval Forces, Vietnam: Saigon

Commanding Officers

Seventh Fleet
V. Adm. Roy L. Johnson   *June 1964*
V. Adm. Paul P. Blackburn, Jr.   *March 1965*
V. Adm. John J. Hyland   *Dec. 1965*
V. Adm. William F. Bringle   *Nov. 1967*
V. Adm. Maurice F. Weisner   *March 1970*
V. Adm. William P. Mack   *June 1971*
V. Adm. James L. Holloway III   *May 1972*
V. Adm. George P. Steele   *July 1973*

Naval Advisory Group, Vietnam
Cpt. William H. Hardcastle   *May 1964*
R. Adm. Norvell G. Ward   *May 1965*

Naval Forces, Vietnam
R. Adm. Norvell G. Ward   *April 1966*
R. Adm. Kenneth L. Vest   *April 1967*
V. Adm. Elmo R. Zumwalt, Jr.   *Sep. 1968*
V. Adm. Jerome H. King   *May 1970*
R. Adm. Robert S. Salzer   *April 1971*
R. Adm. Arthur W. Price, Jr.   *June 1972*
R. Adm. James B. Wilson   *Aug. 1972*

Major Subordinate Units

Seventh Fleet
Task Force 71	Vietnam Patrol Force
Task Force 73	Mobile Logistic Support Force
Task Force 76	Amphibious Task Force
Task Force 77	Carrier Striking Force
Task Unit 70.8.9	Naval Gunfire Support Task Unit

Naval Advisory Group, Vietnam,
and Naval Forces, Vietnam
Task Force 115	Coastal Surveillance Force
Task Force 116	River Patrol Force
Task Force 117	River Assault Force
Task Force 194	Sealords Task Force

2,511 KIA

10,406 WIA

14 Medals of Honor

attentions on the tiny Vietnamese navy that the French had activated in 1952. Between 1954 and 1964, the strength of this force grew from 1,500 men with 4 seagoing ships and 20 riverine vessels to 8,150 men with 44 ships and 208 riverine vessels.

The outcome of the advisory effort did not fulfill American expectations; the Vietnamese navy failed to reach the envisioned level of efficiency. In the words of an official U.S. Navy history: "Political intrigue, cultural differences, and seemingly petty personal disputes divided the officer corps. Senior officers were relatively young and inexperienced. Lack of motivation also pervaded the enlisted ranks. The lack of a modern technological heritage in South Vietnam was reflected in poor maintenance of already-obsolete World War II-vintage ships. All of these factors resulted in a mediocre operational performance."

The frustrations Navy advisers encountered typified the American experience in Vietnam. By late 1959, the South Vietnamese government was steadily losing popularity and the Vietcong were rapidly gaining strength. When John F. Kennedy became president in January 1961, South Vietnam was challenged by a full-scale insurgency.

Kennedy moved to stabilize the situation in South Vietnam by a major expansion of the U.S. advisory and assistance program. By the end of 1963, there were more than 17,000 servicemen in Vietnam. They included 750 naval personnel, including elements of the Pacific Fleet SEAL (SEa, Air, Land) Team. An elite force founded in January 1962 to conduct unconventional warfare at sea and in amphibious environments, SEALs instructed South Viet-

namese frogmen and commandos in their special, deadly skills. In addition MACV had been established in February 1962 to coordinate all U.S. military activities inside Vietnam. It included the Naval Advisory Group, which eventually replaced MAAG's Navy Section.

Despite the escalation of American assistance, the military situation in South Vietnam did not improve during the Kennedy years. There was, nevertheless, no change in policy upon Lyndon Johnson's assumption of the presidency in November 1963. The advisory effort continued to grow, as it had in the past, but with the same disappointing results; always enough to avert disaster, never enough to attain solid success. Then, late in the summer of 1964, an event occurred that ultimately provided the legal basis for the commitment of American combat troops to Vietnam.

In February 1964, South Vietnamese forces began a new program of raids on the coast of North Vietnam, called Operation Plan 34-A, using American-supplied PT boats maintained by advisory personnel. Around midnight on July 30, four boats shelled a pair of North Vietnamese islands in the Gulf of Tonkin. The next morning the destroyer *Maddox* entered the gulf on a Desoto patrol, an intelligence-gathering operation routinely conducted off Asian Communist coasts. Apparently associating the ship's presence with the 34-A raid, on August 2 North Vietnam dispatched three P-4 torpedo boats that attacked the *Maddox* in international waters east of Thanh Hoa. Foreseeing such a possibility, U.S. intelligence had earlier alerted the destroyer to be on the lookout for trouble. At 4:08 P.M., the *Maddox* opened fire on the approaching P-4s and called for air support. In the ensuing twenty-minute action, the *Maddox* damaged all three boats while taking only a single, insignificant hit herself. The P-4s were already retiring when planes from the *Ticonderoga* attacked them and sank one.

A few hours later the *Maddox* was joined by the destroyer *Turner Joy*. Together the two vessels continued the patrol. On the evening of August 3, the South Vietnamese carried out another 34-A operation. The next night both destroyers picked up firm radar contacts, which were interpreted as oncoming PT boats. The *Turner Joy* commenced fire at 10:39 P.M., initiating an action that continued for four hours. Air cover was provided by the *Ticonderoga* and the *Constellation*. Neither destroyer was hit, and although radar indicated that two PT boats were sunk, no wreckage was ever recovered.

Afterward, controversy arose as to whether an attack had actually taken place. Some authorities remain convinced that the radar contacts were nothing more than electronic phenomena and the visual sightings the product of overheated imaginations. Yet, others argue that the PT boat attacks were real.

In any case, President Johnson's reaction was unambiguous. On August 5, sixty-seven aircraft from the *Constel-*

An F–8 Crusader takes off from the deck of the USS Hancock *for a strike against Dong Hoi, North Vietnam, during Operation Flaming Dart I on February 10, 1965.*

lation and *Ticonderoga* launched a retaliatory strike that destroyed or damaged thirty-three of the thirty-four small craft comprising the North Vietnamese navy. Two planes were lost; Lieutenant (j.g.) Richard C. Sather became the first naval aviator to die in the Vietnam conflict and Lieutenant (j.g.) Everett Alvarez, Jr., the first to be taken prisoner. That same day, the administration sent the Tonkin Gulf Resolution to Congress. The passage of this measure on August 7 gave the president a mandate to take whatever steps he deemed necessary in Southeast Asia.

Johnson did not hasten to exercise this authority. In November and again in December, he withheld permission to execute preplanned carrier strikes in retaliation for Vietcong actions in which U.S. servicemen were killed and wounded. On February 7, 1965, however, a mortar attack on the advisers' compound at Pleiku provoked him to order Operation Flaming Dart I, a raid on Dong Hoi by aircraft from the *Coral Sea* and *Hancock*. Flaming Dart II, a reprisal by planes from the *Coral Sea*, *Hancock*, and *Ranger* for the bombing of American quarters at Qui Nhon, followed on February 11.

By then pressure on the president was mounting. The collapse of South Vietnam appeared imminent. On February 12, 1965, therefore, the president approved Operation Rolling Thunder, a limited bombing offensive against military targets in North Vietnam below the nineteenth parallel. The U.S. and South Vietnamese air forces opened the campaign on March 2. Six days later, Marines were landed to guard the U.S. air base at Da Nang. The Vietnam conflict had become an American war.

The Seventh Fleet's carrier striking force, Task Force (TF) 77, launched its first Rolling Thunder raid on March 15, when ninety-four aircraft from the *Hancock* and *Ranger* struck an ammunition depot at Phu Qui. By the end of the year, Task Force 77 aviators had flown 31,000 sorties against the North. Subsequently, the tempo of aerial activity increased until in 1967, 77,000 sorties were launched.

The strength of a carrier's air wing varied from 70 to 100 aircraft. The exact number depended on the capacity of the particular carrier, which ranged from World War II veterans such as the *Ticonderoga*, displacing 33,000 tons, to the nuclear-powered *Enterprise*, displacing 85,600. Most air wings were divided into two fighter and three attack squadrons, plus detachments of reconnaissance and electronic warfare (radar jamming) planes.

Two Navy fighters were used in Vietnam: the single-seat F-8 Crusader and the newer, faster, two-seat F-4 Phantom II. Widely regarded as the finest fighter of its generation, the F-4 gradually replaced the F-8 aboard large carriers and accounted for two-thirds of enemy MiG aircraft downed by the Navy. Its Navy version had what many pilots deemed a serious defect, however; it was armed only with air-to-air missiles, unlike the F-8, which had 20MM cannon as well. Once an F-4's missiles were fired, or if they malfunctioned, speed was its sole defense.

Four types of attack aircraft also saw service. The oldest was the A-1 Skyraider, the fleet's last piston-engined attack aircraft, which had entered service in 1945. Affectionately called the Spad after the World War I fighter, the durable A-1 was withdrawn from combat in 1968, though not before downing two MiG-17s. The A-4 Skyhawk, better known as the Scooter, was a rugged little jet designed in the early 1950s. Including sorties flown by Marine squadrons ashore, it logged more bombing missions than any other naval aircraft in Vietnam. The most advanced attack craft on hand at the start of the war was the new, all-weather, night-capable, high-tech A-6 Intruder, first flown in 1960. The still newer A-7 Corsair II, intended to replace the A-4 Skyhawk, entered combat over Vietnam in December 1967.

Carriers participating in Rolling Thunder operated from a position called Yankee Station, approximately 100 miles off the northern coast of South Vietnam, originally at 16° N 110° E and, after April 1966, at 17° 33'N 108° 30'E. Until August 1966, two or three carriers normally steamed at Yankee Station. Thereafter, three or four ships remained on station. Each carrier was screened by three or four destroyers. Another two destroyers and later a cruiser were routinely deployed as radar pickets between TF 77 and the enemy mainland.

In addition, two destroyers, and later a cruiser, were positioned to recover downed air crew at two advanced

The remains of a North Vietnamese supply depot smolder after an attack by Carrier Air Wing 2 from the USS Midway *on April 30, 1965.*

search and rescue (SAR) stations off North Vietnam. During major operations, one or two armed and armored SH-3A Sea King rescue helicopters from the task force circled over the destroyers, each of which also carried a UH-2 Seasprite helicopter. These measures gave aviators who ejected over the sea a better than 90 percent chance of sleeping in their own bunks that night. One pilot was picked up after only eighty seconds in the water; three were snatched out of Haiphong Harbor. Some of those forced to eject over land were also rescued, often in harrowing circumstances, but few were so fortunate.

Yankee Station was not the only scene of carrier operations. Because of the critical condition within South Vietnam and the scarcity of air bases suitable for USAF jets, shortly after the beginning of Rolling Thunder General William C. Westmoreland requested Seventh Fleet support in attacking enemy forces inside the country. Accordingly, in April 1965 a second operating area, Dixie Station, was established southeast of Cam Ranh Bay. A carrier remained there until August 1966, by which time the Air Force was ready to take over most in-country missions. Between these dates the Seventh Fleet flew one-third of all U.S. sorties over South Vietnam.

North Vietnam never attempted to interfere with TF 77's carrier operations. On occasion, flights of enemy aircraft left the mainland on course for Yankee Station, but they turned back before braving the carriers' combat air patrol (CAP). CAP planes did figure in one action at sea, however. On July 1, 1966, an F-4 on CAP from the *Constellation* spotted three enemy torpedo boats moving toward two destroyers on a SAR station off Haiphong. Aircraft from the *Constellation* and *Hancock* sank them—after which the Navy plucked nineteen North Vietnamese from the water.

Over North Vietnam, Navy fliers ran a gauntlet of fire from small arms, conventional antiaircraft artillery, surface-to-air missiles (SAMs), and sometimes MiG fighters. The enemy fighters were the least of their problems. Of the 328 aircraft lost over the North from 1965 to 1968, only 8 fell in aerial combat, while Navy pilots downed 31 enemy planes, 23 MiG-17s and 8 of their faster cousins, MiG-21s.

Of course, not every loss was the result of enemy action. A malfunction could be as deadly as a SAM. Lieutenant Commander Richard Stratton received proof of this one morning in January 1967, when some Korean War-vintage rockets he fired at a bridge exploded in front of his A-4. The plane's air intakes sucked the debris into the engine, and in a matter of moments Stratton was floating down to six years as a POW. Including the crews of thirty-nine aircraft brought down in Laos and South Vietnam, a total of 454 naval aviators were killed, missing, or captured during these years. An approximately equal number were recovered, and one, German-born Lieutenant (j.g.) Dieter Dengler, performed an almost impossible feat for an American POW in Southeast Asia.

On February 1, 1966, Dengler survived the crash when his A-1 Skyraider was shot down in Laos. But his freedom was short-lived. The following day he was captured by Pathet Lao Communist guerrillas who marched him to a jungle POW camp where he joined other American prisoners. Late in June, the Americans managed to break away from their guards and split up to seek freedom through the dense jungle. Traveling with an Air Force officer, Dengler barely managed to escape a machete-wielding villager who spotted the two men. His companion, however, was killed, and Dengler continued alone, surviving on fruits, berries, and small quantities of rice he had saved while in captivity. On the twenty-second day, near to exhaustion, he managed to spell out an SOS with rocks in a clearing and sat down to await rescue or death. Within hours an Air Force jet spotted his signal and guided a helicopter to him. During his six-month ordeal, Dengler's weight dropped from 157 to 98 pounds.

For all the perseverance and heroism on the part of Navy and Air Force pilots, Rolling Thunder failed to deter North Vietnam from supporting the war in the South. Military personnel blamed this on the restrictions placed on the conduct of the campaign by the Johnson administration, which was fearful of provoking Chinese intervention. In 1965, for example, it was forbidden to bomb within thirty miles of the Chinese border, thirty miles of central Hanoi, and ten miles of Haiphong. Over the years the extent of the restricted zones was gradually reduced, and occasionally permission was given to hit specified targets inside them. Even so, the full potential of American air power was never unleashed during Rolling Thunder.

The big guns

Beginning in May 1965, the Navy added shore bombardment to its Vietnam duties. Ships' guns could reach nearly a third of I Corps and most of the coastal provinces in II and III Corps, too. While any vessel might be called on to deliver supporting fire for forces ashore, those specifically detailed to coastal bombardment were assigned to the Naval Gunfire Support Unit (TU 70.8.9), controlled by the fleet's Cruiser-Destroyer Group. The composition of this unit, which included for a time ships of the Royal Australian Navy, fluctuated greatly. As a rule it included at least one cruiser, four destroyers, an inshore fire support ship (IFS), and two medium landing ships, rocket (LSMRs). Heavy cruisers carried eight-inch guns with an effective range of almost fifteen miles; destroyers, five-inch guns good for thirteen or eight-and-one-half miles, depending on the model. IFSs and LSMRs were armed with five-inch guns and launchers capable of firing 380 rockets a minute for more than five-and-one-half miles. Besides responding to requests for support from units on land, ships also fired on enemy-controlled areas.

The success of the Gunfire Support Unit is reflected in the stark, official statistics of the Navy. In 1965, seventy-two vessels fired 90,000 rounds. The following year, during which TU 70.8.9 operated mainly off I Corps, 250,000 rounds from the fleet devastated 35,000 structures and killed 3,000 troops, almost one-tenth of them on a single day in September when the destroyer *Stormes* shelled enemy positions for three hours. In 1967, the total number of rounds fired for the year increased to 500,000.

Enemy artillery sometimes returned the ships' fire but to little effect. From 1965 through 1967, only two vessels, both destroyers, were hit. Neither was seriously damaged, but two sailors were killed and eleven wounded.

The Navy's shore bombardment was expanded to North Vietnam in October 1966 with the inauguration of Operation Sea Dragon. Conceived as a complement to Rolling Thunder, the campaign was restricted to waters south of 17° 31'N, the latitude of Dong Hoi, until February 1967, after which its reach was extended to the twentieth parallel, just above Thanh Hoa. The Sea Dragon force generally consisted of two to four U.S. and Australian destroyers and a cruiser. Carrier planes helped direct the fire, which was aimed at enemy coastal batteries, radar sites, watercraft, railways, and roads. The North Vietnamese did not hesitate to fire back, often accurately. They hit nineteen Sea

Operation Sea Dragon, March 1967. Left. *A North Vietnamese shore battery round falls short of the destroyer USS* Ingersoll, *though similar fire did damage nineteen Sea Dragon ships between 1966 and 1968.* Below left. *The USS* Canberra *fires a salvo from its eight-inch guns toward on-shore targets.* Below right. *The commanding officer and staff of the* Canberra *review the coordinates of coastal targets.*

Dragon ships from 1966 through 1968, some seriously enough to require yard repairs, but none was sunk.

Amphibious landings have long been the hallmark of Navy and Marine cooperation, and the two services continued that tradition in Vietnam with the commitment of the Seventh Fleet's Amphibious Task Force, TF 76, in 1965. It consisted of a Navy Amphibious Ready Group (ARG) and a Marine Corps Special Landing Force (SLF). The core of the ARG was a helicopter carrier designated an amphibious landing ship (LPH). Other vessels usually included a tank landing ship and an amphibious transport dock or attack transport. The SLF, 2,000 men strong, was composed of a Marine medium helicopter squadron of twenty-four UH-34 Seahorse helicopters aboard the LPH and a Marine battalion landing team (BLT), whose men were distributed among all the ARG ships. Forty-one tracked landing vehicles enabled the BLT to go ashore by sea as well as by air.

TF 76 made its first and probably most successful landing of the war during Operation Starlite on August 18, 1965. Intelligence revealed that the 1st Vietcong Regiment, 1,500 men assembled on the Van Tuong Peninsula, was planning to attack the Marines at Chu Lai. The Marine commanders moved to trap the enemy against the sea. Elements of the SLF helicoptered from the *Iwo Jima* to join two beach-landed Marine and two South Vietnamese battalions blocking the base of the peninsula. Supported by air strikes and naval gunfire, the force killed over one-third of the enemy regiment in a week's fighting and, in the Marines' estimation, left it combat ineffective.

The Vietcong avoided concentrating in coastal areas, and subsequent ARG/SLF operations in 1965 and early 1966 proved less productive. The SLF then conducted a series of inland operations in concert with shore-based units, but in October, increased pressure from North Vietnamese regulars on the Marines in I Corps drew the amphibious force to that region. During 1967, all except one of TF 76's twenty-five landings were made in I Corps. A second ARG/SLF joined in April, expanding the force's capabilities, and helped bring its year-end count to 3,000 enemy dead. In the end, Vietnam saw no large, fiercely opposed amphibious assaults in the tradition of Iwo Jima. The operations of the Amphibious Task Force served primarily as reminders of Navy-Marine combat coordination.

The brown water navy

Vietnam's long coastline became another area of naval action since it provided unlimited opportunities for the North to infiltrate arms and men to the Vietcong. South Vietnamese naval forces tried ineffectively to cut off the flow. After a badly bungled attempt by the South Vietnamese navy to intercept a big shipment of arms at Vung Ro in February of 1965, impatient U.S. Navy officers persuaded MACV, with the grudging approval of the South Vietnamese, to assign American units to the task. These formed the basis of the brown water navy, so named because most operations were conducted on inland waterways.

An operation called Market Time grew out of this decision and initiated joint actions by the South Vietnamese and U.S. naval forces. U.S. Navy planes flew offshore surveillance missions to spot enemy infiltration activities; U.S. surface ships patrolled far offshore to find and intercept would-be infiltrators, while South Vietnamese and Americans manned a barrier of boats close to shore and on inland waters. As constituted by the Seventh Fleet, the U.S. part of this joint force was called the Vietnamese Patrol Force (TF 71), but on July 31, 1965, it was renamed the Coastal Surveillance Force (TF 115) and placed under the command of MACV's Naval Advisory Group.

Originally the Market Time force was composed of destroyers, radar picket escorts, and ocean mine sweepers. These vessels, too large to work in shallow water, were soon supplemented by as many as forty-one cutters manned by the U.S. Coast Guard in its only direct contribution to the war effort. The Navy's new, fifty-foot aluminum-hulled fast patrol craft (PCF) added to the fleet. Better known as Swift boats, PCFs carried a crew of six, a twin .50-caliber machine gun forward, and a .50-caliber machine gun and 81MM mortar piggybacked aft. Serving on them was tough, as they lacked most creature comforts. Broiling hot unless under way, they had no space for eating or sleeping and made for hard cruising in even moderate seas, but they could reach a top speed of twenty-three knots (just over twenty-five miles per hour). The first of the eighty-four Swifts authorized for Market Time reached Vietnam in October 1965.

Between January 1966 and July 1967, Market Time operations searched 700,000 coastal craft, capturing or destroying many enemy junks and sampans, and intercepted 6 North Vietnamese trawlers carrying major arms shipments to the South. Five of these vessels were destroyed and one was forced to turn back. Occasionally these encounters flared into little battles. One occurred off the Mekong Delta on June 20, 1966, when a 120-foot steel trawler greeted the Coast Guard cutters *Point League* and *Point Slocum* with small-arms and mortar fire. The cutters pursued and drove the trawler aground in flames.

Meanwhile, the Navy had launched Operation Game Warden, the first time since America's Civil War that its ships campaigned on inland waters. Controlled initially by the Naval Advisory Group, Game Warden was designed to wrest from Vietcong control some of the 3,000 nautical miles of waterways in the Mekong Delta and the Rung Sat Swamp between Saigon and the sea. By the time the River Patrol Force (TF 116) was activated on December 18, 1965, the Navy had already procured new river patrol boats (PBRs), which reached Vietnam in March 1966. They were thirty-one-foot, plastic-hulled boats powered by water-jet propulsion engines giving them a speed of up to twenty-eight-and-a-half knots. They carried a crew of four

and a standard armament of a twin .50-caliber machine gun forward, a single .30-caliber aft, and a rapid-fire 40MM grenade launcher amidships. The conning station and gun positions were protected by ceramic armor capable of stopping a rifle bullet, but that was all. Enemy rockets and recoilless rifle rounds could penetrate, but fortunately, at very close range—the situation in which most engagements occurred—often failed to arm and punched through PBRs without exploding.

Twenty boats comprised a river division, with PBRs generally patrolling in pairs. During daylight hours they conducted inspections of river traffic. Most searches were uneventful, but booby traps were an ever-present danger. One sailor opened a bilge compartment to confront an extremely irritated poisonous snake whose tail had been nailed to the keel. After dark, PBRs on ambush assignments tied up in dense brush beside riverbanks in hopes of surprising Vietcong trying to cross. "That was," a PBR officer recalled, "a form of Russian roulette." Despite the dangers they faced, an intense team spirit among PBR crews and a sense of shared responsibility bred of serving in such small units kept morale high. Although between 1966 and 1969 one out of three PBR sailors was wounded, one in five volunteered to extend his tour.

Game Warden forces included more than PBRs. In May 1966, Mine Squadron 11, Detachment Alpha (later redesignated Mine Division 112), became a part of TF 116, primarily to keep open the Long Tau shipping channel to Saigon. The SEALs also came under the command of TF 116, and by mid-1968, eight fourteen-man SEAL platoons were usually active in Vietnam. Finally, on April 1, 1967, Game Warden, previously supported by Army- or Navy-operated Army helicopters, gained its own with the creation of the Helicopter Attack (Light) Squadron (HAL) 3.

With a peak strength of 140 PBRs between 1966 and 1968, the River Patrol Force was much too small to cover all the delta waterways. It did, however, secure the major rivers. In 1967 alone it made 400,000 searches; captured, destroyed, or damaged 2,000 Vietcong watercraft; and inflicted 1,400 casualties on the enemy while suffering 414 of its own. General Westmoreland believed that, whereas before 1965 the Vietcong obtained 70 percent of their supplies by maritime infiltration, Market Time and Game Warden reduced that figure to 10 percent after 1966.

Shortly after the deployment of the River Patrol Force, the Navy obtained the approval of the Joint Chiefs of Staff for a change in the command structure in Vietnam. Since the absorption of MAAG by MACV in May 1964, activities within Vietnam had been controlled by the chief of the Naval Advisory Group, while those offshore came under

the command of the Seventh Fleet. On April 1, 1966, a new command, Naval Forces, Vietnam was established to direct the operations of the brown water navy. Headed by an admiral designated as commander, Naval Forces, Vietnam (COMNAVFORV), it assumed responsibility for the Coastal Surveillance and River Patrol Forces and support activities in II, III, and IV Corps. Operations in I Corps were controlled by the commander of the III Marine Amphibious Force there, and the Seventh Fleet continued its offshore activities.

The Navy's brown water war escalated in 1967 with the creation of the Army-Navy Mobile Riverine Force (MRF). A joint command designed for deployment in the Mekong Delta, where every operation was necessarily amphibious, the MRF was modeled after the *Dinassauts* (*Divisions Navales d'Assaut*) that the French had employed during their Indochina War. The MRF's naval component was called the River Assault Force (TF 117), while the Army component consisted of the 2d Brigade of the 9th Infantry Division, later reinforced by the 3d Brigade. TF 117 included two and, after mid-1968, four river assault squadrons, 400-man units equipped with seven or eight Monitors and twenty-six heavily armed armored troop carriers (ATCs). The Monitor was the capital ship of the MRF, a small but densely armored vessel with a crew of eleven. Most carried a 40MM and 20MM cannon, a .50-caliber machine gun, two grenade launchers, and an 81MM mortar. A water cannon with a jet so powerful it could demolish concrete bunkers and—on craft nicknamed "Zippos"—a flame thrower, which could shoot a stream of napalm for 150 meters, sometimes replaced the big gun.

Although TF 117 was activated by COMNAVFORV on February 28, 1967, the riverine force did not begin operations until early summer. Typically, a river assault squadron and one or two infantry battalions would work together from a floating base formed by a cluster of barracks ships and supporting vessels. Going into action, Monitors and assault support patrol boats led the troop carriers to the landing site, after which all craft would deliver covering fire while the infantry waded ashore. Once the troops were on land, the vessels moved to take up blocking positions across the enemy's line of retreat. The MRF's first major operation, on May 15, 1967, successfully demonstrated these tactics. Two battalions pushing inland from landing sites on a small river called the Rach Ba Rai encountered two Vietcong companies that withdrew to the east, toward the Rach Tra Tan. On reaching the river, the Vietcong found their crossings blocked by Monitors and ATCs. After several attempts to break through, they pulled back to the west, where about 100 were killed in action with the advancing infantry.

A PBR crew from the River Patrol Force inspects sampans on the Go Cong River in November 1967. In that year alone Task Force 116 searched 400,000 vessels.

A supporting role

While combat operations garnered most of the attention, many other naval activities were performed behind the scenes. The Navy managed the enormous logistical effort necessary to support the American presence in Vietnam. Approximately 95 percent of all supplies and 99 percent of the ammunition and fuel used by U.S. forces came by sea. To keep these materials flowing through the 6,900-mile life line from the American West Coast, the Navy's Military Sea Transportation Service built up a fleet that by mid-1967 consisted of 527 vessels, ranging from World War II freighters to modern, roll-on/roll-off vehicle carriers chartered from private shipping companies.

The offshore Navy's own needs were satisfied by the Service Force, U.S. Pacific Fleet, a squadron of which functioned as the Seventh Fleet's Mobile Logistic Support Force (TF 73). The supply of forces inside Vietnam was handled by the Naval Support Activity (NSA), Da Nang and NSA, Saigon. NSA, Da Nang, established on October 15, 1965, to support forces in I Corps, soon became the Navy's largest overseas logistic facility. NSA, Saigon, activated to replace an earlier organization on May 17, 1966, was responsible for providing support to naval forces in the other corps areas.

Among the responsibilities of NSA, Da Nang was the care of I Corps' sick and wounded. A naval hospital opened in 1965 and was repeatedly enlarged. Perhaps the most dramatic experience in it was the removal of a live 60MM mortar round from the chest of a South Vietnamese soldier by a surgeon assisted by an ordnance disposal expert. In February 1967, the 721-bed hospital ship *Repose*, fresh out of Reserve Fleet mothballs, arrived at Da Nang to augment the existing facilities. The *Repose* provided care for 33,000 patients, including 9,000 battle casualties, before returning to the U.S. in March 1970. A second hospital ship, the *Sanctuary*, joined the *Repose* in April 1967 and remained in Vietnamese waters until April 1971.

Another important support role of the Navy was played by its Seabees (construction battalions). While small Seabee technical assistance teams had been in Vietnam since 1963, larger units started arriving in 1965 to undertake major projects for U.S. forces. Over the next three years, Seabee strength in Vietnam grew from a battalion of 600 men to a brigade of 10,000. Seabees developed port installations at Da Nang and elsewhere; improved and maintained roads; and built airfields, bridges, barracks, fortifications, warehouses, and other facilities. Their work was often done under fire; by 1968, fifty-seven Seabees had been killed in action.

In fact, the first member of the naval service to be awarded the Medal of Honor in Vietnam was a Seabee, Construction Mechanic Third Class Marvin G. Shields. Shields belonged to a nine-man Seabee detachment sent to the 1st Special Forces camp at Dong Xoai, 100 kilometers northeast of Saigon. On June 10, 1965, the eleven Green Berets and 400 native troops holding the camp were assaulted by a Vietcong regiment with an estimated strength of 2,000. The Seabees—all of whom were eventually hit—contributed valiantly to the defense. Seven hours after the

---

A heavily armored Monitor, a member of the Navy's Riverine Assault Force (TF 117), streams fire on a potential enemy ambush site in the Mekong Delta, July 1968.

attack began, the camp commander called for a volunteer to help him knock out a machine gun that was sweeping the compound. Shields, already wounded twice, responded quickly. Moving forward with a 3.5-inch rocket launcher, the two men destroyed the gun, but Shields was mortally wounded while returning to his position.

Thirteen more Medal of Honor recipients from the Navy followed Shields during the war. Three, two of them posthumous, went to hospital corpsmen and one posthumously to a chaplain attached to the Marines; three, one posthumous, to members of riverine forces; three to SEALs; and three to aviators, including one to a heroic POW.

By the end of 1967, naval forces had been deployed in a wide range of combat and support activities. So when the enemy launched the Tet offensive on January 30 and 31, 1968, the U.S. Navy was ready to play a significant role in the riposte. Along the coast the Gunfire Support Unit, quickly enlarged to twenty-two ships, recorded its highest rate of fire of the war; heavy cruisers averaged 800 rounds a day. In the delta, units of the River Patrol and Mobile Riverine Forces acted as fast-moving fire brigades, reinforcing threatened positions and helping recapture those that had fallen. At Ben Tre, PBRs and Seawolves checked the advance of Vietcong who had broken into the city during the thirty-six hours it took ground troops to arrive. Offshore, Market Time patrols discovered five enemy trawlers en route to resupply the attackers; two turned back, one was run aground and scuttled by her crew, and two were sunk. In the north the aircraft of TF 77 were diverted from Rolling Thunder to support the Marines in I Corps, where the Special Landing Force was rushed ashore for the same purpose. By the end of February, the Tet offensive had been crushed. An officer of the Gunfire Support Unit recalled that, "after Tet, there was nothing left to shoot at."

In the aftermath of the offensive, President Johnson chose to restrict the U.S. air war over North Vietnam in the hope of starting peace negotiations. For the Navy, this resulted in the constriction and then the cancellation of Rolling Thunder and Sea Dragon. For the next three years the Seventh Fleet's guns were fired only at targets inside South Vietnam. TF 77's planes ranged wider, attacking traffic on the Ho Chi Minh Trail in Laos as well as providing support in the South.

In November 1968, when Richard Nixon was elected to the presidency promising to bring peace with honor, the policy he adopted in pursuit of that goal was Vietnamization. Implementing the naval role in Vietnamization was youthful Vice Admiral Elmo R. ("Bud") Zumwalt, Jr., who had become COMNAVFORV in September 1968 at age forty-seven. He called his program ACTOV, for accelerated turnover to Vietnam, personally picking the acronym because it sounded like "action." ACTOV was basically an intensification of the original advisory and assistance effort that, though never abandoned, had been eclipsed by

En route to the Binh Thuy naval base on October 6, 1968, Secretary of the Navy Paul R. Ignatius (right) confers with two aides and Admiral Elmo R. Zumwalt, Jr., COMNAVFORV (second from right).

the U.S. Navy's own entry into the war. Under Zumwalt, it became the top priority of Naval Forces, Vietnam.

ACTOV did not signal an immediate end to American operations within Vietnam. Rather, it was counterpointed by another major offensive initiative—SEALORDS, the Southeast Asia Lake, Ocean, River, Delta Strategy. Within weeks of arriving in Vietnam, Zumwalt concluded that while Market Time was preventing appreciable infiltration from the sea and Game Warden was doing the same on the big rivers of the Mekong Delta, large quantities of arms were still reaching the enemy over the Cambodian border via a network of streams and canals extending from Tay Ninh, just above the Parrot's Beak, to Rach Gia on the Gulf of Thailand. SEALORDS, or TF 194, was designed to stop this traffic.

Acting in conjunction with the South Vietnamese navy and allied ground forces, TF 194 began its operations in October 1968. It was composed of units drawn from the brown water navy's other task forces and supported in the air by the Seawolves and, later, the new OV-10 Bronco counterinsurgency aircraft of Light Attack Squadron (VAL) 4, the Black Ponies. By the spring of 1969, SEALORDS had established an effective blockade of the waterways along the Cambodian border.

SEALORDS then moved into its second phase, expanding to the full length of Vietnam. In April, U.S. and South Vietnamese craft began pushing into the most remote regions of the delta around the Ca Mau Peninsula, carrying the war into former enemy havens. That same month, SEALORDS extended its operations northward to support

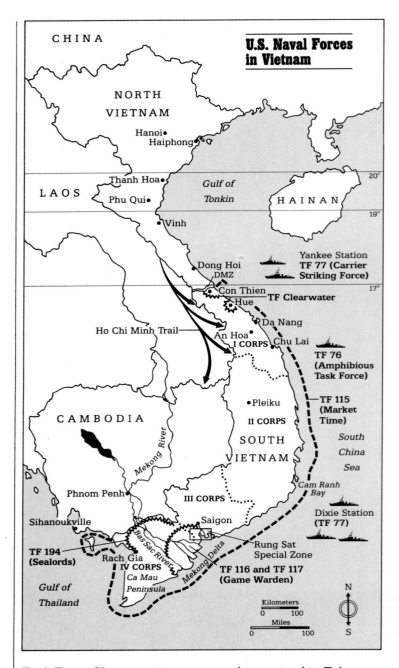

U.S. Naval Forces in Vietnam

month went by without the transfer of a unit, a base, or a mission to South Vietnamese forces. Between 1968 and 1970, the strength of Naval Forces, Vietnam, decreased from 38,000 to 16,750 men, while that of the South Vietnamese navy increased from 18,000 to 32,000. The Mobile Riverine Force ended its service in June 1969, and the River Assault Force was deactivated in August. Full responsibility for SEALORDS began to fall on the South Vietnamese in March 1970. Task Force Clearwater turned over the last of its inshore combat vessels in July. Market Time did so in September. In December, the River Patrol Force was disestablished and COMNAVFORV's remaining riverine craft—517 in all—were transferred to South Vietnam. Solid Anchor, the last American element of SEALORDS, changed hands in April 1971.

Like the riverine forces, the blue water navy remained active as ever in the immediate aftermath of Tet. Its punch was strengthened by the appearance of the battleship *New Jersey* in September 1968. A veteran of World War II and Korea, the ship had been recommissioned to add the weight of its nine sixteen-inch guns to the bombardment forces. Each of those guns could hurl a shell weighing up to 2,700 pounds for twenty-three miles with great accuracy. Together with other secondary armament, the *New Jersey* had eight times the firepower of a heavy cruiser. That firepower was put to particularly good use in the six hours before dawn on February 22, 1969, when nonstop shelling broke up a heavy attack on a Marine outpost just south of the demilitarized zone. In his thanks to the battleship's skipper, the post commander concluded, "If it hadn't been for the *New Jersey*, they would have zapped our ass."

Beginning in 1969, however, the Seventh Fleet began to reduce the scale of its operations. When the *New Jersey* went home for a routine refit in April, the ship wound up back in mothballs. The Amphibious Task Force made its last landing in September. By 1971 the usual strength of the Gunfire Support Unit had dwindled to three ships, the number of carriers on station to two, and monthly attack sorties from the 1968 average of 5,000-6,000 to 1,000-2,500. An exception occurred in March of that year, when 5,000 missions were flown in support of South Vietnam's disastrous thrust into Laos, Operation Lam Son 719, but the trend was clearly down.

Meanwhile, the Vietnamization of the land war was all but complete. The last Marines withdrew from I Corps in 1971, and by March 1972 fewer than 10,000 U.S. combat troops were left in Vietnam. Then on March 30, North Vietnam launched its Easter offensive, a massive, conventional invasion across the DMZ into South Vietnam. As the extent of the onslaught became evident, U.S. forces moved to aid ARVN by air and naval action, and on April 2, President Nixon authorized the first sustained bombing of North Vietnam since November 1968.

The Seventh Fleet contributed powerfully to the sudden expansion of the American war effort. While forces already

Task Force Clearwater, a command organized in February 1968 to maintain control of the most important rivers in I Corps. Two months later SEALORDS entered the struggle for the Michelin Plantation north of the capital by patrolling the Saigon River. In June it also expanded its presence in the Ca Mau Peninsula by establishing a mobile pontoon base, Sea Float (later renamed Solid Anchor), on the Cua Lon River. At the end of its first year, SEALORDS had captured or destroyed more than 500 tons of enemy supplies and killed 3,000 troops at a cost of 186 friendly KIAs and 1,451 wounded. The following spring SEALORDS units participated in the attack on North Vietnamese staging areas during the American and South Vietnamese incursion into Cambodia.

Even as these operations were taking place, ACTOV was winding down the Navy's brown water war. Hardly a

on station at the opening of the offensive supported the South Vietnamese defending I Corps, reinforcements were rushed to Vietnam from points as far distant as the U.S. eastern seaboard. By the end of May, the number of carriers on station had risen to six, the greatest concentration of naval airpower in the war. Besides flying missions over the South, their aircraft seconded Air Force B-52s in Operation Linebacker raids on North Vietnam. A simultaneous increase of the fleet's surface ships soon brought to as many as twenty the number of cruisers and destroyers ranging the coasts of the two Vietnams. In the North, shore batteries often returned the Navy's fire and before the war's end hit sixteen ships, although none seriously.

The bombing of North Vietnam brought about a resumption of aerial combat, little of which had occurred since 1968, as MiGs rose in futile attempts to defend Hanoi and Haiphong. On May 10, Lieutenant Randy Cunningham and his radar intercept officer, Lieutenant (j.g.) Willie Driscoll, scored their third, fourth, and fifth victories to become the first American aces of the war. Altogether, from May 6, 1972, to January 12, 1973, TF 77 aviators downed twenty-three MiGs in air battles in which only five Navy planes were lost. These victories raised the Navy's

wartime total to fifty-seven enemy aircraft destroyed.

To further increase the pressure, President Nixon made a decision in early May that Navy leaders had long advocated: he approved the mining of North Vietnam's harbors. On May 6, A-6s from the *Coral Sea* carried out Operation Pocket Money, dropping magnetic-acoustic mines along the approaches to Haiphong. Other ports soon received the same treatment. The mines were set to arm themselves in three days. In the interim, news of the action was broadcast to the world, and the Navy established a "notification line" patrolled by U.S. vessels equipped with tape recordings in a dozen languages to warn inbound ships.

The effect was immediate. In 1971, 350 Soviet ships had discharged a million tons of cargo in North Vietnam. After the mining, not a single sizable vessel entered or left a North Vietnamese port for the remainder of the war. An officer on a destroyer arriving to join the operations off the North noticed, "The Tonkin Gulf had changed since my last

Returning from their last mission in June 1972, the jets of Attack Carrier Air Wing 15 approach the USS Coral Sea. *The lead group's slot position is vacant in honor of dead and missing pilots.*

trip in 1969. Whereas before it had been filled with foreign-flag ships on their way to Haiphong to unload, the brownish waters were now utterly devoid of any shipping other than the haze grey of American warships." North Vietnam had finally been denied access to the sea.

The combination of U.S. air and naval power and the ARVN's generally staunch resistance halted the Communist drive by the end of April. In June ARVN was able to begin a counteroffensive that recaptured much of the lost territory. Apparently convinced of the impossibility of winning the war while the U.S. remained a party to it, in August the North Vietnamese moderated the demands that had held the Paris peace talks in gridlock for four years.

By early October a settlement seemed imminent, and on the twenty-third President Nixon suspended attacks on the North above the twentieth parallel. But when the peace talks again broke down in December, Nixon responded by authorizing Operation Linebacker II. Between December 19 and 29, TF 77 aircraft accompanied USAF B-52s and F-111s into the densest air defense in the world in a series of devastating raids concentrated along the sixty-mile corridor from Haiphong to Hanoi. Most of the restrictions that had hamstrung Rolling Thunder were lifted, and laser- or television-guided "smart" bombs struck targets deep inside both cities. Enemy batteries fired 1,242 surface-to-air missiles, bringing down four carrier planes along with Air Force aircraft. By December 27, however, the enemy defenses had been exhausted; only one aircraft went down that day and none thereafter. Peace talks resumed in January, and on the twenty-third the Paris agreement was signed, ending America's Vietnam War.

Naval Forces, Vietnam and the Naval Advisory Group were disestablished on March 29, 1973. Since 1950, 2 million Navy men had served in Southeast Asia; 2,511 had died there. The POWs freed in Operation Homecoming included 138 naval aviators. Another 36 were known to have perished in captivity and 600 remained missing, presumed dead.

The fall of South Vietnam and Cambodia in the spring of 1975 added a postscript to the Navy's participation in the Southeast Asian conflict. Hours before Communist forces entered both countries' capitals, the Seventh Fleet was called on to extract U.S. diplomats and citizens and politically compromised local nationals. Helicopters were used in both cases. Operation Eagle Pull, the evacuation of Phnom Penh, took place on April 12; Frequent Wind, the evacuation of Saigon, on April 29 and 30. It was a bitter duty for the men of the Seventh Fleet who had fought for a quarter-century in Indochina to deny the Communists the victory that their last operations now had to acknowledge.

In April 1975, with the fall of South Vietnam imminent, refugees scramble from the U.S. Merchant Ship Green Port *onto a barge flanked by the Panamanian tug* Pawnee.

Bibliography

I. Books and Articles

Anderton, David A. *The History of the U.S. Air Force.* Crescent Bks., 1981.

"As US Infantry Units Depart Brigade Fills Police Vacuum." *The Roundup,* October 1970.

Babb, Capt. Wayne A. "The Bridge: A Study in Defense." *Marine Corps Gazette,* July 1971.

Banks, 1st Lt. Al. "Eleven Days on Vinh Loc." *Rendezvous with Destiny,* Winter 1968–1969.

"The 'Battle Born' Brigade." *The Roundup,* June 1971.

Beech, Keyes. "I'm Happy to Have Them Out." *Chicago News,* June 11, 1966.

Bergerson, Frederic A. *The Army Gets an Air Force.* Johns Hopkins Univ. Pr., 1980.

Blair, Clay. *Ridgway's Paratroopers: The American Airborne in World War II.* Dial Pr., 1985.

Blakey, Scott. *Prisoner at War: The Survival of Commander Richard A. Stratton.* Anchor Pr./Doubleday, 1978.

"The Bloody Checkerboard." *Newsweek,* May 23, 1966.

Blumenthal, Ralph. "U.S. Copter Pilots Taking Some of Worst Fire of War." *New York Times,* February 12, 1971.

Bond, Ray, ed. *The Vietnam War: The Illustrated History of the Conflict in Southeast Asia.* Crown, 1979.

Bowen, SSgt. Bob. "Two Walks." *Leatherneck,* November 1969.

Browne, Malcolm W. *The New Face of War.* Bobbs-Merrill, 1968.

"Bullets Flicked Past Soldier and Killed His Commander." *Baltimore Sun,* September 21, 1965.

Burton, 2d Lt. Bruce. "Eagle Flights." *Thunder,* February 1970.

"Can Choppers Be Vietnamized?" *Newsweek,* March 15, 1971.

Cassidy, Lt. Gen. William F. "The Army's Engineers in Vietnam: A Record Unsurpassed." *Army,* October 1967.

Caufield, Maj. Matthew P. "India Six." *Marine Corps Gazette,* July 1969.

Christmas, Maj. Ron. "A Company Commander Remembers the Battle for Hue." *Marine Corps Gazette,* February 1977.

Clark, Everett. "Army Aviation Set to Hurdle Size Limits." *Aviation Week,* March 12, 1956.

Croizat, Col. Victor (Ret). *The Brown Water Navy: The River and Coastal War in Indo-China and Vietnam, 1948-1972.* Blandford, 1984.

Dalby, Col. Marion C. "Combat Hotline." *Marine Corps Gazette,* April 1969.

———. "Task Force Hotel's Inland Beachheads." *Marine Corps Gazette,* January 1969.

Davis, 1st Lt. Crane. "Bridge at Cam Le." *Marine Corps Gazette,* February 1970.

Davis, Maj. Gen. Raymond, and 1st Lt. Sheridan W. Bell III. "Combined Operations with ARVN." *Marine Corps Gazette,* November 1969.

Davis, Maj. Gen. Raymond, and 1st Lt. Harold W. Brazier II. "Defeat of the 320th." *Marine Corps Gazette,* March 1969.

Davis, Maj. Gen. Raymond, and Capt. R. O. Camp. "Marines in Assault by Helicopter." *Marine Corps Gazette,* September 1968.

Davis, Maj. Gen. Raymond, and 1st Lt. James L. Jones, Jr. "Employing the Recon Patrol." *Marine Corps Gazette,* May 1969.

Drendel, Lou. *The Air War in Vietnam.* Arco, 1968.

Emerson, Gloria. "Saigon's Copter Pilots Are Criticized." *New York Times,* March 5, 1971.

"Engineers Fight as Infantry to Halt VC." *Castle Courier,* February 24, 1968.

"Engrs. Beat Off VC Ambush." *Castle Courier,* December 2, 1967.

Fall, Bernard B. *Hell in a Very Small Place: The Siege of Dien Bien Phu.* Lippincott, 1967.

"First Log." *Dynamo,* Winter 1969.

"From First to Last." *Newsweek,* December 27, 1971.

Galvin, John R. *Air Assault: The Development of Air Mobile Warfare.* Hawthorne Bks., 1969.

Gavin, Lt. Gen. James M. "Cavalry, and I Don't Mean Horses." *Harper's,* April 1954.

"Golden Hawks." *Newsweek,* October 2, 1967.

Goldsberry, CWO Jay G. "Always in a Hurry: Dustoff." *Hawk,* November 1969.

Gorland, Sp4 Stan. "A Bit About First Log." *Dynamo,* Special Issue, 1970.

Griminger, Lt. Col. Charles O. "The Armed Helicopter Story." *US Army Aviation Digest,* July/August 1971.

Gunston, Bill. *Helicopters at War.* Chartwell Bks., 1977.

Halberstam, David. *The Best and the Brightest.* Random, 1972.

Hammond, Lt. Col. J. W. "Combat Journal," parts 1 and 2. *Marine Corps Gazette,* July/August 1968.

Hannum, SP4 Art. "Sky Trackers." *Hawk,* September 1970.

"The Helicopter War." *U.S. News and World Report,* November 23, 1970.

Herring, George C. *America's Longest War: The United States and Vietnam, 1950–1975.* John Wiley and Sons, 1979.

Hines, William. "How Two Hundred and Sixty Encircled GIs Beat Seven Hundred Reds." *Washington Star,* September 25, 1966.

Hopper, Capt. John L., as told by Capt. William F. Dismukes. "Eyewitness to Valor." *U.S. Army Aviation Digest,* n.d.

"How Aviation Proved Itself: In Combat." *Armed Forces Management,* February 1966.

Howze, Gen. Hamilton H. "Tactical Employment of the Air Assault Division." *Army,* September 1963.

Hymoff, Edward. *The First Air Cavalry Division in Vietnam.* M. W. Ladd, 1967.

Jaunal, Sgt. Maj. Jack W. "One Large Success in a Lost War." *Marine Corps Gazette,* November 1978.

"Just Say It Was the Comancheros." *Newsweek,* March 15, 1971.

Karnow, Stanley. *Vietnam: A History.* Viking, 1983.

Kinnard, Lt. Gen. Harry W. O. "A Victory in the Ia Drang: The Triumph of a Concept." *Army,* September 1967.

Krulak, Victor. *First to Fight: An Inside View of the U.S. Marine Corps.* U.S. Naval Inst., 1984.

Krumpa, Peter J. "U.S. Officer Describes Viet Battle." *Baltimore Sun,* September 21, 1966.

Lewy, Guenter. *America in Vietnam.* Oxford Univ. Pr., 1978.

Littauer, Raphael, and Norman Uphoff, eds. *The Air War in Indochina.* Beacon Pr., 1972.

McAllistar, G. J. "Army Puts New Stress on Air Mobility." *Aviation Week,* March 15, 1954.

McArthur, George. "One Hundred and First Airborne 'Guerrillas' Whip Viet Cong with Own Weapons." *Commercial Appeal,* June 29, 1967.

McNamara, Robert S., and Gen. Earle G. Wheeler. "The Prospects for Army Airmobility." *Army,* March 1963.

Marcellino, SP5 Mike. "Nighttime Terror from the Skies." *Hurricane,* November 1968.

Marshall, S.L.A. *Battles in the Monsoon.* Morrow, 1967.

———. *Bird: The Christmastide Battle.* Cowles Book Co., 1968.

———. "The Truth About the Most Publicized Battle of Vietnam." *Harper's,* January 1967.

Merron, Richard. "One Hundred and First Airborne Troops Are Firemen of Viet War." *Courier-Journal,* July 14, 1966.

Mersky, Peter, and Norman Polmar. *The Naval Air War in Vietnam, 1965–1975.* Nautical and Aviation, 1981.

Mertel, Col. Kenneth D. *Year of the Horse—Vietnam.* Exposition Pr., 1968.

Millett, Allan. *Semper Fidelis: The History of the U.S. Marine Corps.* Macmillan, 1980.

Miskin, J. Robert. *The U.S. Marine Corps Story.* Paddington Pr., 1979.

Murphy, Jack. *History of the U.S. Marines.* Bison Bks., 1984.

Myers, Maj. Donald J. "The Pacification of Cam Lo." *Marine Corps Gazette,* October 1969.

"Narcos Hurt Pushers." *The Roundup,* May 1971.

Nichols, Nick. "Sky Cavalry Comes of Age." Unpublished manuscript, 1986.

Nicoli, Maj. Robert. "Fire Support Base Development." *Marine Corps Gazette,* Sept. 1969.

"One Hundred and First Earns 'Grand Nomad' Title." *Nashville Tennessean,* July 21, 1966.

"One Hundred and Seventy-Sixth AHC Rescue Near Tien Phuoc Rates Twenty-One Impact Awards." *Falcon,* April 9, 1969.

"One-Sixth of an Era." *Hawk,* Summer 1972.

"Only Way to Go . . . ." *Army Digest,* August 1968.

Palmer, Dave Richard. *Summons of the Trumpet: U.S.-Vietnam in Perspective.* Presidio Pr., 1978.

Pearson, Brig. Gen. Willard. "Day and Night Battle in Relief of an Outpost." *Army,* March 1967.

———. "Find 'em, Fix 'em, Finish 'em." *Army Digest,* December 1966.

Peatross, Brig. Gen. O. F., and Col. W. G. Johnson. "Operation Utah." *Marine Corps Gazette,* November 1966.

The Pentagon Papers. 4 vols. Edited by Senator Mike Gravel. Beacon Pr., 1971.

Peterson, Iver. "Copter Pilots Over Laos Invasion Question the Risks." *New York Times,* March 7, 1971.

Poe, Perry. "How's Air Mobility?" *Army,* June 1963.

Porter, Gareth, ed. *Vietnam: A History in Documents.* New American Library, 1981.

"Relief Force Battling to Aid of GIs Caught in Red Trap." *Detroit Free Press,* June 11, 1966.

Richardson, GySgt. Herb. "Meade River." *Leatherneck,* April 1969.

Ripley, Major John W. "Tiger Tale." *Marine Corps Gazette,* June 1977.

Rowny, Maj. Gen. Edward L. "After the Air Mobile Tests." *Army,* May 1965.

"Saigon's Choppers: A Crash Waiting to Happen." *Time,* March 29, 1971.

"Sharks Down Reds." *Falcon,* February 16, 1969.

Sharp, Adm. U.S. Grant (Ret). *Strategy for Defeat: Vietnam in Retrospect.* Presidio Pr., 1978.

Shawcross, William. *Sideshow: Kissinger, Nixon, and the Destruction of Cambodia.* Simon and Schuster, 1981.

Shulimson, Jack, and Maj. Edward F. Wells. "First In, First Out: The Marine Experience in Vietnam, 1965–1971." *Marine Corps Gazette,* January 1984.

Simmons, Brig. Gen. Edwin H. *The United States Marines, 1775–1975.* Viking Pr., 1976.

Smith, Jack P. "Death in the Ia Drang Valley." *Saturday Evening Post,* January 28, 1967.

Smith, Col. Richard B. "Leatherneck Square." *Marine Corps Gazette,* August 1969.

Stanton, Shelby L. *Anatomy of a Division: The 1st Cav in Vietnam.* Presidio Pr., 1987.

———. *The Rise and Fall of an American Army: U.S. Ground Forces in Vietnam, 1965–1973.* Presidio Pr., 1985.

———. *Vietnam Order of Battle.* Galahad Bks., 1986.

Stillwell, Paul. *Battleship New Jersey: An Illustrated History.* Naval Inst. Pr., 1986.

Stockdale, Jim, and Sybil Stockdale. *In Love and War: The Story of a Family's Ordeal and Sacrifice During the Vietnam Years.* Bantam, 1985.

Street, Sgt. James F. "A Little Help from Above." *Octofoil,* April/May/June 1969.

Summers, Col. Harry G., Jr. *Vietnam War Almanac.* Facts on File Publications, 1985.

Sweetman, Jack. *American Naval History: An Illustrated Chronology of the U.S. Navy and Marine Corps, 1775- .* Naval Inst. Pr., 1984.

"Ten Thousand and Four Hundred Troops Being Flown to Vietnam." *Baltimore Sun,* December 6, 1967.

Thompson, Sir Robert, consulting ed. *War in Peace: Conventional and Guerrilla Warfare Since 1945.* Harmony, 1982.

Topping, Seymour. "Airborne Brigade Arrives." *New York Times,* July 30, 1965.

Uhlig, Frank, Jr., ed. *Vietnam: The Naval Story.* Naval Inst. Pr., 1986.

Utter, Lt. Col. Leon N. "Solid Contact for 2/7." *Marine Corps Gazette,* April 1966.

Vance, Cyrus R., and Gen. Earle G. Wheeler. "Air Mobility as the Army Command Sees It." *Army*, June 1963.
Vanderpool, Col. Jay D. "We Armed the Helicopters." *U.S. Army Aviation Digest*, June 1971.

Wakefield, Lt. Col. Donald S. "US Military Helicopter Operations." *Interavia*, July 1970.
Walt, Lewis W. *Strange War, Strange Strategy.* Funk and Wagnall, 1976.
Westmoreland, Gen. William C. *A Soldier Reports.* Doubleday, 1976.
"Westmoreland Tells Airborne, 'Live Up To Your Legend.' " *Army Reporter*, December 30, 1967.
"Why Helicopter Losses Are Up." *U.S. News and World Report*, May 19, 1969.
Wilson, George C. "Army Continues to Push for More Helicopters." *Aviation Week*, November 30, 1964.
Woolsey, SP4 Jim. "Mutt and Jeff." *Hawk*, January 1969.

Zich, Arthur. "A Commander Went Looking for Trouble." *Life*, July 8, 1966.
Zumwalt, Adm. Elmo R., Jr. (Ret). *On Watch: A Memoir.* Quadrangle/New York Times, 1976.

II. Government and Government-Sponsored Reports

Berger, Carl, ed. *The United States Air Force in Southeast Asia, 1961–1973.* Office of Air Force History, 1977.
Christmas, Capt. G. R. "A Company Commander Reflects on Operation Hue City." In *The Marines in Vietnam, 1954–1973*, edited by Brig. Gen. Edwin H. Simmons. U.S. Marine Corps, 1985.
Collins, Lawton S. *Training and Development of the South Vietnamese Army.* Department of the Army, Vietnam Studies Series, 1978.
Davis, 1st Lt. Gordon M. "Dewey Canyon: All Weather Classic." In *The Marines in Vietnam, 1954–1973.* U.S. Marine Corps, 1985.
Dictionary of American Naval Fighting Ships. 8 vols. Naval History Division, 1959–1981.
Eckhardt, Maj. Gen. George S. *Command and Control, 1950–1969.* Department of the Army, Vietnam Studies Series, 1974.
Emmet, 2d Lt. Robert. *A Brief History of the 11th Marines.* U.S. Marine Corps, 1968.
The 1st Marine Division and Its Regiments. U.S. Marine Corps, 1981.
Fulton, Maj. Gen. William B. *Riverine Operations: 1966–1969.* Department of the Army, Vietnam Studies Series, 1973.
Heiser, Lt. Gen. Joseph M., Jr. *Logistic Support.* Department of the Army, Vietnam Studies Series, 1974.
Hooper, V. Adm. Edwin B. *Mobility, Support, Endurance: A Story of Naval Operational Logistics in the Vietnam War, 1965–1968.* Naval History Division, 1972.
Hooper, V. Adm. Edwin B., et al. *The United States Navy and the Vietnam Conflict.* Vol. 1, *Setting the Stage.* Naval History Division, 1976.
Johnstone, Maj. John H. *A Brief History of the First Marines.* U.S. Marine Corps, 1968.
Lavalle, Maj. A.J.C., ed. *Airpower and the 1972 Spring Invasion.* USAF Asia Monograph Series, vol. 2, monograph 3, n.d.
McCarthy, Brig. Gen. James R., and Lt. Col. George B. Allison. *Linebacker II: A View from the Rock.* USAF Asia Monograph Series, vol. 6, monograph 8, n.d.
Marolda, Edward J., and Oscar P. Fitzgerald. *The United States Navy and the Vietnam Conflict.* Vol. 2, *From Military Assistance to Combat, 1959–1965.* Naval Historical Center, 1986.
Marolda, Edward J., and G. Wesley Pryce III. *A Short History of the United States Navy and the Southeast Asian Conflict, 1950–1975.* Naval Historical Center, 1984.
Nalty, Bernard C. *Air Power and the Fight for Khe Sanh.* Office of Air Force History, 1973.
Neel, Maj. Gen. Spurgeon. *Medical Support of the U.S. Army in Vietnam, 1965–1970.* Department of the Army, Vietnam Studies Series, 1973.
Nguyen Duy Hinh, Maj. *Lam Son 719.* Indochina Monographs, U.S. Army Center of Military History, 1979.
Pearson, Lt. Gen. Willard. *The War in the Northern Provinces, 1966–1968.* Department of the Army, Vietnam Studies Series, 1975.
Ploger, Maj. Gen. Robert R. *U.S. Army Engineers, 1965–1970.* Department of the Army, Vietnam Studies Series, 1974.
Rienzi, Maj. Gen. Thomas M. *Communications-Electronics, 1962–1970.* Department of the Army, Vietnam Studies Series, 1985.
Santelli, James S. *A Brief History of the Fourth Marines.* U.S. Marine Corps, 1970.
Shore, Capt. Moyers S. II. *The Battle for Khe Sanh.* U.S. Marine Corps, 1977.
Shulimson, Jack. *U.S. Marines in Vietnam: An Expanding War, 1966.* U.S. Marine Corps, 1982.
Shulimson Jack, and Maj. Charles M. Johnson. *U.S. Marines in Vietnam: The Landing and the Buildup, 1965.* U.S. Marine Corps, 1978.
Simmons, Brig. Gen. Edwin H., ed. *The Marines in Vietnam, 1954–1973.* U.S. Marine Corps, 1974.
Telfer, Maj. Gary L., et al. *U.S. Marines in Vietnam: Fighting the North Vietnamese, 1967.* U.S. Marine Corps, 1984.
Thayer, Thomas C. "How to Analyze a War Without Fronts: Vietnam 1965–1972." *Journal of Defense Research*, 7B, Fall 1975.
The Third Marine Division and Its Regiments. U.S. Marine Corps, 1983.
Tilford, Earl H., Jr. *Search and Rescue in Southeast Asia.* Office of Air Force History, 1980.
Tolson, Lt. Gen. John J. *Airmobility, 1961–1971.* Department of the Army, Vietnam Studies Series, 1973.
U.S. Army Combat Developments Command. *Debriefings of Vietnam Returnees.* September 1968, September 1969, and September 1971.
U.S. Congress. Senate. Committee on Armed Services. Hearings Before the Preparedness Investigating Subcommittee. *Military Pilot Training Requirements and Inventories.* 90th Congress, 1st sess., May 11, 1967.

III. Unpublished Government and Military Sources
The following documents are available through Dept. of the Army, Office of the Adjunct General. Most can also be found at the U.S. Army Military History Institute, Carlisle Barracks, Pennsylvania.

Combat After Action Reports
1st Cavalry Division (Airmobile)
 Operation Masher/White Wing: 25 January–6 March 1966.
 Operation Crazy Horse: 16 May–5 June 1966.

 Operation Jeb Stuart III: 17 May–3 November 1968.
 Operation Toan Thang II: 21 November 1968–16 February 1969.
1st Brigade, 1st Cavalry Division (Airmobile)
 Operation Pershing: Battle of Tam Quam, 6–20 December 1967.
 Battle of Quang Tri: 31 January–6 February 1968.
3d Brigade, 1st Cavalry Division (Airmobile)
 Operation Thayer II: 25 October–16 December 1966.
 Song Re Valley Operation: 1–20 August 1967.
1st Battalion, 7th Cavalry, 1st Cavalry Division (Airmobile)
 Ia Drang Valley, Operation: 14–16 November 1966
 14th Military History Detachment, 1st Cavalry Division (Airmobile)
 Operation Hue: 2–26 February 1968.
 Operation Liberty Canyon: 26 October–20 November 1968.
101st Airborne Division (Airmobile)
 Airmobile Operations in Support of Operation Lam Son 719: February 1971– April 6 1971. 2 vols.
 Operation Nevada Eagle: 19 April 1969.
1st Brigade, 101st Airborne Division
 Operation Gibraltar: 8 October 1965.
 Operation Hawthorne (informal): 30 June 1966.
2d Brigade, 101st Airborne Division (Airmobile)
 Operation Vinh Loc: 3 October 1968.
Operational Reports—Lessons Learned
 1st Cavalry Division (Airmobile), three-month periods ending April 1968 and July 1970.
 1st Aviation Brigade, three-month periods ending January 1967 and October 1970.
Senior Officer Debriefing Reports
 Maj. Gen. Olinto M. Barsanti
 Maj. Gen. Allen M. Burdett, Jr.
 Maj. Gen. John J. Hennessey
 Maj. Gen. Robert N. Mackinnon
 Maj. Gen. Thomas M. Tarpley
 Maj. Gen. John M. Wright
 Maj. Gen. Melvin Zais
Miscellaneous Documents
 1st Air Cavalry Division. "Seven Month History and Briefing Data (September 1965–March 1966)."
 14th Military History Detachment, 1st Cavalry Division (Airmobile). "The Shield and the Hammer: The First Cavalry Division (Airmobile) in War Zone C and Western III Corps, 1968–1969."
 Sykes, Capt. Charles S. *Interim Report of Operations of the First Cavalry Division (Airmobile): July 1, 1965 to December 31, 1966.* Office of Information and History, Headquarters, 1st Cavalry Division (Airmobile), 1967.
 101st Airborne Division (Airmobile) *Historical Summary of the Battle of Dong Ap Bia (Hamburger Hill): 10–20 May 1969.*
U.S. Army Military History Institute, Carlisle Barracks, Pa.
 Oral History Collection
 Lt. Gen. Jean E. Engler
 Gen. Hamilton H. Howze
 Lt. Gen. Harry W. O. Kinnard
 Gen. Frank T. Mildren
 Lt. Gen. Bruce Palmer
 Brig. Gen. George P. Seneff
 Gen. Robert R. Williams
 Lt. Gen. John M. Wright
 Unit History Collection
 Division Histories
 1st Cavalry Division (Airmobile), Office of Information and History, Unit Histories:
 (#2) "Attack on LZ Bird: 27 December 1966."
 (#5) "Operation Irving: 2–24 October 1966."
 (#6) "The Battle of Hoa Hoi: 2–3 October 1966."
 (#7) "The Battle of Charlie 1st of the 5th: 21 November 1966."
 (#8) "Operation Bullseye VI: 27–31 January 1967."
 (#10) "Operation Lejeune: 6–22 April 1967."
 (#11) "The Battle of Phu Ninh: 11 March 1967."
 (#12) "Hill 534: 14–15 August 1966."
 (#13) "The Battle of An Qui: 30 May–1 June 1967."
 "The Battle of LZ Pat: 9 August 1967."
 "The Battle of Tam Quan II: 14–16 December 1967."
 101st Airborne Division (Airmobile)
 101st History of the Screaming Eagles.
 Brigade Histories
 History of the Third Brigade (ABN) 101st Airborne Division. May 1973.
 McKenzie, Maj. Robert H. *The First Brigade in the Republic of Vietnam: July 1965–January 1968.*
 Battalion Histories
 History of the 307th Combat Aviation Battalion, 1 August 1967–30 June 1968.
 2d Battalion, 502d Infantry. *Unit History: 1 January to 31 December 1965.*
 Company Histories
 Goebel, Capt. Ernest W. *History of the 128th Aviation Company,* 12 July 1965–31 December 1965.
 History of the 116th Aviation Company, 5 July–31 December 1965.
 History of the 361st Aviation Company, 1 January–31 December 1968.
 Supplement to the History of the 336th Assault Helicopter Company, 1 January–31 December 1967.

IV. The authors have consulted the following newspapers and periodicals:
Army: Army Digest; Army Times; Army Reporter; Time; Falcon; First Team, 1968–1972; *First Team* (division yearbook); *Infantry; Newsweek; New York Times; Rendezvous with Destiny; Screaming Eagle; U.S. News And World Report.*

Picture Credits

Cover Photo
AP/Wide World

Command and Control: MACV and the Support Commands
p. 7, George Silk—LIFE Magazine, c. 1966, Time Inc. p. 8, top, U.S. Army. pp. 8, bottom, and 9, Philip Jones Griffiths—Magnum. p. 10, left, U.S. Army; right, Co Rentmeester—LIFE Magazine, c. 1966, Time Inc. p. 11, left, Dick Swanson—LIFE Magazine, c. 1966, Time Inc.; right, Ian Berry—Magnum. p. 12, Larry Burrows—LIFE Magazine, c. 1964, Time Inc. p. 13, top, AP/Wide World; bottom, Larry Burrows—LIFE Magazine, c. 1963, Time Inc. p. 14, U.S. Army. p. 15, top, U.S. Army; bottom, Larry Burrows Collection. p. 16, U.S. Army. p. 17, top, U.S. Army; bottom, Shelby L. Stanton Collection. pp. 18-19, U.S. Army. p. 20, top, U.S. Army; bottom, Mark Jury. p. 21, top, Charles Bonnay—LIFE Magazine, c. 1967, Time Inc.; bottom, Mark Jury. p. 22, U.S. Army. p. 23, top left, David Burnett—LIFE Magazine, c. 1972, Time Inc.; top right and bottom, U.S. Army.

The Limits of Air Power: 7th Air Force
p. 25, Charles Moore—LIFE Magazine, c. Time Inc. pp. 26, 28-30, 34-35, 37, U.S. Air Force. p. 38, Thomas Billhardt, Berlin, GDR. p. 41, AP/Wide World.

Field Dress
pp. 42-48, Illustrations by Donna J. Neary.

The War Along the DMZ: 3d Marine Division
p. 51, Larry Burrows—LIFE Magazine, c. 1966, Time Inc. p. 52, Bill Eppridge—LIFE Magazine, c. Time Inc. p. 54, Paul Schutzer—LIFE Magazine, c. 1965, Time Inc. p. 55, p. 56, top, Co Rentmeester—LIFE Magazine, c. Time Inc. p. 56, bottom left, Larry Burrows Collection; bottom right, Larry Burrows—LIFE Magazine, c. Time Inc. p. 58, AP/Wide World. p. 60, UPI/Bettmann Newsphotos. p. 61, U.S. Marine Corps. p. 62, UPI/Bettmann Newsphotos. p. 65, AP/Wide World. p. 68, U.S. Marine Corps. p. 69, UPI/Bettmann Newsphotos.

1st MAW
pp. 70-74, U.S. Marine Corps. p. 75, Terrence Spencer—LIFE Magazine, c. Time Inc. pp. 76-79, U.S. Marine Corps.

The Village War: 1st Marine Division
pp. 81-82, 84, 86, 88-89, U.S. Marine Corps. p. 90, AP/Wide World. p. 92, U.S. Marine Corps. p. 94, top, UPI/Bettmann Newsphotos; bottom, Don McCullin—Magnum. p. 95, AP/Wide World. p. 97, U.S. Navy. p. 99, U.S. Marine Corps.

Dominion Over the Skies: 1st Aviation Brigade
p. 101, Shelby L. Stanton Collection. p. 102, U.S. Army. p. 104, Bunyo Ishikawa. pp. 105-6, U.S. Army. p. 107, c. Fred Ward—Black Star. p. 108, U.S. Air Force. p. 110, AP/Wide World. p. 112, Shelby L. Stanton Collection. pp. 114, 116, U.S. Army.

The Sky Cavalry: 1st Cavalry Division (Airmobile)
p. 119, U.S. Army. p. 121, Co Rentmeester—LIFE Magazine, c. Time Inc. p. 125, UPI/Bettmann Newsphotos. p. 126, U.S. Army. p. 127, Bunyo Ishikawa. p. 128, U.S. Army. p. 131, UPI/Bettmann Newsphotos. p. 132, p. 133, top, U.S. Army; p. 133, bottom, Co Rentmeester—LIFE Magazine, c. Time Inc. p. 135, U.S. Army. p. 136, AP/Wide World. p. 137, U.S. Army.

Combat Assault
p. 138, U.S. Army. p. 140, UPI/Bettmann Newsphotos. p. 141, top, Martin Stuart-Fox—TIME Magazine; p. 141, bottom, p. 142, Co Rentmeester—LIFE Magazine, c. 1965, 1966, Time Inc.

The Nomads of Vietnam: 101st Airborne Division
pp. 145, 148, U.S. Army. p. 150, S. Sgt. John R. Baird, U.S. Marine Corps. p. 152, Larry Burrows—LIFE Magazine, c. 1966, Time Inc. p. 155, U.S. Army. p. 156, Shelby L. Stanton Collection. p. 159, AP/Wide World.

The Navy's Elite
pp. 161-63, Co Rentmeester—LIFE Magazine, c. Time Inc. pp. 164-67, U.S. Navy.

Command of the Sea: Seventh Fleet
pp. 169-70, 172-73, U.S. Navy. p. 175, c. R.D. Moeser. p. 177, U.S. Navy. p. 178, c. R.D. Moeser. pp. 180-81, 183-84, U.S. Navy.

Map Credits

All maps prepared by Diane McCaffery. Sources are as follows:

p. 9—Department of the Army.

p. 59—*The Rise and Fall of an American Army: U.S. Ground Forces in Vietnam, 1965–1973* (by Shelby L. Stanton); copyright 1985 by Presidio Press; used by permission. "Combat Hotline," (by Col. Marion C. Dalby); copyright 1969 by *Marine Corps Gazette*; used by permission.

p. 123—*Anatomy of a Division* (by Shelby L. Stanton); copyright 1987 by Presidio Press. Used by permission.

p. 182—*American Naval History* (by Jack Sweetman). Copyright 1984 by Naval Institute Press; used by permission.

Unit Charts—based on data from *Vietnam Order of Battle* (by Shelby L. Stanton). Copyright by *U.S. News & World Report, Inc.*, updated and reprinted by Kraus Reprint and Periodicals, Route 100, Millwood, New York, 10546, published by arrangement with The Atlantic Monthly Press.

Acknowledgments

In addition to acknowledging the kind assistance of the following people, Boston Publishing Company gives special thanks to George Daniels, former executive editor at Time-Life Books, for his guidance and support.

Dan Crawford, head, Reference Section, U.S. Marine Corps History & Museums Division; Lieutenant Commander Thomas F. Cutler, U.S. Navy; Lieutenant Commander Noel A. Daigle, U.S. Navy; Master Sergeant Roger Jernigan, Reference Services Branch, Office of Air Force History; David Keough, U.S. Army Military History Institute, Carlisle Barracks, PA; Colonel Rod Paschall, director, U.S. Army Military History Institute, Carlisle Barracks, PA; Major Robert F. Saikowski, U.S. Marine Corps; Commander Robert Shenk, U.S. Naval Reserve; Brigadier General Edwin Simmons, commander, U.S. Marine Corps History & Museums Division; John Slonaker, chief, Historical Reference Branch, U.S. Army Military History Institute, Carlisle Barracks, PA; Douglas G. Smith, former fire control officer, USS *Turner Joy*; Dr. Richard Sommers, archivist, U.S. Army Military History Institute, Carlisle Barracks, PA; Commander Paul Stillwell, U.S. Naval Reserve.

Index

Note on U.S. Military Unit Organization

The following chart summarizes the general organizational structure of the U.S. Army and Marine Corps in Vietnam, with the approximate number of men in each unit. One notable difference between the Army and the Marine Corps was their use of the regimental command structure. After World War II the Army eliminated the regiment (except in the case of armored cavalry) and replaced it with the comparably sized brigade, composed of various battalions of former regiments. The battalions retained their regimental designations for purposes of historical continuity (for example, 1st, 2d, and 3d battalions, 22d Infantry) but were usually scattered to different brigades. Marine Corps battalions remained organized into regiments except for a few unusual circumstances, though Marines did not officially use the word "regiment"; hence the 1st Marines (a regiment) comprised the 1st, 2d, and 3d battalions, 1st Marines.

Army and Marine Corps Structure

Unit	Size	Commanding Officer
Division	12,000–18,000 troops or 3 brigades	Major General
Brigade/ Regiment	3,000 troops or 2-4 battalions	Colonel
Battalion/ Squadron	600-1,000 troops or 3-5 companies	Lieutenant Colonel
Company/ Troop	150-160 troops or 3-4 platoons	Captain
Platoon	40 troops or 3-4 squads	Lieutenant
Squad	5-10 troops	Sergeant

Names, Acronyms, Terms

AAA—antiaircraft artillery.

Agent Orange—a chemical defoliant widely used in Vietnam to deny jungle cover to the enemy. Named after the color-coded stripe painted around the barrels in which it was stored.

ARVN—Army of the Republic of (South) Vietnam.

Brown Water Navy—division of the U.S. Navy that conducted most of its operations on Vietnam's inland waterways.

CAP—combat air patrol. Assignment of fighter aircraft to provide cover for strike aircraft.

CIDG—Civilian Irregular Defense Group. Project devised by the CIA that combined self-defense with economic and social programs designed to raise the standard of living and win the loyalty of the mountain people. Chief work of the U.S. Special Forces.

CINCPAC—Commander in Chief, Pacific.

civic action—term used by U.S. military forces for pacification programs in South Vietnam.

COMUSMACV—Commander, United States Military Command, Vietnam.

Corps—organizational unit of two or more divisions designed mainly for control of combat operations. U.S. established four corps tactical zones in South Vietnam: I Corps (northern provinces), II Corps (northern highlands and adjacent lowlands), III Corps (southern highlands and adjacent lowlands), and IV Corps (Mekong Delta).

COSVN—Central Office for South Vietnam. Communist military and political headquarters for southern South Vietnam.

DMZ—demilitarized zone. Established by the Geneva accords of 1954, provisionally dividing North Vietnam from South Vietnam along the seventeenth parallel.

FAC—forward air controller. Low-flying pilot who directs high-altitude strike aircraft engaged in close air support of ground troops.

GVN—Government of (South) Vietnam.

Ho Chi Minh Trail—network of roads and pathways through the jungles and mountains of Laos and Cambodia that served as the principal NVA infiltration route of men and materiel into South Vietnam.

Huey—nickname for UH–1 series of helicopters.

JCS—U.S. Joint Chiefs of Staff. Consists of chairman, Army chief of staff, chief of naval operations, Air Force chief of staff, and Marine commandant. Advises the president, the National Security Council, and the secretary of defense.

KIA—killed in action.

LAW—M72 light antitank weapon. A shoulder-fired 66MM rocket with disposable fiber glass launcher.

LOCs—lines of communication. Land, water, and air routes along which supplies and reinforcements move from rear bases to troops in the field.

LOH—light observation helicopter. Also known as a "Loach."

LZ—landing zone.

MAAG—Military Assistance Advisory Group. U.S. military advisory program to South Vietnam beginning in 1955.

MACV—Military Assistance Command, (South) Vietnam. Commanded U.S. forces in Vietnam.

MACV-SOG—Studies and Observation Group. Conducted unconventional warfare, including cross-border missions in Laos, Cambodia, and North Vietnam throughout the Vietnam War.

Main Force unit—regular forces of NVA/VC military.

medevac—medical evacuation of wounded or ill from the field by helicopter or airplane. Also name given to the evacuating aircraft.

MiG—Soviet-designed fighter aircraft developed by Mikoyan and Gurevich.

montagnards—the mountain tribes of Vietnam, wooed by both sides because of their knowledge of the rugged highland terrain and for their fighting ability.

MRF—Mobile Riverine Force. Joint Army-Navy command formed in 1967 to direct amphibious operations in the Mekong Delta.

NCO—noncommissioned officer.

NVA—U.S. designation for North Vietnamese Army. Officially PAVN (People's Army of Vietnam).

OCS—Officers' Candidate School.

OPCON—operational control. Authority granted to one unit over others not organic to it. OPCON was normally granted for a specific operation.

pacification—unofficial term given to various programs of the South Vietnamese and U.S. governments to destroy enemy influence in the villages and gain support for the government of South Vietnam.

PBR—Patrol Boat, River.

PCF—Patrol Craft, Fast. Also known as Swift boats, PCFs were fifty-foot, aluminum-hulled boats that were capable of reaching a speed of twenty-three knots and could navigate in shallow waters.

POL—petroleum, oil, and lubricants.

POW—prisoner of war.

RF/PF—South Vietnamese Regional and Popular Forces. Paramilitary units organized to provide provincial and rural defense. The U.S. nickname Ruff-Puffs is derived from the abbreviation.

ROK—Republic of (South) Korea.

Rome Plow—large tractor with a bulldozer blade, especially developed for land-clearing operations. Also called a "jungle-eater."

RPG—rocket-propelled grenade.

RRF—ready reaction force. Organized within the 1st Cavalry Division (Airmobile), the RRF conducted normal operations but on a moment's notice could be mobilized and helilifted into another battle zone.

SAC—Strategic Air Command. Branch of the USAF that carried out long-range air operations against vital target systems to destroy an enemy's ability or will to wage war.

SAM—surface-to-air missile.

sapper—NVA/VC commando.

SAR—search and rescue.

Seabees—U.S. Navy engineers. Derived from "C.B.s" (construction battalions).

SEAL Team—SEa, Air, and Land Team. Elite U.S. Navy force of highly trained commandos skilled in underwater, airborne, and ground combat.

SLF—Special Landing Force. A Marine batallion serving as the ground troops of the 7th Fleet's Amphibious Task Force.

slick—transport helicopter that lacked guns, giving it a slick exterior.

sortie—a single aircraft flying a single mission.

Special Forces—U.S. soldiers, popularly known as Green Berets, trained in techniques of counter-insurgency warfare.

Swift Boat—see PCF.

TAOR—tactical area of responsibility. A specific area of land where responsibility for security is assigned to the commander of the area.

III MAF—III Marine Amphibious Force. MACV's Marine component, commanding all Marine activities in Vietnam. Headquartered in I Corps, it was the equivalent of an Army Field Force.

USARV—U.S. Army, Vietnam. The largest of MACV's component commands, USARV exercised administrative and logistical command of Army units.

VC—Vietcong. Originally derogatory slang for Vietnamese Communist; a contraction of Vietnam Cong San (Vietnamese Communist).

VCI—Vietcong infrastructure. Local Communist apparatus, responsible for overall direction of the insurgency including all political and military operations.

Vietminh—coalition founded by Ho Chi Minh in 1941. Absorbed by the Vietnamese Communist party in 1951.

VNAF—(South) Vietnamese Air Force.